MITCHUM

IN HIS OWN WORDS

MITCHUM

IN HIS OWN WORDS

INTERVIEWS WITH ROBERT MITCHUM BY

CHARLES CHAMPLIN
DAVID FROST
DICK LOCHTE
JERRY ROBERTS
RICHARD SCHICKEL

EDITED BY JERRY ROBERTS

FOREWORD BY ROGER EBERT

LIMELIGHT EDITIONS
NEW YORK

First Edition June 2000

Copyright © 2000 by Gerald Roberts

All rights reserved under International and
Pan-American Copyright Conventions.
Published by Proscenium Publishers Inc., New York.

Manufactured in the United States of America.

Interior design by Mulberry Tree Press, Inc.
(MulberryTreePress.com)

Library of Congress Cataloging-in-Publication Data
Mitchum, Robert.
    Mitchum : in his own words / interviews with Robert Mitchum by Charles
    Champlin ... [et al.] ; edited by Jerry Roberts ; foreword by Roger Ebert.
    p. cm.
    Includes index.
    Filmography:
    ISBN 0-87910-292-6
    1. Mitchum, Robert—Interviews. 2. Motion picture actors and actresses—
    United
    States—Interviews. I. Champlin, Charles, 1926- II. Roberts, Jerry, 1956- III.
    Title.

PN2287.M648 A5 2000
791.43'028'092—dc21
[B]

00-035716

Dedicated to the inspiration
for change and nerve

CONTENTS

Preface 9

Acknowledgements 13

Foreword by Roger Ebert 14

Introduction 21

Interview with David Frost, 1970 33

Interview with Richard Schickel, 1971 57

Interview with Dick Lochte, 1973 79

Interviews with Charles Champlin,

    1988 and 1994 99

Interview with Jerry Roberts, 1991 114

Mitchum Quotes & Excerpts 157

Quotes & Excerpts on Mitchum 177

Chronology 205

Filmography 212

Index 245

   Photo sections follow pages 32 and 160

PREFACE

One of Robert Mitchum's final wishes was that he didn't want his family to contribute to any new or envisioned last-word biography. He was emphatic on this point. In 1991, when I was at work on my first book about him, a career collation, I suggested that a collection of Q&A-format interviews he had done for radio and television would make a substantial second volume as something of a companion oral history. But Mitchum more than suggested, with his singularly persuasive vocal force, that one project ought to be completed before another is started, especially for a first-time author. I then dropped the oral history idea, finished the first book and went on to other endeavors.

It seems appropriate in his permanent absence to resurrect that rare voice of sharp humor, intellectual grounding, sardonic edge, measured iconoclasm, idiosyncratic cool and coal-mine acoustics. His preserved words can fill part of the vacuum left when Mitchum drifted off on us and went to the big snooze without proper notice and with an absence of fanfare. When he died on July 1, 1997, of complications from lung cancer and emphysema, it was one day prior to the death of his one-time costar, James Stewart, whose passing was justifiably treated with a week-long national last hurrah. The Stewart testimonies upstaged any second-wind eulogies of Mitchum, even though one newspaper columnist went so far as to theorize that the demises of the dual icons—and co-stars, coincidentally, of the 1978 remake of *The Big Sleep*—represented a moment to contemplate the great bright (Stewart) and dark (Mitchum) sides of the movies' expressions of the American character.

But Mitchum got what he wanted. He turned up his collar and sidestepped into the alley of entertainment history. He was cremated and his ashes were scattered at sea off the California coast by his family from aboard the Santa Barbara schooner "Spike

Africa." A small wake followed. And that was it, as he used to say. One of the most recognized movie stars finally fulfilled his boyhood dream to be invisible. As critic Andrew Sarris wrote in 1973, "He was self-propelled toward a very private destiny in a very small corner of the universe."

No big tributes were organized like the one in 1987 for the passing of the actor's old pal, John Huston, at which Mitchum called up from his memory bank of dialects and imitations a casual impression of the director to the delight of the wake's gathering at the Directors Guild of America. When the actor was informed of Huston's death that August, Mitchum replied with a statement that surely would have had Huston's approval, "All I can say is they'd better drive a stake through his heart."

Any last call for *habeas corpus* in Mitchum's case—to whack a two-by-four into one of the all-time chests—is long gone, as his residue spikes the oceanic cocktail. And there's no one to imitate *that* voice—in humor, style, directness or pitch. Mitchum was, as journalist Bob Thomas wrote in the 1980s, "an endangered species"—now extinct. He was a lone operator who sustained a big-time gig for the better part of a century in a tinsel landscape where 35-year-old dinosaurs crash to their own ashes on a daily basis. And the voice was a calling card all its own. Even though "Beef, it's what's for dinner" echoes yet as Mitchum's last big annunciation in popular culture, plenty more of his stories, analyses, zingers and japes are preserved on the following pages.

He was at times the taciturn grump and profane crank that the obits were keen to recall. And he always said that nothing bored him more than talking about himself, which usually was what everyone else wanted the warhorse to jaw about. Part of the cantankerous rep came from an intolerance of presumption and phony baloney. "There's nothing Mitch loves better than to let one of those big-lipped guys blubber his way through a long talk that makes no sense and then sail into him," the late Frank Sinatra once said. If anyone tried to be pretentious, the late director Edward Dmytryk said, Mitchum "would put them down, and very hard. He didn't give a damn about their feelings."

Although he openly viewed the movie business with skepticism, and cynicism lolled in his cadence by rote, Mitchum usually sought humor in any situation. Because he was a slab of beefcake, played violent roles, owned a very publicly aired rap sheet, favored the sauce and splintered a tavern or three, there was a press tendency to see him mostly as Hollywood's bad boy and rarely as the great actor he was.

It was an easy way to pigeonhole a guy who fit no definable context and, in the process, largely distort who he actually was to a public ever ready to digest the next renegade's *mea culpa*. If he intimidated some directors, co-workers, journalists and barroom slackers just by being Mitchum, and they didn't look past the 1,000-mile squint, pile driver's shoulders and bass baritone growl to see in him the perpetual humorist and perceptive quick study, then the hell with it. But he liked to tell about the time Humphrey Bogart assessed him as a jester and put-on. "I think they get a little upset about being put on," Mitchum said. "Bogart used to do that all the time. He was a funny guy. Really a funny guy. He told me that one time. He said, 'You know, Mitch, the difference between us and the rest of those guys is that we're funny.'"

Mitchum, the funny guy, the one who told me that amusement was one of his favorite words—"my whole life, really," he said— is certainly evident on these pages. The tough guy is here along with the cynic, too, and the put-on and the iconoclast and the intellect. But the funny guy seems to crop up on almost every other page. Humor was essential to his spirit. His contrariness was a part of it. When Howard Hawks told him that he doesn't appear to give a damn about a scene, then ends up being "the hardest working so-and-so I've ever known," Mitchum grinned and told the great director, "Don't tell anybody."

Mitchum once said that he rarely smiled for photographers because he "looked like a fox in a henhouse." He developed one of the great deadpan deliveries of all time. He could have a listener rolling off the couch doubled up in laughter, while he sipped coffee to outwait the noise. Because of the screen scowls of his reluctant private eyes and pistoleros, it's fitting that the great sportswriter, Jim Murray, could once describe Mitchum's countenance as resembling an "alpine crag." But it's just as true to the man to re-call another journalist's description after the actor completed an obvious tall tale: "He shrugs and grins his slow grin," William Hall once wrote, "the big face breaking up reluctantly, like a cliff being dynamited."

The following interviews and quotes contain a great deal of movie lore about a great many people, from Frank Sinatra to Marilyn Monroe to David Lean to John Wayne to 101 others, and reveal a lot about how, why and with what resources many fa-mous movies were made. These talks also tell us a lot about Robert Mitchum, actor, man and unavoidably funny guy. His words about hitching rides on freight trains and surviving the Great Depression and putting incarcerations behind him to be-come a top movie star qualify as a strange yet distinctly American 20th century story. As for the screen presence who critic Roger Ebert said "embodies the soul of film noir"—who often portrayed that dark side of the American character—he's here, too. The night in Mitchum's voice gave a formidable sound to stories of the night in postwar movies. To me, this book is another make-up piece for the absence of the fair shake due to Mitchum that mainstream Hollywood never got around to giving him.

To place events in Mitchum's life in context, a filmography and a chronology are provided at the back of the book. Also pro-vided is a section of stand-alone quotes on a wide range of sub-jects by Mitchum from other interviews and statements. Another section of quotes about Mitchum from others is included just so he doesn't have all the say.

As complex and multi-dimensional as Mitchum may have made even the thinnest roles just by showing up, his voice was always one of great clarity and authority. And it almost reverberates yet—between the lines and at appropriately odd instances—on the fol-lowing pages.

ACKNOWLEDGEMENTS

I thank the journalists who generously allowed me to collate their talks with Robert Mitchum into this volume. And I thank Roger Ebert for the gracious provision of the foreword.

I also thank Erwin Frankel Productions, Ltd., of New York City for allowing me the use of Richard Schickel's interview for the *Sound on Film* syndicated radio series. Likewise, Group W Productions of Los Angeles, through its general counsel, Cornell Chulay, graciously allowed me to reprint David Frost's television interview conducted for the syndicated *The David Frost Show*. Dave Holland of the Lone Pine Film Festival generously supplied me with a videotape of one of Charles Champlin's interviews. Thanks, too, to Eliot Ephraim in Chicago.

Thanks also go to Mrs. Dorothy Spence Mitchum, whose dedication and kindness helped lead to an earlier book I wrote on Robert Mitchum, without which this book would not have been possible. I also want to thank Christopher Mitchum and Robert's sister, Julie Mitchum, for their kind words and their diplomacy.

Portions of this book's introduction originally appeared on Microsoft's Cinemania on-line web site, once based at Redmond, Wash., and in the summer 1997 issue of *Final Take*, the film journal published at Mission Viejo, Calif. Personal thanks go to Don Lechman, James Robert Parish, Wil Haygood, Doug List, Steve Gaydos, Charles Champlin, Joe Bensoua, Alain Silver, Melvyn B. Zerman, Mort Janklow and Joe McBride for their help, encouragement and goodwill.

FOREWORD
BY ROGER EBERT

[Editor's note: Roger Ebert originally wrote this piece for *The New York Times* in 1971, when Robert Mitchum was in Pittsburgh for location shooting on *Going Home*. The story also appeared in the *Chicago Sun-Times*, *Los Angeles Times* and elsewhere. Mostly a three-way conversation in a car, the piece seems an appropriate introduction to the actor's freestyle brand of conversation, inherent sense of humor and relaxed approach to getting lost on the way to jail.]

The sky hung low and dripping over the Sheraton Motor Inn, and Robert Mitchum hunched his shoulders against it and scooted around to the other side of the Mercury, slamming the door against the rain.

"I bought some of that lime spray," he told his friend Tim Lawless, who was in the driver's seat. "Maybe she'll go for some of that lime spray."

"Lime spray," Tim said. Then he started the car and guided it down a ramp and onto a highway, turning left, which was, as it turned out, a fateful decision.

"This is, I would say, relaxing work," Mitchum said. "They don't push you too hard. While you're resting, they say, would you mind carrying these anvils upstairs?"

"Jesus, what a lousy, crummy day," Tim said.

"And here it is only two in the afternoon," Mitchum said. "Reflect on the hours still before us. What time is the call for?"

"They're looking for you around 2:30, quarter to three," Tim said. "You got it made."

"You know the way?" Mitchum said.

"Hell yes, I know the way," Tim said. "I was out here yesterday. Sons of bitches, picking locations way the hell the other side of hell and gone. . . ."

"Look at those kids," Mitchum said.

Three or four kids had parked their motorcycles at an intersection and were sitting backwards on the seats, in the drizzle, watching traffic.

"Kids hanging around street corners," Mitchum said wonderingly, as if that were a sight he didn't see much anymore. "Oogling, drooling . . . ."

"Drooling," Tim said.

"Oogling," Mitchum said. "What do we gotta shoot this afternoon? We gotta jam our butts into those little cells again?"

"Those are the smallest cells I've ever seen," Tim said. "Can you imagine pulling solitary in one of those?"

"I did five days of solitary once, when I was a kid," Mitchum said. "In Texas. Of course, in Texas, you might as well be in as out . . . ."

"You did solitary?" Tim said.

"I liked it," Mitchum said. "You read about Alvin Karpis, up in Canada, they finally let him out after 40 years or something? Son of a bitch walks outside, and the guy who put him in is still there. J. Edgar. Son of a bitch does 40 years, the least we could do for him is not have J. Edgar still sitting there when he gets out a lifetime later . . . ."

"Karpis?" Tim said.

"I guess he was a real mean mother at one time," Mitchum said.

The wipers beat back and forth against the windshield, and on the sidewalks people put their heads down and made short dashes between dry places. We were in Pittsburgh now, and the smoke and fog brought visibility down to maybe a couple of blocks.

"I'm glad we're shooting inside today," Tim said. Mitchum whistled under his breath, and then began to sing softly to himself: "Seventy-six trombones led the big parade . . . ."

"With a hundred and ten cornets in the rear," Tim sang, banging time against the steering wheel. "A hundred and ten? Is that right?" Tim said after a while.

"All I know is the 76 trombones," Mitchum said. "I don't have time to keep pace with all the latest developments."

"So how long you been in Pittsburgh?" I asked.

"I was born here," Mitchum said, "and I intend to make it my home long after U.S. Steel has died and been forgotten. I intend to remain after steel itself has been forgotten. I shall remain, here on the banks of the Yakahoopee River, a grayed eminence . . . . I used to come through here during the Depression. I don't think the place has ever really and truly recovered . . . ."

He reached in his pocket for a pipe, filled it carefully, and lit up. "I find myself talking to the kids," he said. "And they say . . ."

He broke off as a Mustang with two girls in it pulled up next to the Mercury at a stoplight. Through the window on his side, he mouthed a warm suggestion. "Hey, baby, you want to . . ." The Mustang pulled away. "They don't have lip readers worth a damn in this town," Mitchum said. "But the kids. I was talking about the kids. They say they figure they owe the community about two more years, and then they're pulling out, before they're flung headlong into despair."

"I don't think we went through a tunnel yesterday," Tim said.

"Well, we're going through a tunnel now," Mitchum said.

"Are you sure we're supposed to be on 79, and not 76?" Tim said.

"I think I'm sure," Mitchum said. "We were either supposed to sing 'Seventy-six Trombones' to remind us to take 76, or to remind us not to, I'm not sure which . . . ."

"You're not leading me down the garden path, are you, Bob?" Tim said.

"Route 79," Mitchum said. "Maybe it was 76. Or . . . Route 30?"

"This is the goddamn airport road," Tim said. "Look there."

"Steubenville, Ohio," Mitchum said. "Jesus Christ, Tim, we're going to Steubenville, Ohio. Maybe it's just as well. Make a left turn at Steubenville and come back in on the Pennsylvania Turnpike . . . ."

"Ohio's around here somewhere," Tim said.

"I've always wanted to make a picture in Ohio," Mitchum said. "Maybe I have. I was bitten by a rowboat once in Columbus . . . ."

There were three lanes of traffic in both directions, and Tim held grimly to the wheel, trying to spot a sign or an exit or a clue.

"The Vesuvius Crucible," Mitchum said. "Pull off here and we'll ask at the Vesuvius Crucible. If anybody ought to know where they are, the Vesuvius Crucible ought to."

Tim took the next exit and drove into the parking lot of the Vesuvius Crucible. Mitchum rolled down the window on his side and called to a man inside the office: "Hey, can you tell us how to get to the Allegheny County Workhouse?" Mitchum said.

"The what?" the man said.

"The Allegheny County Workhouse," Mitchum said.

"Hell, they closed that down back here six months ago," the man said. "It's empty now."

"We just want to visit," Mitchum said. "Old times' sake."

The man came out into the yard, scratching himself thoughtfully. "The Allegheny County Workhouse," he repeated. "Well, buster, you're real lost. You turn around here and go right back to downtown Pittsburgh. Take the underpass. When you get to downtown Pittsburgh, ask for directions there."

"How wide are we off the mark?" Mitchum said.

"Buster," the man said, "you're 38 or 40 miles away from where you should be."

"Holy shit," Mitchum said.

"I'm telling you," the man said, "they shut the workhouse down back here six, seven months ago. You won't find anybody there."

"Thanks just the same," Mitchum said.

Tim drove up to the expressway overpass and came down pointed at Pittsburgh. "We should have taken Route 8," he said.

"Sorry about that," Mitchum said. "There's a road to Monroeville. Ohio's around here somewhere . . . ."

"Nice countryside," Tim said. "You ought to buy it and build yourself a ranch."

"I could be the biggest rancher in Pittsburgh," Mitchum said. "Get up in the morning and eat ham and eggs in my embroidered pajamas. Some girl broke into the motel, did you hear about that? With a pair of embroidered PJs?"

"Embroidered?"

"A great big red heart right over the rosette area," Mitchum said. "I've got an idea. Maybe we should hire a cab and have it lead us to the Allegheny County Workhouse."

"I don't even think we're in Allegheny County," Tim said.

Mitchum hummed "Seventy-six Trombones" under his breath and filled his pipe again.

"This is your first picture since *Ryan's Daughter*, right?" I asked him. The picture was *Going Home*, with Mitchum as a man who murdered his wife years ago, gets out of prison, and is confronted by his son.

"There's a funny thing about that," Mitchum said. "At the same time I was reading this script, I was also reading a script about a jazz musician in San Francisco. So I ask myself, do I want to play a jazz musician in San Francisco, or do I want to go out on location in some godforsaken corner of McKeesport, Pennsylvania, and live in a motel for two months? No way. No way. So these two guys come in and we have a drink or two, and I sign the contract. On their way out, I say I'll see them in San Francisco. I thought they looked a little funny. Do you know what I did? I signed up for the wrong fucking movie."

"Here's Route 8 right now," Tim said.

"That's Exit 8, not Route 8," Mitchum said.

"We're going to be real late," Tim said. "Real late."

"They can rehearse," Mitchum said. "They can practice falling off stairs, tripping over lights, and shouting at each other in the middle of a take."

The car was back in the tunnel again now, heading the other way. Tim came down through a series of cloverleafs and found himself back on Route 79, headed for the airport.

"I'm lost," he said. "Baby, I'm lost."

In desperation, he made a U-turn across six lanes of traffic and found himself on an up-ramp going in the opposite direction, with a cop walking slowly across the street toward him. Mitchum rolled down the window. "Roll down your window," he told Tim. "Let's get a breeze in here." He shouted to the cop: "Hey, chief! We're lost! We been 40 miles out in the country and here we are headed right back the same way again."

"What are you doing make a U-turn against all that traffic?" the cop said. "You could go to jail for that."

"Hell, chief," Mitchum said, "that's where we're trying to go. We been looking for Allegheny County Workhouse for the last two hours."

"They closed that down back here six months ago," the policeman said.

"We're shooting a movie out there," Mitchum said.

"Hey, you're Robert Mitchum, aren't you?" the cop said.

Mitchum pulled his dark glasses down on his nose so the cop could see more of his face, and said, "We are so lost."

"I tell you what you do, Bob," the cop said. "You take this underpass and follow the road that curves off on your left before you get to the bridge."

"Thanks, chief," Mitchum said.

Tim drove onto the overpass, followed the road that curved off on the left before he got to the bridge, and groaned.

"We're back on Route 79 heading for the airport," he said.

"Jesus Christ," Mitchum said. "Screw that cop. Screw that cop and the boat that brought him."

"Now we gotta go back through the tunnel," Tim said. "I'm upset. I am really upset." On the other side of the tunnel, Tim pulled over to a State Highway Department parking lot and backed into it down the exit ramp. A state employee came slowly out of a shed, wiping his hands on a rag.

"Ask that guy," Mitchum said. "Offer him a certain amount to lead us there with a snowplow." Tim got out and got some instructions from the state employee. Their essence seemed to be: Go back that way.

Tim tried it again, back through the tunnel, across the bridge, down the overpass to the red light, where a police squad car was stopped in front of the Mercury. Mitchum jumped out of the car and hurried up to the squad car for instructions. He got back just as the light turned green.

"You'll see a sign up here that says Blawnox," he said. "That's what we need. Blawnox."

"I'm out of gas," Tim said.

"I got a letter from John Bryson today," Mitchum said. "John's in Dingle, in Ireland. Where we shot *Ryan's Daughter*?"

"I am really upset," Tim said.

"According to John," Mitchum said, "they've formed a Robert Mitchum Fan Club in Dingle. The membership is largely composed of unwed mothers and their brothers."

"Where the hell are we?" said Tim.

"That's what happens when you shoot on location," Mitchum said. "It's nothing but a pain in the ass."

He began to whistle "Seventy-six Trombones" again, softly, but not too softly.

INTRODUCTION

After more than 120 feature and television films and miniseries and a dozen-plus contretemps that made the papers and added to his rap sheet and for which he did time behind bars, Robert Mitchum helped promulgate the Hollywood logic that perpetually tells us the down-and-out shall find redemption on the screen. In real life, he was one of the rare rounders to thrive from and through down-and-out status.

His endurance is partially a result of that rough-road mystique. He was also fascinating for being a strange ranger in one of the most image-conscious businesses of them all. He was a man of many contradictions, a hugely skeptical and sarcastic cat on the pop-culture fringe who also managed to be one of the hardest working and most in-demand star performers in history.

And every self-styled rebel riding his star's course across the astral firmament, from Brando to Sean Penn, should take a moment to pay respects if he hasn't already, because their unofficial god-daddio—the first cool dude to go big time in Hollywood and one of the seemingly least concerned about that status—swims with the fishes: cremated, canned and scattered at sea in 1997. Big Bad Bob, who filled the hipster's role by rote and shrug, and got busted on a reefer rap in 1948 to ignite the first big postwar Hollywood scandal, opted out of the pine overcoat for the complete freedom in death that he so coveted in life.

Any discussion of Mitchum's place in film history isn't helped by the man's own deeply ingrained sardonicism, developed out of the experience of fame and success, infamy and failure. He became a movie star out of obscurity in 1945 when William A. "Wild Bill" Wellman selected him to play the second lead in the classic war picture, *The Story of G.I. Joe.*

This chance arrived after stunt work and bit parts and a collage of harsh experience. He lived in four or five states as a child after his half-Blackfoot Indian, half-Scotch-Irish father was killed between coupling boxcars in a 1919 railroad accident at Charleston, South Carolina. During the Depression, he contracted pellagra from malnutrition and gangrene from a Georgia chain-gang shackle (the conviction was for vagrancy in Savannah during a hobo roundup; he escaped after a month). For years he crisscrossed the nation as a boxcar bum, hiding from railroad detectives, sleeping in barns, digging ditches, washing dishes, mining coal in Pennsylvania, working a salvage boat out of Massachusetts, prizefighting in Nevada, operating a punch press in Ohio, doing a longshoreman's labor at the American-Hawaiian docks in Long Beach, California.

To understand Mitchum the actor is to know that three years after his rise to fame, his public branding as "Big Bad Bob" for his 1949 conspiracy conviction connected to the marijuana frame-up and jail sentence (he was exonerated after the L.A. County district attorney conducted a follow-up investigation), instilled in the man's senses of humor and irony a reluctance to publicly express any seriousness about his talent or films. He thought he was ruined and had failed his young family. When his pictures became more popular than ever after his two-month stint at Wayside Honor Farm in the California hills, irony settled in for good.

Mitchum on Mitchum: "They want it bad, I do it bad . . . Like an old whore, you know, I got nothin' to get ready. Show up and do it . . ." Add one: "[The movie fan] thinks, if that bum can make it, I can be President. I bring a ray of hope to the great unwashed." Add two: "I used to wear the same raincoat in every picture. They just changed the leading lady and said, 'Roll 'em.'" Husbandry came into play—Mitchum said his two acting styles are "with and without a horse," and he extolled the performing of Rin Tin Tin: "That was a mother dog, so there can't be too much of a trick to it."

But great directors knew better. Mitchum was of "the calibre of Olivier, Burton and Brando, capable of *King Lear*," John Huston wrote. His showing up "can make every other actor look like a hole in the screen," Sir David Lean said. He was "one of the finest,

most solid and real actors we have in the world" claimed
Wellman. Fred Zinnemann put him "almost in the same class as
Spencer Tracy." Charles Laughton averred that he would "make
the best Macbeth of any actor living."

Writing about Mitchum the actor always ends up as a defense,
making a case. "How can I offer this hunk as one of the best actors in the movies?" asks critic David Thomson in *A Biographical
Dictionary of Film*. But among dozens of routine genre exercises,
the record shows an abundance of brilliant, deeply felt performances crafted by an invisible and seemingly effortless style that
has gone undetected for half a century. It often came in films that
few people saw upon their initial release. No other star actor has
had as many of his old pictures reevaluated and upgraded by re-
visionist criticism. *When Strangers Marry* (1944) has been singled
out as a model of the efficient studio B-movie; *Pursued* (1947)
counts as the first psychological western; *Out of the Past* (1947)
as the epitome of film noir; *Angel Face* (1952) as another noir
benchmark; *Blood on the Moon* (1948), *Track of the Cat* (1955),
The Man With the Gun (1955) and *The Wonderful Country*
(1959) as atypical and complex character westerns about unusual
loners; *His Kind of Woman* (1951) as a surprising compendium
of frisky innuendo; *The Lusty Men* (1952) as the greatest rodeo
picture, an identity that does it no justice; the now exalted *The
Night of the Hunter* (1955) and *Cape Fear* (1962) as brilliant pre-
sentations of psychosexual villains; and Mitchum's most personal
film, *Thunder Road* (1958), as the archetype for the four decades
of car-crunching pictures that followed.

These films, combined with those generally accepted as his
best—the ones that also won praise in their day—confirm him as
one of the greatest of all Hollywood star actors: *Thirty Seconds
Over Tokyo* (1944), *The Story of G.I. Joe, Crossfire* (1947), *Not
as a Stranger* (1955), *Heaven Knows, Mr. Allison* (1957), *The
Enemy Below* (1957), *Home From the Hill* (1960), *The
Sundowners* (1960), *The Longest Day* (1962), *El Dorado* (1967),
Ryan's Daughter (1970), *The Friends of Eddie Coyle* (1973),

Farewell, My Lovely (1975), *The Yakuza* (1975), *The Last Tycoon* (1976) and the remake of *Cape Fear* (1991).

Independent, opaque to most, a self-contained operator who never had a personal publicist and once claimed he was politically registered as "a Druid," he often allowed the audience "a shared understanding that he's a man acting in material conceived for puppets," critic Pauline Kael wrote. Mitchum rarely evinced any character continuity from film to film. His familiarity has been in the bourbon-smooth cadence, the hooded eyes and the enormous chest that seemed to require a distinctive walk—the bow-legged "Mitchum ramble"—to keep his feet centered beneath it. He was an anti-persona, "reborn" in each role, according to critic Andrew Sarris, even though it was usually another pistolero or soldier or private eye.

Although Mitchum never dominated a decade or genre, he has come in retrospect to signify the shadowy world of film noir more than any other actor. The broad visage in the coat and hat, with wafting cigarette smoke and languid eyes—an image and style and mood representative of his Jeff Bailey in *Out of the Past*—stands tall in the iconography of postwar American films, when prosperity brought with it feelings of Cold War paranoia and vulnerability, and corrosion caught up with urban growth. Mitchum is a premium mood element in the poetry of the tough-guy mosaic of the American night. He belongs with hard liquor, chain-smoking hooligans, circumspect women, nightclubs and the law of the concrete, where the solution often meant compromise. He should have played Philip Marlowe long before *Farewell, My Lovely*.

Even though he was the central figure in most of his pictures, Mitchum nearly always seemed to conjure a sense of detachment that could make Bogart seem like a Kiwanis Club cheerleader. And Mitchum walked through many movies as if the camera wasn't turned on: *My Forbidden Past* (1951), *White Witch Doctor* (1953), *Foreign Intrigue* (1956), *The Angry Hills* (1959), *The Way West* (1967), *The Amsterdam Kill* (1977), *Agency* (1979), *Believed Violent* (1990). But the actor's outsider status lies beyond intellect, effort and story line.

"Robert Mitchum has . . . assurance in such huge amounts that he seems almost a lawless actor," Kael wrote in 1971. "He does it all out of himself. He doesn't use tricks and stratagems of clever, trained actors. Mitchum is *sui generis*. . . . There is no other powerhouse like Mitchum. . . . he's still so strong a masculine presence that he knocks younger men off the screen. His strength seems to come . . . from his dependence on himself."

He was a package of raw power held in check by the knowledge of what he can and mostly can't do in the world. "That's the point," he said in 1964. "These pictures—I can do them and walk away from them. It's all finished and I never have to see them—and I'm not that *involved*. Furthermore, I don't let anyone down. I don't want that responsibility. I don't want that deep involvement." Two decades later, gone to the bank again in hired-gun style, he allowed: "I always thought I had as much inspiration and tenderness as anyone in the business. I always thought I could do better. But you don't get to do *better*, you get to do *more*."

Mitchum's importance to film history sneaked up on us via his sheer endurance and was underscored by his unlikely television superstardom in what would be the twilight of most careers. In the most expensive and far-flung productions ever undertaken in the medium—*The Winds of War* and *War and Remembrance*—Mitchum was the bellwether for 50 hours of prime time World War II, playing the globe-trotting naval officer, Pug Henry. When the sequel debuted in 1989, Mitchum was 72.

He fought that same war many times. At the end of the battle for Omaha Beach at the close of *The Longest Day*, he heaves away a stogie for a replacement and flags down a Jeep out of the epic convoy behind him and says to the driver, "OK, run me up the hill, son." His general's sense of weariness, the job-done sigh and acceptance of some new task ahead all issue through Mitchum's body language and been-there look. That weariness is everywhere in Mitchum's work and immediately identifiable as part of his appeal to both men and women.

The screen Mitchum was a damned tired guy; we've been tired, too. On the mean streets in the 1970s, The Man was on his back as he traveled the underworld as ex-con Harry Graham in *Going Home* (1971), was forced into duplicity from pressures on both sides of the law as the title low-level racketeer in *The Friends of Eddie Coyle*, and was hired out a few times to find the girl, twice as Marlowe—*Farewell, My Lovely* and the lousy *The Big Sleep* (1978)—and as Harry Kilmer, sent into the Tokyo underground in *The Yakuza*. Eddie Coyle is among his most representative roles, a character shot through the solar plexus by a lifelong series of cruddy jobs and facing the new fear of another jail term. When Eddie answers a bartender's casual greeting inquiry with a weary "I've been better," it echoes from Mitchum with profound truth.

The Yakuza was a mid-late-career example of a film that inspired British author Bruce Crowther to write in the book *Film Noir*, "Of them all, Mitchum is so steeped in the sardonic characteristics of old noir icons that he brings echoes of those old movie roles to everything he does, on screen and off." Sydney Pollack, who directed *The Yakuza*, said, "I was concerned with trying to get on film the essence of this character who had been marinated by life, which is the feeling you get when you look at Mitchum's face. You have the sense of a man who has seen it all and been through it all."

And has gotten plowed in countless bars. And known too many women. Big Bad Bob's somnambulistic lids had a way of languorously letting the lust seep out: scanning Jane Russell's sinuous form in *His Kind of Woman* and *Macao* (1952); as the Caribbean boat captain-for-hire, Felix, going after Rita Hayworth in the aptly titled *Fire Down Below*; as Curt Bridges, the mountain pioneer, stealing his brother's wife in *Track of the Cat*; and comfortably remorseless as Old Man Bibic, seeking the favors of his son's girl in *Maria's Lovers* (1985).

Hayworth, Ava Gardner, Shirley MacLaine and Sarah Miles are on the short list of stars who were supposed to have done the primal mambo with studly Bob, even though his marriage to the former Dorothy Spence lasted for 57 years until his death. When his profligate African drifter, Joe Moses, wakes up at the outset of *Mister Moses* (1965) and immediately induces a young woman he's never met to lie to her fiancé about him, her agreeability is entirely believable. The screen's Ol' Sleepy Eyes was the ultimate rogue, but never more coolly and easily than when he was looking to get inside a skirt. When he casually allows to Jane Russell in *His Kind of Woman* that she would be "a handy thing to have around the house," she and the audience get the drift with a warm current of electricity.

The actor was an egalitarian screen lover. "Of all the postwar actors—Kirk Douglas, Burt Lancaster, Richard Widmark—only Mitchum immediately figured out how to be a man's man and a woman's man at the same time," wrote critic Carrie Rickey, who figured him for "a hipster John Wayne." Three decades after she co-starred with him in *The Last Time I Saw Archie* (1962) and *Man in the Middle* (1964), actress France Nuyen, in an effort to describe Mitchum, paused, upturned her palms before her emphatic face and declared, "Is *man*!" A fan magazine called him "The Man With the Immoral Face," and a natural air of coital *in-flagrante delicto* pervaded many of his screen characters.

The thousand-mile stare, which threatened to disappear into a snooze at any moment from the sleepiest eyelids that the screen ever saw, could combine potently with a clinch, as it did in *Out of the Past*, in which Mitchum delivers one of the most fatalistic and dame-intoxified lines ever uttered in movies. "Baby, I don't care," he whispers to Jane Greer's denial of theft as he kisses her, having found in her wiles a force to shake his bruised torpor. "Bob Mitchum is so sleepily self-confident with the women that when he slopes into clinches you expect him to snore in their faces," wrote critic James Agee of *Out of the Past*.

Mitchum's catnip status for women came a little crummy and dangerous around the edges. He was someone whom nice girls had dirty fantasies about in the heyday of such studio-polished and clean-fingernailed types as Van Johnson and Tyrone Power. He was a walking example of the realist's ambivalence and complexity next to the blocks of righteous granite presented by John Wayne, Gregory Peck, Charlton Heston and almost every other major star on the next marquee. The elemental emotional force inherent in *Cape Fear*, for example, relies almost as much on the polarity of the Mitchum/Peck reputation dynamic as it does on the obscenity of Max Cady's sinister campaign of terror.

The galoot took his lumps. During the pot scandal, Jane Greer wrote some fan-mag damage control that said Mitchum "really hurt when he hurt." Kilmer's Tokyo reunion with an old flame in *The Yakuza* is given a haunting pall by Mitchum's eyes and gestures. Those eyes truly are evocative windows to the soul in *Out of the Past*, *Angel Face* and *Heaven Knows, Mr. Allison*. The recognition and complexity of the love expressed by his Jeb Rand for the woman who was raised as his sister in *Pursued* and by his Jeff McCloud for his best friend's wife in *The Lusty Men* is better served by the glances of this great less-is-more disciple than by the dialogue.

When his Paddy Carmody comes into the bedroom near the end of *The Sundowners* to tell his wife he lost the family nest egg by gambling it away at the horse track, he defines with few words the shame and regret of a hundred irresponsible husbands and fathers—the kind of role that Mitchum confessed he played in real life as what he called an "absentee father." His title Marine in *Heaven Knows, Mr. Allison* is an excellent rendition of none-too-bright yet natural resourcefulness. Hiding in a cave for months on a Japanese-held Pacific island during World War II with Deborah Kerr's attractive nun, Allison learns the hard lesson of falling in love with someone who can't return that love the way he wishes, and Mitchum makes us believe in the deep hurt.

When his Captain Walker explains to war correspondent Ernie Pyle why he writes individual letters to parents of the infantrymen who were killed under his command in *The Story of G.I. Joe*, the moment not only won him his only Academy Award nomination, but struck to the heart the way few film scenes have on the sorrow of death in war. When Walker is later brought down a mountain as a corpse, slung over the back of a mule, the sorrow, loss and irony are doubly jolting. Calling Mitchum's work "an extraordinarily haunting performance," Sarris wrote, "This scene is still a convulsive emotional experience not because of any lingering idolatry of a dead G.I., but because Mitchum's exquisite stillness in death is the result of his expressive stoicism in life."

To select a best performance is tough. To select even a dozen is tough. Several are distinctive unto themselves. His performance as the recovering drunk sheriff J.P. Harrah in *El Dorado* is easily his best comic work as he trades barbs with John Wayne. His portrayal of East Texas land baron Wade Hunnicutt in *Home From the Hill* is a potent collage of big-money arrogance and domineering machismo, traits that refract through all of the actor's rugged strengths the character's underlying failures as a husband and father.

His Preacher Harry Powell in *The Night of the Hunter*, with "HATE" tattooed on one hand, "LOVE" on the other, has come in retrospect to be regarded as a unique masterpiece of evil. The self-mockery in the role—Mitchum essence—goes a long way in converting this child-stalking killer into a walking obscenity. Mitchum later instilled a great deal more surface malice into his Max Cady. Today, it's a prerequisite for every big-style action picture to have a showy villain's role, but in the immediate postwar decades, no big star was more willing to depart from the conventional studio-steered good-guy course and be the complete lout than Mitchum, who has had an easy way of looking as if he knew where the bodies were buried. And no one in movie history did it more often, with more complexity, conviction and realism.

For most of his career, Mitchum was a big, serviceable stallion who, in his servitude to RKO Radio Pictures in the late 1940s and early '50s, liked to call himself Howard Hughes's "horseshit salesman." From the 1940s through the '70s he was considered among the top choices for starring roles in all of the action genres—he turned down *The Defiant Ones, Gunfight at the O.K. Corral, The Misfits, Dirty Harry, The Long Goodbye, Atlantic City*, and films that eventually won best actor Academy Awards for Lee Marvin, Gene Hackman and George C. Scott: *Cat Ballou, The French Connection* and *Patton*, respectively.

Many critics over the years seemed to have a love-him or hate-him policy, until the '70s when *Out of the Past* and *The Night of the Hunter* were rediscovered and accorded with the mantle of cult status that *Thunder Road* had already accrued in a world far removed from film criticism, the boondocks of the Southern ozoner circuit. *Thunder Road*, the only film Mitchum conceived—he wrote the original story and also produced and starred—concerns a moonshiner, Luke Doolin, who eludes authorities, operates by night and gains a folk reputation while remaining true to himself and his chosen way of life. If that sounds a lot like Mitchum, it's certainly not coincidental.

In the '80s and '90s Mitchum shifted his career to mostly TV movies and miniseries with the same seemingly careless attitude that once prompted him to say that the only difference between him and other actors was that he had spent more time in jail. The general critical thrashing he got for what one reviewer called his "calcified" performance in *War and Remembrance* was like a return to the old days, when longtime film critic Bosley Crowther treated him like a slob on the pages of *The New York Times*.

In some cases, the press gave the "Big Bad Bob" label a ride and in others Mitchum provided grist for the mill with a right hook or umpteenth glass of hooch. He knocked out top-10 heavyweight prizefighter Bernie Reynolds in a 1951 tavern rumble in the Red Fox Bar of the Alamo Hotel in Colorado Springs, where he had gone to make *One Minute to Zero* (1952). He drove away from a Los Angeles police officer who tried to arrest him for speeding in 1953. He was fired off *Blood Alley* by Wellman in 1954 and *Rosebud* by Otto Preminger in 1974. He beat up five sailors in a Tobago bar in 1956. He hung a producer upside-down from a lamppost in 1959.

He told a Tokyo press conference to "remember Pearl Harbor" in 1975. He got rowdy at press sessions for *That Championship Season* (1982) and had to settle a lawsuit out of court and do a stint in the Betty Ford dry-out tank. He was accused of anti-Semitic remarks in *Esquire* in 1983. Mitchum may hold the Hollywood record for most front-page appearances in the *Los Angeles Times* for incidents that have nothing to do with performing for the cameras. Headlines in the *Times* and elsewhere over the years include "Mr. Bad Taste and Trouble Himself," "Hollywood Roughneck," "Pose With Starlet Puts Mitchum in Doghouse," "Mitchum Begins Behind-Bars Role," and "Roverboy Robert Mitchum." In 1954 *Photoplay* asked, "Why Can't Mitchum Behave Himself?"

His youngest son, actor and producer Christopher Mitchum, explained his father's worldview: "When you start with nothing and you prepare to end up with nothing, you have nothing to lose. And it gives you a basis to be true to yourself. And that's the way he is: he's true to himself."

In the final analysis, Robert Mitchum's assessment that he did *more* and not *better* doesn't fly. He did both in ample amounts. He was an actor of almost limitless range relying on his own perceptions and pragmatism to present us with signposts to truths to understand people.

Of all of the stars to have risen as outsider figures in Hollywood, no one of his magnitude was more fringe-dwelling. His skepticism kept him remarkably uncommitted and protected. His posture was to not give a shit. And that, wrote Roger Ebert, "inspires response." People are attracted to someone who doesn't appear to care. It helped keep Mitchum a star for much of the history of motion pictures. The mystique, the demonstrated talent and the renegade ethos made him attractive to filmmakers looking to anchor a picture with his sort of unflappable nonchalance.

Where many actors believe they are contributing to art, Mitchum always refused to acknowledge any real importance in acting, except that it supported his family. But this attitude ennabled him to come in clean and facile and without baggage for each role. Career? "If I agree and they send a check and a plane ticket, I show up," he maintained. Whether by design or not, this path preserved him as a cult figure rather than an ordained great on the order of many stars whose careers don't stack up to his— Kirk Douglas, for instance.

Mitchum will be an eternally unsung actor, but the record shows he belongs on the short list of the great movie stars as well as that of the great movie actors.

In 1989, Mitchum provided an impromptu summation of his career and talent: "I've got the same attitude I had when I started. I haven't changed anything but my underwear. I've played everything except midgets and women. People can't make up their minds whether I'm the greatest actor in the world—or the worst. Matter of fact, neither can I. It's been said that I underplay so much, I could have stayed home. But I must be good at my job. Or they wouldn't haul me around the world at these prices."

As usual, a sense of truth and deep sarcasm pervaded the answer. And as usual, he understated the case.

Robert Mitchum,
Los Angeles,
September 1948

Pursued, 1947, with Teresa Wright

Out of the Past, 1947, with Jane Greer and, below, with Kirk Douglas

Actor Held in Narcotics Raid on Eve of Youth Program Talk

**Robert Mitchum,
Lila Leeds and
Companions
Arrested**

From the
Los Angeles Examiner,
September 1, 1948

The Lusty Men, 1952, with director Nicholas Ray

Angel Face, 1952, with Jean Simmons

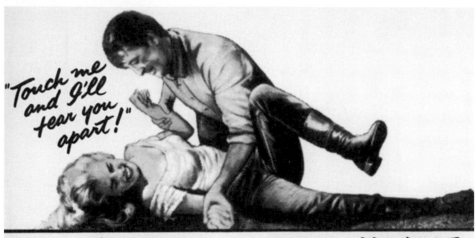

"Touch me and I'll tear you apart!"

Robert **MITCHUM** TAMES *Marilyn* **MONROE**

in 20th CENTURY-FOX'S **RIVER of NO RETURN**

Color by TECHNICOLOR

SIG. **CinemaScope** SIG.

in the Wonder of 4-TRACK, HIGH FIDELITY STEREOPHONIC SOUND

River of No Return, 1954

Night of the Hunter, 1955

Heaven Knows, Mr. Allison, 1957,
with Deborah Kerr

INTERVIEW WITH DAVID FROST

In 1970 after his return from Ireland, where he made *Ryan's Daughter*, Robert Mitchum agreed to be the sole guest for the entire 90 minutes of television's *The David Frost Show*. It was syndicated from flagship station WNET in New York to stations coast to coast that were affiliated with Group W Productions. Along with another 90 minutes he allotted ABC's *The Dick Cavett Show* two years later, it was his longest continuous nondramatic TV appearance. Much of the value in the talk comes from the actor's concentration on his life before acting.

DAVID FROST

David Frost is a British television personality and humorist who, after transferring the 1964 London success of *That Was the Week That Was* to NBC, joined Group W with the syndicated *The David Frost Show* in 1969. He made headlines in 1975 when he secured exclusive TV interviews with former President Richard M. Nixon, which aired in 1977. His books include *The Americans*; *David Frost, an Autobiography*; *David Frost's Book of Millionaires, Multimillionaires and Really Rich People*, and *I Gave Them a Sword: Behind the Scenes of the Nixon Interviews*.

David Frost: We're delighted to welcome for 90 minutes today Mr. Robert Mitchum. [music up, applause] Thank you. We welcome today the star of so many varied and great movies—everything from *Thirty Seconds Over Tokyo, His Kind of Woman, The Night of the Hunter, Heaven Knows, Mr. Allison, The Enemy Below, The Hunters, Home From the Hill, The Sundowners, Cape Fear, El Dorado* to now *Ryan's Daughter*. We welcome Mr. Robert Mitchum. [applause] As you can hear, everybody says welcome.

Robert Mitchum: It's a very neat audience—isn't it?

Frost: Very neat audience. Very good to have you with us, I must say. Reading about the lives of everyone who's been on this program, it sounds to me as though you've had perhaps the most interesting childhood of them all.

Mitchum: Had I read it, I might find it so.

Frost: Do you think it's true?

Mitchum: I don't know; I haven't read it. [audience laughter]

Frost: You've never read it?

Mitchum: No.

Frost: Go right back in to the beginning. What's the very first thing you can remember?

Mitchum: Birth.

Frost: Really?

Mitchum: Yes.

Frost: Do you really remember it?

Mitchum: Yeah. I remember the agonies of birth.

Frost: How did you manage to live through it?

Mitchum: I was encouraged by an elder sister and my mother, and a spanking doctor. They still had spanking doctors then. I was born in Bridgeport, Connecticut. And it disappeared and I went on.

Frost: Wonderful. When did you move south, in fact? When did the family moved to the South?

Mitchum: Well, actually we sort of vacillated between New England and Florida—as far south as Florida. My father is from South Carolina. And I went to high school here in New York. I went to Haaren High School, 10th Avenue and 59th Street. It was a finishing school to end all. [audience laughter] They had monitors on the door to keep you in. True.

Frost: Really?

Mitchum: Oh, yeah, because you'd flee at any given opportunity. I tried to transfer up to George Washington [High School]. And they wouldn't let me in because I was from Haaren High School. They said, "We've heard about those cats. No way." I had gone to school in Delaware. My family had lived in Florida and South Carolina, as I said. My father was from South Carolina. And I had gone to school in Philadelphia and Delaware, and in Connecticut. And finally there was just no way out [of Haaren], so I took off and I got as far as Savannah, Georgia. I was, I think, 15, and I wound up on the chain gang in Savannah.

Frost: How did that happen?

Mitchum: Very simple, really. They just reached out and grabbed me and put me on a chain gang.

Frost: You hadn't done anything particularly to annoy them?

Mitchum: I'm sure I had. I was charged with the common crime of poverty. I was a dangerous and suspicious character with no visible means of support, which is a common charge of vagrancy. You know, begging. I probably asked a kind lady for a crust of bread or something, and they whacked me out. And I didn't want them to put me on a punk farm, so I told them I was 19 and they put me on a real grown-up gang. And I stayed there until it got dull and I split.

Frost: Forgive me for not knowing—what's a punk farm?

Mitchum: A juvenile farm.

Frost: You didn't want that? That would have been boring?

Mitchum: No. I was an abraded 15, and I thought I'd fare better among the men, so I elected to do that and they agreed. And they accepted my version of my own age and gave me a little time to fatten me up on the Brown Farm. I got out of there and I came back to Delaware to heal up. That was in the fall. And the following April, I left and went to California, went out there on a freight train. It was a popular form of transportation in those days.

Frost: But how long were you actually on that chain gang, Bob?

Mitchum: No longer than it takes to tell. I wasn't there more than a week or two or three. But I really don't remember. It was a very short time. I mean, maybe as much as 30 days, but at any rate, I got out of it.

Frost: What did you actually have to do during that time?

Mitchum: Well, we built roads. I remember one day we were working on a road, clearing out a swamp, and a woman called the captain and she had a big pile of brush in the front yard. She asked if he could loan her a few of the convicts to come and clear out that brush because it was full of rattlesnakes underneath—and there are no days that you're going to go in and do that. But like that, we just worked on the road, cracking up things.

Frost: What sort of guys were the other guys on the chain gang? What had they done?

Mitchum: Charmers all. I suppose they were victims of their own circumstances. I really don't know. I remember one of the friendliest was a pusher, a trustee, a guy who kept getting busted for making whiskey. He was making whiskey illegally and they kept throwing him in—fellow named Polk. And there was my sort of guardian angel, who was a transferee from the state of Florida, and he was in for murder. And he just saw to it that nothing bad happened to me. He took care of me.

Frost: Your guardian angel.

Mitchum: Well, yeah. He taught me to sell bunks for a quarter apiece, because there was no place to sleep. The joint was overcrowded. And any time a tankful of fish would come in, I'd sell them a bed here, a bed there, for a quarter apiece. It wasn't my bed. So, they had to fight the guy that was in the bed. But meanwhile, I got the quarter—right?

Frost: And the guys who were in charge of you and in control of you—what do you remember of them?

Mitchum: There was my immediate sort of duty or detail captain—they called him Captain Friend. Actually his name was Freundt. But in Savannah, Georgia, it was "Friend." He used to sit there all day long with an old broken Panama and a 30-30 across his knees. He said [Southern drawl], "The reason y'all boys is here is 'cause y'all don't believe in God. Ya'll ain't got the Holy Spirit." He said, "You know, I rode with Teddy's boys up San Juan Hill down in Cuba. Messing around down there I got the gonorrhea in my eyes and went blind. And I dropped down on my knees and I prayed to God for my sight. You think I can't see, take off across that field." [audience laughter]

Frost: Were there any other characters like that who you remember from those days? Because that's absolutely fascinating.

Mitchum: Well, of course, I had very little else to do but study characters. I was sort of a traveling witness. I didn't have a trade and I didn't have a little box of tricks. I had nothing to sell. And I was principally concerned with keeping myself undetected and alive. And naturally, you know, you met characters everywhere. As I said, I made nine trips back and forth across the country on freight trains. And I thought, doesn't everyone? Right after I got off the chain gang, I had a little scar on my leg, because they had tied me up for a day or two and it got infected. There was a traffic cop on the street in Washington, [D.C.], and I said, "Look, I got a little trouble with my foot. Now, don't throw me in jail because I just got out of jail." He said, "Go on over there." He went into a Thompkins [sic] restaurant and he sat down with bowl of soup, then he took me to a hospital. And I lay there in the hospital after they had examined my foot and they were talking about amputating it, and I quietly got up and put my clothes on and split that joint. I went back to Delaware and my mother boiled my foot—you know, made a little broth out of it. And I was on crutches when I met my wife, and I didn't want to tell [her family] that I had hurt my leg on a chain gang, because I thought they'd look at me with some horror. So, I told them that I had hurt my leg jumping freight trains, because, I figured, everybody did that. Really, that was my scope. That following spring, I went to California. And I learned to catch them on the fly at 30 miles an hour, and to unload them, and I met a lot of characters. I think probably one of the most sinister cities in the country was Birmingham, Alabama. And that railroad yard in Birmingham was not to be believed. I came in there one time and there was a sort of blue-jawed Georgia boy who had "Wanted" written all over him. He had on a pair of bib overalls and a cap and [he was] a bad mother. Some cat chose him out of the corner of the boxcar at some stop, like Anniston,

Alabama. That two of them got out of the boxcar and the big rangy cat stuck up his hands like Marquis of Queensberry rules and the other cat whipped out a .38 blue steel pistol. He said, "Where's your pistol? I thought you wanted to fight." And he pistol-whipped him until the train left. I learned something then.

Frost: What did you learn then?

Mitchum: Well, I learned that if you come to fight, be ready to die, because that cat couldn't understand this child coming up with his fists. Anybody that's going to fight has got to have a pistol. It makes it all even. I liked him. He was kind of a romantic character. He kept his end of it up.

Frost: What sort of guys were riding the freight trains along with you?

Mitchum: Everyone. I met teachers, bankers—honestly. Not necessarily all losers, but people who were displaced largely by circumstance, the Depression. And it was not depressing. They were hopeful. They were strong, honestly. A lot of times there were so many bums running on the boxcars that the crews couldn't walk the tops. They would have to get off and walk the sides, because there was no room. A freight train would carry 300 or 400 of them.

Frost: You said they weren't all losers. At that time what were you thinking you'd do yourself? Was it already your ambition to be an actor, or did you think of yourself as a loser or potential winner at that point—or what?

Mitchum: Oh, no. I just felt that I wasn't quite ready. Obviously, I had no clear concept of myself. I didn't know if I had any potential. And all I wanted to do was eat enough to be strong enough to survive. I had no particular notion. I was an appreciator, largely. But not a very active participant.

Frost: Which came first, meeting your wife, whom you mentioned, or your first acting job?

Mitchum: Meeting my wife. I was 16 years old when I met her. She was 14.

Frost: Really?

Mitchum: Yes. They busted me right out of the county.

Frost: They what?

Mitchum: Nothing. [audience laughter] That's just an old Southern expression.

Frost: Where did you meet her?

Mitchum: I met her in Camden, Delaware, on a blind date in the back of a Model A Ford.

Frost: Where did you go on your blind date?

Mitchum: Just around, you know—round and around. Four-cylinder Ford, long on gas. Had to get her home by 10 or something. Just around. But she smelled all of that liniment on my foot and it attracted her. Kept telling her that she was making a wrong move, but you can't tell them.

Frost: It was going to be a long term—

Mitchum: Oh, I said then, "This is it. I can't get hung up and I don't want to fool around anymore. So this is it. You stay there. I'll be back." That's the way it was.

Frost: You were 16. You had done all your fooling around?

Mitchum: No, not right there. We had too much to do. "I don't want to digress and I don't want to run up any blind alleys and I don't want to dance and fool around. You stay there, I'll be back." And she was there. And I came back.

Frost: How long afterwards did you come back?

Mitchum: Well, I kept coming back. I kept jumping off freight trains. Every time I'd come back, they'd button up the town. They'd say, "God, here it comes again." And finally, it got to be kind of a public disgrace. I was 22 and in Florida and I went to some sort of charity affair where you sign a chit and I had a generous hostess. And I had $11 and I signed for one and I thought one was a penny, because it was the Penny Fair at the Four H Club in Palm Beach. Actually, I had signed up for $1,100. I didn't know that. I would have had to drown myself [if I lost]. Anyway, I won. I won $2,300 and there was a freeze in Florida and all the trains were booked. I got on a Greyhound bus in an ice cream suit and a Panama hat, and I fell on my nose in Philadelphia in four feet of snow, stoned. And I checked into the YMCA. I never lived there. I went and lived in this girls' dormitory where my [future] wife was staying. These broads walked by and looked at me sleeping on the couch, you know, [while there were] cats reaching through the window all the time. And that was it. So she said, "Look, you know you're footloose and you don't have too much direction, you don't have too much sense—but you can be valuable." Because I had worked and I had made money at it if I chose. And she said, "I think you ought to marry me." And I said, "I agree." I didn't know how to bring it up, you know. OK, so that was it. She was working for the Penn Mutual Life Insurance Company and she quit her job. And I blew the whole stash on all her friends. We went to Jersey because you couldn't get a belt in Philadelphia and I was a swinger, right?—in my ice cream suit in March. So, I blew the whole stash. We went down to Delaware and I borrowed $5 from the guy and we got married.

Frost: In Delaware.

Mitchum: Yes [Dover]. Ignatius Cooper, justice of the peace—at large, or something like that—esquire. They have a square system. It said, "Licenses, dogs, hunting, marriage: $2." Solid. And that was it. We got married in the kitchen in the odor of burnt cabbage.

Frost: Best $2 bargain you ever had?

Mitchum: I think so, yeah. I don't know what would have happened to me otherwise. Now that they had shut up the railroads, I had trouble—right?

Frost: How long have you been married?

Mitchum: About 30 years. [audience applause] Is that the magic number?

Frost: Yes, yes. You've just won two weeks free on a freight train. And what's made your marriage work and last where so many haven't?

Mitchum: Oh, I don't know. I don't know why so many haven't. I suppose with us it's a mutual forbearance, that's all. I think we have each continued to believe that the other will do better tomorrow.

Frost: That's a great slogan. We've got to the stage when you got married and so on. Is that when you headed back to California to search for fame and fortune and all that stuff?

Mitchum: No. I went back there because my mother had a house there [in Long Beach]. And I had been living out there more or less since I was 16.

Frost: Before you got your first acting part, what were the other jobs you did, Bob?

Mitchum: Oh, name it. I worked at Lockheed. I was a sheet metal worker. I boxed. I was a shoe salesman. I shipped out, I sailed.

Frost: How much boxing did you do—how many fights?

Mitchum: Enough to get hit. That discouraged me.

Frost: That's the thing I never really understood about boxing, the way the average boxer just takes blows that would knock other people down.

Mitchum: I knew too many really good fighters. My brother [John Mitchum, who became a character actor, most notably as Clint Eastwood's partner in the *Dirty Harry* movies.] actually was the family boxer. I just wanted to stay out of the way, that's all.

Frost: Did you see boxers who were really damaged by boxing?

Mitchum: Oh, yes. I've known lots of boxers who have been damaged permanently, but I continued. You know, the repetition of blows is like a coagulation system, so that everything stops for a time and it eventually deadens whole areas of the brain. And I don't say that I'm immune to it. I get a little goosy myself now and then.

Frost: You did enough boxing? You're glad you stopped?

Mitchum: Just enough to convince me that I was a lover. And there was no market for that.

Frost: When did you decide you'd have a go at acting?

Mitchum: Well, my wife was pregnant and I needed $500 and I was probably a better deterrent to the American war effort than Tojo [Japanese prime minister during World War II], because I was working at Lockheed gluing airplanes together inexpertly. And I felt very badly about that, because they were instruments of death. Not only that, but the plane was obsolete. And they had a big contract for the airplanes we were building. They had a contract with the British, and Britain really was sort of on its knees, in a very difficult position. To what would appear to be a dying nation, we were selling obsolete airplanes. And guys that would fly them across the channel had a big slogan: "You couldn't knock them down." Well, they couldn't do much, very inefficient. But that's all the British had. And I didn't believe in that at all. Finally one night I threw a clamp across the room and hit the foreman on the head.

Frost: Did he object?

Mitchum: No, I got a medical discharge from Lockheed. They said, "Why did you hit him?" I said, "You won't understand." There was a girl typing up the thing. She said, "I understand. I very well understood it." And she said, "Why don't you do what you can do?" So actually, in a fit of sort of embarrassed desperation, I became a movie actress. So I went out and tossed my golden locks. I had hair down to my hips, you know, just as an economy measure. And I borrowed a suit from a working actor. And I went over and saw [producer Harry] "Pop" Sherman and a guy named Dick Dixon and Bill Boyd in the Hopalong Cassidy series. And they said, "Yeah, he looks a little crafty around the eyes. Yeah, he looks a little ugly, a little mean." So, I thought I was going to be the handsome—the juvenile. They said, "Don't shave and don't cut your hair until you hear from us." So, I went out and got $100 a week and all the horse manure I could carry home. And I got thrown off every horse—I mean, flat, bam, gone. But I made it, you know—a lot of beard, very little dialogue. And I just kept right on going, never looked back.

Frost: "A lot of beard, very little dialogue." What year would that be about?

Mitchum: June 1942.

Frost: And from there you branched out into . . .

Mitchum: I just never looked back. When the decision came, I figured, well, I couldn't, you know, wax somebody out in an alley. If I robbed a bank, they'd know me. They'd say, "Hey," because I didn't venture too far from my own neighborhood. I figured if

I went in and tapped a bank, they'd say, "Hey, Bob, somebody will follow you home." So I figured the next closest thing was to become just a public nuisance. So I became a movie actress.

Frost: Why do you always say "movie actress"?

Mitchum: What's the difference? [audience laughter] I never looked back. In I figured if Rin Tin Tin could make it, I was a cinch.

Frost: And so it proved. There were war films—*Thirty Seconds Over Tokyo* and *The Story of G.I. Joe.*

Mitchum: Well, at that time, anybody who was not in the Army, they just threw in a picture. I came at a very fortunate time. It was the era of the ugly leading man. They had done with all of those sort of flashy waitressy types and here I came, all broken up. I was the first in line.

Frost: And after *The Story of G.I. Joe*, you got jobs?

Mitchum: During, as a matter of fact. I was a big movie star at $30 a month. But, you know, it was OK.

Frost: And didn't you go to war?

Mitchell: No, I was a rectal inspector.

Frost: I know I shouldn't, but . . .

Mitchum: I was in the infantry, and the infantry didn't really have time for me, because they didn't need any more heroes. But at any rate, I went down to Fort MacArthur [San Pedro, Calif.] to be discharged. And I ran afoul of a colonel down there who was in the medical department. I used to have to take guys out on the field because the general down there decreed all the ingoing or outgoing personnel on the post should have close-order drill, they should be daily drilled. So they sent me to drill officers. So I go in the BOQ—the bachelor officers' quarters—and I said, "Who's in charge?" And a guy would say, "Me," or they point to somebody. And I say, "You've just completed two hours of close order drill on a hot, dusty parade ground—sign here." So, this one cat says, "Is that the way you execute your orders, soldier?" And I said, "Every chance I get, sir." And he racked me up about it. I said, "Fine—if the colonel cares to march . . ." So, I took them out. These are a bunch of doctors and they're falling all over each other, and they march, you know—I turn on them, give them about four hours. The next morning I had to fall out at, like, 4:30 or 5 o'clock in the morning and reported to this cat and he kept me at attention all the time. He said, "How would you like to be an assistant to the chief orthopedic examining surgeon?" And I said, "I can't stand the sight of blood, sir." He said, "I doubt you'll see very much blood." [audience laughter]

He said, "Anybody with a pair of lungs and copy of the Field Manual can drill field soldiers." He said, "Your talents are being wasted in the Army." Anyway, I had to report to the Kentucky captain-doctor, and from that date forward—up to 900 people a day—I said, "Turn around, bend over, spread your cheeks." I said, "Ah-oh, you still got your 1942 license plates," and I would do accents . . . Russian accent, Japanese. And they'd go up and complain. And they'd say, "There's a maniac down there who's peeking up people," you know. [audience laughter]

I finally wrote my own discharge. I'll tell you about that if anybody is interested. I wrote it, stamped it, everything—the fastest discharge on record, 11 minutes. Right? Hardship case. So, everybody else is trying to get out, too. They say, "How do you do it?" And I'm not going to tell right then, because all those doctors are trying to get out. So, anyway, I finally created enough nuisance so they were willing to let me go.

Frost: They were willing to let you go, but you still had to discharge yourself?

Mitchum: They found me very amusing, I guess. They kept trying to commission me. They were going to send me to Fort Benning, Georgia. Did you ever see a fat second lieutenant in the infantry? No way. No mother way. Before his first meal, the bum is dead. There's no way.

Frost: So, you discharged yourself out in 11 minutes flat?

Mitchum: Exactly. I had a suit hanging in the locker room, and a bottle of Scotch and I was out. And I was under contract to RKO. I mean, it was kind of in abeyance, because I was under contract when I went in the Army. And by the time I sobered up, I was in a Marine uniform and I'm down at Five Points [near Albuquerque] in the Marine Corps and I'm in a picture. And I don't know where I am, really—flat don't know where I'm at. And a guy is going [snaps fingers], "Take 17." And the next guy to me said, "If you quit fooling around, those numbers wouldn't get so high." I didn't know where I was. I thought I was in combat somewhere. I put on that suit, grabbed that Scotch bottle, Jack, and the next thing I knew, I was on salary.

Frost: Do you remember the name of the film?

Mitchum: *Till the End of Time.*

Frost: Bob, you've made several very successful pictures with Deborah Kerr. And we've got scenes from two of them—two rather different bedroom scenes, one from *Heaven Knows, Mr. Allison* and the other from *The Sundowners*. I don't think you've seen this.

Mitchum: Identical performances.

Frost: Identical performances?

Mitchum: I'm sure.

Frost: Well, let's take a look at the first, coming up right now, from *Heaven Knows, Mr. Allison*. [film clip] Do you enjoy seeing old films of yours?

Mitchum: I rarely do.

Frost: What do you think when you're watching yourself, for instance, when you were watching then?

Mitchum: I remember the experience.

Frost: What was the experience?

Mitchum: I was down at Tobago, which is very pleasant, with Deborah, with Johnny Huston. And I enjoyed it—a pleasant and rewarding experience. I was in England, as a matter of fact, when a guy came up to me and said, "My name is Ozzie Morris." And I said, "Hello." And he said, "Do you suppose that we could run some tests Saturday." I said, "I guess so." I didn't know what he wanted—Wassermann tests, what?—I didn't know what the hell. So I said, "Yes, I guess. As far as I'm concerned, go ahead on." He said, "No, no, with you." I said,

"What do you mean?" He said, "We'd like to do some camera tests and wardrobe tests, and that sort of thing." For what? He said, "I'm John's cameraman." I said, "John who?" He said, "John Huston." I said, "Well, good luck." I still didn't know. He said, "You know nothing about this?" I said, "No, I don't." So, anyway, Saturday came and they put me in a couple of uniforms. Meanwhile, I guess somebody had sold me to Twentieth Century-Fox, but they had neglected to tell me. So they had a company sitting down there at Tobago, Trinidad and Tobago. The whole company sitting there, waiting—John, Deborah, etal. But nobody had told me about it. And I said, "Do you mind, really?—I'd like to at least be asked, not shoved down the line." I suppose the agent said, "Forget it, I'll deliver him." But it wasn't like that. I said, "I'd like to have a signed contract before I leave." They said, "Oh, you'll get it." And it usually shows up, like, 30 days after the picture is finished. I said, "No more days like that."

I signed a contract at the airport. Once I got to Trinidad, I discovered I had also signed away my house, my everything else, which we straightened out. But they were sitting down there waiting. And I came in in a very odd circumstance, because no one had told me about it. I got a long cable from my agent. I had an agent then. And he was in Haifa, Tel Aviv, and he sent me a long, detailed, "on-the-other-hand" cable, like David Selznick used to dictate, you know, say, "Maybe . . . well . . . um-m-m . . . in any case, well, on the other hand," like that. This all goes into the cable—these interruptions and hesitations. And he never ceased to tell me that the cable had cost him something like $430. Well, that had nothing to do with me at all.

But anyway, I went down there and made the film and I enjoyed it very much, because one of the few things that John ever said to me, one time—the first time I was in a scene—he had said, "How is it, kid? How is that? How is it for you?" I said, "It's OK with me, John—if something didn't fall down or the light didn't break, it's all right with me." I said, "Look, wait a minute. I just got off this island," because I had just

made a picture there with Rita Hayworth [*Fire Down Below*].
I said, "I had just got off this island and I'm anxious to get off
it again. You know, I'm not hung up. If you like it, print it. You
know, you're the boss. What the hell . . ." And everybody
froze, because, you know, they were all the subjects of the great
John Huston. And John said, "Swell, kid, swell." And the only
other time he said anything to me was in a scene after the
bombing. I looked over at him and he said, "Even more, kid, I
think even more." And I said, "Really, John?" He said, "Yes,
kid, I think even more. You can do it more." And that's the
only time he spoke. It was marvelous. And Deborah and I have
such rapport that they could put the camera in Hong Kong and
she can be in Switzerland and I am here and we can phone it
in. [audience laughter]

Frost: Let's take another look at that rapport in *The
Sundowners* . . .

Mitchum: Yes, she's beautiful in that. [film clip] [applause]

Frost: Where was that shot?

Mitchum: Australia and England. We worked in Australia mostly.

Frost: Those are two very different scenes with Deborah.

Mitchum: Identical performances, right? [audience laughter]

Frost: By Robert Mitchum?

Mitchum: Yes, the same thing.

Frost: Do you do the same performance all the while?

Mitchum: All the time. Change costumes. [audience laughter]

Frost: How would you describe the regular, identical performances
you give?

Mitchum: Well, you show up about eight o'clock and get on the
set at about nine. They say, "Face in that direction—say this."
And clock out at six.

Frost: Sounds relaxed.

Mitchum: Mmm.

Frost: How would you describe the characters you usually play?
What should one look for in the classic Mitchum character?

Mitchum: The wardrobe. [laughter] [applause] It's key to the
piece, isn't it?

Frost: Yes, yes, it is, isn't it? What's the wardrobe you wear in your newest and latest, David Lean's *Ryan's Daughter*?

Mitchum: It would be quite acceptable right now. It's like six-button coats, which I tried to get [costume designer] Jocelyn Rickards to bring over here, because I need them and I can't stand still for those fitters. And I had a pair of shoes, hobnail boots. They were mismatched. One was two sizes too small and the other was two sizes too large. And David said, "Would you walk like a farmer, like a man accustomed to walking over soil?" And I said, "Well, I am a farmer, David." [In the decade prior to the film, Mitchum lived primarily on a Maryland farm.] What the hell . . . We had a little difficulty because I speak American; David speaks English. I understand English but he doesn't understand American, unfortunately.

Frost: Oh, that's bad.

Mitchum: Well, it's not serious. I'm adjusted to it, but he never really got adjusted to the differences.

Frost: We've got some pictures of you in the movie. There's one of Robert Mitchum in action. [on-screen stills]

Mitchum: There you are. There's the wardrobe.

Frost: Classical performance with the wardrobe. How long did you spend in Ireland on the picture?

Mitchum: I was there, from, I think, the 10th of February or the 17th of February until early November, it seems to me, although Trevor Howard told me that I abandoned them all in October, which may be true. I think it was about nine months.

Frost: And I gather while you were there in Ireland you met that magnificent specimen of the Irish courage, who was here with us, Christy Brown. [Brown is the famed Irish author who was born with cerebral palsy and, 19 years after this interview, was portrayed in an Academy Award-winning performance by Daniel Day-Lewis in the adaptation of Brown's *My Left Foot*.]

Mitchum: Yes, yes. Our company solicitor is a man named Joe Grace, who is from Wexford. And Joe practices law out of Tralee and is a marvelous man, a very eloquent fellow. In the heat, we went out and had a few jars, you know. And I have some friends who are paraplegics and have no use with their legs. And one of them is a big cat, 245 pounds, and I have to wheel him around in a wheelchair. And he's very delicate around the lower back, around the coccyx, because if he snaps again, then he's really had it. So, at the same time, you can't be too delicate in a wheelchair, because it's a matter of balancing, like a furniture mover. So Christy found out that I was at least acquainted with movement, with handling people in wheelchairs, so he felt confident. And we were both drunk, let's face it, with all those Irishmen going from pub to pub. So Joe said, "Your man, Christy, he's written a book." So I thought, what sort of a book?—cat sitting here stoned, all twisted up. And I thought something by a child in crayon, as dim as I am. And it dawned on me that he was a very inquisitive and assimilative man. And I said, "You mean to tell me—all through your life— that people have propped you up against the wall like a piece of furniture, and that they say, 'Ah, go on, give old Christy a drink, giving him a jar,' and they just talked in front of you, because they thought you were not receptive?" "Yeah," he said. "Yeah, man."

Frost: It was one of the most . . .

Mitchum: Very juicy.

Frost: . . . inspiring programs I've ever done.

Mitchum: His eye and his ear are so beautiful. I could communicate with him. He didn't have to talk. I could talk with him, you know. A beautiful man.

Frost: He came on here and he talked, and he was such a lesson to everybody, because at one point I was asking him what he had learned, really, in life. And he said . . .

Mitchum: He couldn't care less.

Frost: Well, he also said that he learned to live life to the full, and when a guy like him can say that, it's just inspiring.

Mitchum: Well—what else? He's not hanging on. He's got no fingernails to hang on with. There he is. He's got to do the best he can. His way. Marvelous. I really find him to be a very rewarding, enormously rewarding, human being.

Frost: Very much.

Mitchum: I think people should take heart from people like that. I was amazed by his ear when I finally read his book. I was just humbled by his talent. Truly.

Frost : It's a remarkable talent. You came back to Hollywood after the war, and then very soon—what?—in 1948, you got into trouble years ahead of your time, didn't you? You got into trouble for smoking pot.

Mitchum: No, I didn't. I was convicted of conspiring to possess. [audience titters] I don't know what it means. I was in that house for seven minutes. They broke the door down, and I figured I'd go quietly. Not like I was a virgin. It was trip number 11 for me—various infractions of the statutes—walking against the lines, stepping on the grass, sassing the cops—jazz like that. But they had had the house bugged for five months, and they had a cast of characters that they wanted to drag across the stage, and I didn't think it was worth it. And I said, "I'll do six months on this ear. Any more than that, I'll be quarrelsome about it." And that was it. I was convicted of a felony, count of conspiracy, and submitted without defense on transcript. And after all the heat died down, I resubmitted on transcript, and it was wiped out. Nobody cared about that, you know, that I was innocent.

Frost: It was wiped out?

Mitchum: Of course, yeah. No evidence. I got dumped, like they say. [Los Angeles Superior Court Judge Clement D. Nye entered a "not guilty" plea in place of Mitchum's earlier plea of "nolo contendere" on January 31, 1949, and expunged the case from the records.]

Frost: But I mean you were "conspiring to possess." Which means what? That you weren't smoking pot?

Mitchum: I don't know what it means. I was convicted of conspiracy.

Frost: How long were you in jail?

Mitchum: I think I got 60 days on the condition that I get sentenced to six months. It was like Palm Springs without the riffraff. [audience laughter]

Frost: Did you meet some more characters?

Mitchum: Yeah, a few. That's the place to meet them—isn't it? The bucket?

Frost: Can you remember any that you met at that time?

Mitchum: Suddenly, I was sort of a cause célèbre, and I couldn't understand that at all. All the cats said, "Are you joking, man? They pay you nine billion dollars a minute, and now you've topped out, and then you don't know why?!" I didn't know, I really didn't know. So, I got letters from chicks in Colorado, age 14, and say, "I live with my ugly uncle and he beats me, and I got nowhere to go." So, all the pimps used to grab those letters and figure, "Well, I'll be out later and check up on that." And so I met those, all the pimps. They tried to rack me up while I was in the joint, and they had a few movers in there. Guys would come in and say, "Hi!," you know, like a radio emcee . . . [audience laughter] They'd come and say, "I'm here for a non-support," I mean, something easy. And they tried to rack me over. And I just said, "No." I eventually said, "Take me out of the clean fresh air [Wayside Honor Farm, near Castaic, California] and put me back in the tank, man." I can see them coming. So they put me back in the joint.

Frost: Did that affect your career when you came out?

Mitchum: Oh, enormously, yeah. I got out and went back to work. Make it easy on yourself, you know. The only thing is, I had to resign from the local scout troop, and stuff like that. [audience laughter]

Frost: In the 1950s you had some celebrated run-ins with, among other things, *Confidential* magazine, wasn't it? You won a great action against them, didn't you?

Mitchum: They were sort of running unbridled. And they published a story concerning me which was totally unfounded, had absolutely no basis in fact at all. And we sued them—we got passed an act of Congress to deprive them of mailing privileges. But they were disenfranchised from using the mails, because there is no such thing, obviously or apparently, as a libel law in this country. And when I brought the case before the attorneys, they said, "You know, it's going to cost you money." I said, "Well, somebody's got to do it." So I did it. Because otherwise, they'd be feeding on people and blackmailing people.

Frost: What did they say? Did they say anything about you that looking back on it amuses you?

Mitchum: No. It was dull and really unimaginative. And it was untrue. Was totally untrue. [The May 3, 1955, edition of *Confidential* printed a story under Charles Johnson's byline that Mitchum crashed a party thrown by Charles Laughton in Santa Monica, California, stripped nude, splattered himself with catsup and announced he was a hamburger.]

Frost: So, you won that one?

Mitchum: I didn't win anything. The people won it, and I instrumented it. I financed it and I processed the suit. But I did it in the public interest, truly, because, after all, once it'd been published, it's just like the other case, the exoneration means nothing. It's only the press, you know, that means something. And say, we squashed that mother, Paul Walker. Put him down. When he gets back up again, that's not news. So, I figured if it could happen to me, it could happen to people who are probably less prepared to fight against it. So, I just fought in that order, that's all.

Frost: You've done so many surprising and different things in your career. One of the things you did, of course, in addition to all of the acting, was the singing as well, with that record that was a tremendous hit, "Little Old Wine Drinker Me."

Mitchum: That was kind of a joke. I was a lyric arranger and music arranger, and I picked up a tune that I had just overheard on the radio. I was going to take it up to Dean Martin, and Dean was out of town. So, they said, "Why don't you do it?" And suddenly I found myself in Nashville, Tennessee, doing, like, 12 songs that I'd never heard of. It was, again, a gig. And so, finally, I think a year or so later, I was going to Mexico, and these guys all showed up from Nashville, and they say, "Well, we're ready." I say, "You're ready for what?" They said, "We're ready to put out another one." I said, "What are you talking about?" They said, "Man, that record went all over the world." I said, "But we did that." They said, "But, man, that made a lot of [money]." And I just left them standing there. I didn't go there to challenge Sinatra.

Frost: Frank Sinatra once said that you're the most musical man who doesn't do music full-time that he's ever met. Do you remember "Little Old Wine Drinker Me"? Do you remember it now?

Mitchum: No. [audience laughter]

Frost: Don't you? If we were to say we might be able to find the music, do you think you might remember it?

Mitchum: It's a burden. [applause]

Frost: Would you like to do it for us?

Mitchum: It's on your head.

Frost: All right. [piano]

Mitchum: You're going to have to come on a lot stronger than that with the music. [louder piano] [singing]:

I'm praying for rain in California.
So the grapes can grow and they can make more wine.
And I'm sitting in a honky in Chicago
With a broken heart and a woman on my mind.
I ask the man
Behind the bar
For the jukebox;
And the music
Takes me back to Tennessee.
And when they ask, "Who's the fool
In the corner?"
Crying, I see.
Little old wine drinker me.
[applause]

Frost: Great! And I'm sure we'd like to say that—right on the spur of the moment—that performance—congratulations! That was really . . .

Mitchum: Thank you.

Frost: Don't you agree? [applause]

Mitchum: I disagree.

Frost: Modesty will get you nowhere, actually. You've done so many surprising things. I read, when you were younger you read poetry, didn't you? You once quoted some poetry you wrote when you were 15.

Mitchum: I once quoted?

Frost: You once quoted a poem—you quoted the poem in 1964, and you said, "Oh yes, I was Bridgeport's resident poet. Or whatever. You wrote it on a postcard to your mother when you were 15. And it said,

> Trouble lies in sullen pools along the road I've taken
> Sightless windows stare the empty street
> No love beckons me save that which I've forsaken
> The anguish of my solitude is sweet.

Do you remember that?

Mitchum: Yeah.

Frost: Good.

Mitchum: I mailed that from the chain gang on a penny postcard to my mother.

Frost: Did you really?

Mitchum: Yes, I didn't get it for years and years later. They never sent it.

Frost: Did you write many poems?

Mitchum: I am sure I did. You can find them in the men's rooms in filling stations all over the country. [audience laughter]

Frost: And do you still write them? In those places? And others?

Mitchum: Yes, in those places. More objectively.

Frost: Let's take a look at another scene from your magnificent career. *Home From the Hill* coming up. [film clip] [applause]

Frost: That was a scene from *Home From the Hill* with you very much as the father there. What sort of father are you yourself, do you think? Have you been a disciplinarian?

Mitchum: No, hardly. I'm sort of an absentee father. [Like] my father [Mitchum's father was killed between coupling box-cars in a 1919 accident at Charleston, South Carolina]. Truly, I don't . . .

Frost: Are there rules about being a good father, do you think?

Mitchum: Oh, I should think so, yes. I do subscribe to them, morally, but, unfortunately, I don't fulfill them.

Frost: How often have you done movies with that magnificent father figure to us all—how often have you done movies with John Wayne?

Mitchum: Just one.

Frost: Is that just the one? *El Dorado?* [Two, actually, as the two actors were the main stars of *The Longest Day*, but had no scenes together.]

Frost: And we've got a scene and from it right now, a very brief glimpse of *El Dorado*, with John Wayne and Robert Mitchum. [film clip] [applause] Robert, as you look over your life, so far, is there anything, if you—in the words of the old phrase—had your time over again, is there anything you'd change?

Mitchum: I don't think I'm qualified to answer that. I mean, the results speak for themselves, the mistakes and the stubbed toes and the scars. You know, everything just works out. I've been enormously helped. I continually renew my faith in people, truly. I've found that's my best bet. Oh, yeah, I've tried it with trees and trucks and everything, but people come out best. They're the best kissers, anyway. [audience laughter] Right? I don't think I should be prepared by any step-by-step process. I've found that the abuse of communications has been detrimental. I think most of my follies have been largely laid to the telephone, which I regard as an instrument of the devil. But, because I say, "Yeah, un-hunh, OK, fine, yeah . . ." Anything. I'll say anything and hang up the phone. I'll go for anything, just to get away. But honestly, I think it gets better all the time. As we all do, I regard myself as an instrument in the betterment.

Frost: Well, whatever your suspicions of the telephone, stick with television anyway. You've given us a terrific 90 minutes.

Mitchum: You're very kind.

Frost: Bob Mitchum, thank you very much indeed.

[applause]

[music]

INTERVIEW WITH RICHARD SCHICKEL

Recorded before a live audience of mostly students at Columbia University in New York, this installment of *Sound on Film*, a series of interviews with movie-making personalities, was released in April 1971, when *Ryan's Daughter* was still in wide release. *Sound on Film* was produced by Erwin Frankel Productions in association with Columbia University Radio and syndicated nationally to college and university AM and FM stations. In this talk, Mitchum contemplates fame, directors and his take on the process of acting.

RICHARD SCHICKEL

Richard Schickel has been film critic of *Time* magazine since 1972 and was film critic of *Life* from 1965 until 1972. He is the author of books on Douglas Fairbanks Sr., Marlon Brando, Cary Grant, James Cagney, Clint Eastwood and other film figures. Schickel has held a Guggenheim Fellowship, has lectured on art history and is a writer-director of television documentaries. His books include *Matinee Idylls: Reflections on the Movies; The Disney Version; Intimate Strangers: The Culture of Celebrity; The Men Who Made the Movies; D.W. Griffith: An American Life; His Picture in the Papers*, and *Schickel on Film*.

Announcer: *The Story of G.I. Joe . . . The Night of the Hunter . . . Thirty Seconds Over Tokyo . . . Till the End of Time . . . Heaven Knows, Mr. Allison . . . The Sundowners . . . Thunder Road . . . Not as a Stranger . . . Cape Fear . . . Two for the Seesaw . . .* The list seems endless—the list of screen credits for one of Hollywood's most durable motion picture personalities, who has played leading roles in more than 60 movies and personifies an image that is tough, virile, indifferent, casual—always casual. His film career began when he played a villain in a

Hopalong Cassidy western. That was in the early 1940s. Now, in the early 1970s, his background, training and experience have been brought together to cast him in a role considered by many to be against type—as the gentle, diffident school-teacher in David Lean's newest film, *Ryan's Daughter*. During this coming hour we focus on the man and his past—in this radio visit with Robert Mitchum. [music] This is *Sound on Film*, another in a series of broadcasts on films and the people who make them. Today, *Sound on Film* program No. 14, "Mitchum: Reflections," with the veteran Hollywood star of *Ryan's Daughter*, looks back on his enduring screen career, in a talk with *Life* movie reviewer Richard Schickel. In addition to his weekly column in *Life*, Mr. Schickel is the author of the highly acclaimed *The Disney Version* and a contributor to *Harper's*, *The New York Times Magazine*, *Commentary* and other publications. He has also written *The Movie Crazy Years*, currently on view as part of National Education Television's series on the 1930s.

Schickel: Well, Robert Mitchum, you're out doing something you very rarely do, which is plugging a picture. You said before we went on the air that you didn't quite know why you were doing it. But I did read somewhere that maybe you kind of like the picture.

Mitchum: I haven't seen the picture—but it augurs well, I think, based on the personnel involved in it and in the preparation of it and the general execution. It speaks or at least suggests an ex-cellence in it. I just hope it's as good as I feel it is.

Schickel: The reputation of David Lean is as a very meticulous craftsman. Is that true? Is he a very careful and slow shooter?

Mitchum: It's rather difficult to explain because I'm sure that David has a notion—he has a vision—of each scene or each se-quence. And he is, I'm sure, totally convinced that no one else has. He finds it very difficult to accept anyone else's devotion or anyone else's interest as his own. Because, in effect, you start a picture with David, take a deep breath, and you don't exhale for a year—until it's all over. No laughter is permitted, no levity, oh no. It's all holy writ. Actually, David, in his grouping, is great. He has a great visual sense and he's an enormously sensitive man. Again, I say, it's rather difficult to explain or to judge. Of course, he is meticulous. You watch him behind the camera and he picks up a paint brush, or he suggests a shading on a door, odd things like that.

Schickel: Would you say his sensibility is primarily a visual sensibility? I once talked with Fred Zinnemann. He tries to find what he calls a visual nucleus to the film. Famous were those train tracks in *High Noon*—cut to the clock—and so forth. Do you think that Lean is that way primarily—a visual sort of person— or do you think he is attracted to literary ideas?

Mitchum: Not necessarily literary ideas. But [a movie] is really, intrinsically, a motion picture, a moving picture. It's very easy to run out of patience with David. We would stand for, literally, weeks on the beach waiting—four miles from the bathroom— waiting for sea gulls.

Schickel: Waiting for exactly the right kind of cloud formations?

Mitchum: Exactly. For right cloud formations and for sea gulls. And we had two prop men out there tossing dead fish to the sea gulls, baiting them in. They'd bait them in and then it appeared that we had sea gulls in the interior shots. Finally, David went about eight reels—and he came up screaming [Lean imitation], "It's like a bloody aviary! There's nothing but bloody sea gulls." There were too many sea gulls. [laughter] He comes to work in the morning, he begins a scene with—I think—really no preconceptions, or at least no established or announced concept.

Shickel: Is that so? Because the film looks so carefully . . .

Mitchum: But, you see, first he shoots the picture. Then he takes a look at it. Then he shoots again. And then he takes a look at that. And then he finally shoots it. So, it's a bit expensive.

Schickel: This is not necessarily a high-budget picture, is it? It's a relatively small canvas for Lean, at any rate.

Mitchum: Yeah. But this was "the little film" that David had always wanted to do. He said, "I want to do a little, quiet love story in Ireland." And this is it.

Schickel: It's now cost how many millions?

Mitchum: About $12 million, $13 million. If we had shot in a phone booth, we'd have 400 people in attendance. We just dragged this whole, ridiculous circus around with us everywhere we went. By the time I left I think we had demolished something like 35 vehicles. We could have shot *Gone With the Wind* on the transportation budget alone. [laughter]

Schickel: For an actor, isn't this rather difficult? Actors have told me that one of the biggest problems with movie—especially location—shootings is keeping your energy up. You know, with these long delays. And keeping your attention focused. Is that a problem for you or not?

Mitchum: I don't know. I suppose the result speaks for that. David just doesn't countenance that at all. He doesn't recognize that.

Schickel: You just better be there . . .

Mitchum: Yes, and ready. For instance, we're on the beach and we have a wind machine blowing a salt gale at you about 75 miles an hour, and he wants you to register anxiety or anguish. Nothing you can do. If you gap your mouth open, you're blown up. [laughter] Come out your ears. And your eyes are closed, because they're full of salt water and sand. Of course, he's behind the camera. He doesn't feel that. He doesn't understand what your problem is. Somebody asked me about getting on with David. I have great respect for him and I like him. And of course, your reward is in pleasing the director, really. And I guess he was pleased. I demonstrated at least some efficiency. I think it would really canker him if I did it in one take because . . .

Schickel: It would go against his whole grain.

Mitchum: Exactly. Because he didn't have time to indoctrinate, to instill, his own vision.

Schickel: He has said, in the press, that he thinks it's your finest performance. And he has, after all, seen it. Does he give you line readings?

Mitchum: No, not at all. No. He said very little to me. He directs rather through scorn. He directs by contempt. [laughter] First of all, I'm an American. Then, when I arrived, he said, "I didn't know you were so large." I said, "Well, I'm not really." I kind of hunkered down and he padded everybody else up. Basically, our problem was that he speaks English, and I speak American. And I understand English, but he doesn't understand American. I started off with a pair of boots that were varying sizes—one was two sizes smaller than the other—and it was too small. And the other one was too large and the larger one had two nails in it. I couldn't get them off. They were just nailed to my foot. And I'd say, "You know, it alters my gait." And David would say, "What's he *on* about?" I said, "These bloody boots. I can't walk." "What's he talking about?" He never did understand. Finally, after about five months, the wardrobe master, Johnny Briggs, said, "I don't know if you know it or not, Mr. Mitchum, but you have been wearing the wrong size boots since this film began." I said, "Do *I* know?" And the dresser, Jack Gallaher, said, "Well, of course, his feet do bleed sometimes, but we take them off when we get the opportunity. Between takes, we take them off. Of course, sometimes his feet are bleeding." And David never understood what my problem was. Like I was speaking Polish to him.

Schickel: So, some of the anguish you get into your role is due, at least in part, to small boots. [laughter] You have in the past often expressed a degree of contempt for some of the films you've been in. Which is a contempt, I think, some of us don't entirely share. Are there films, in fact, other than this one, which you look back on with a certain fondness?

Mitchum: Oh, sure. Many of them. I suppose I hold the same feeling that David does—anyone in any business—that the attempt warrants at least a total aspiration. I think that a motion picture should be as good as it possibly can. I do think that there's too much wasted. When you talk about contempt for past efforts—not really. I just regarded a lot of them as wastes of time. And I think that's a public cheat. I don't believe in that. When I was under contract to RKO, and they would come up with one picture after another, I just wore the same suit all the time, kept the same dialogue. They just changed leading ladies, that's all. And I said, "Look, people pay $1.40"—or whatever it was at the time—"for a key to the closet. They open the closet and the horse manure falls out. And faithfully they return, and the same thing happens. Finally, they're defeated and they no longer buy the key." I said, "What happens then?" They said, "Well, then we get a new boy. Figure, by that time you're smarter and you've gone on. Then we get a new boy. We've got an awful lot of the horse manure to sell." I understand it— their plight—and their rather pragmatic approach to it. But I think it's demeaning, and I never felt that I should be party to a public cheat. That's all.

Schickel: In this picture, Lean has also said that he felt that he cast you against type, in the sense that you play, I gather, a rather shy and diffident character. It doesn't seem to me, in fact, entirely against type. I'm not sure you're diffident, but you have some reputation for being relatively shy.

Mitchum: I guess he meant as opposed to what was considered a popular image—which I've never been able to pin down or to identify. I haven't been able to analyze any popular image. But, I guess he felt that—and I am sure he is right. I don't know that the casting was David's idea, or if it was [screenwriter] Robert Bolt's or Sarah's [Miles, Bolt's then wife]. I'm sure that they fought it out bitterly.

Schickel: Is it true that you turned the picture down when it was first offered to you?

Mitchum: Yes.

Schickel: Why did you do that?

Mitchum: Well, I would have turned down anything. I had just had it—lost all taste for it. I found myself doing something like five pictures in a row. I don't even know what I was doing in them. I mean, they were not really worthwhile. Somebody would come up and nudge me in the ribs and say, "Wanna hear the deal?" I'd say, "No, I don't wanna hear the deal; I couldn't care . . ." "You've got 40 percent of the music." "I can see people running around whistling that," you know, from an unseen film. [laughter]

Schickel: Isn't it true that in the sort of "New Hollywood" that an awful lot of what one might term creative energies go into making the deals? It was years ago that Samuel Goldwyn said that it takes more time to make Mary Pickford's deals than it does to make her pictures. It seems to me, if anything, that that's probably gotten worse rather than better.

Mitchum: I'm sure. That's another thing I find abhorrent: that the whole machinery—which smacks largely of chicanery—is the prime mover. I mean, that's the reason for making a film.

Schickel: Shuffle all those papers around, and figures.

Mitchum: Yeah. In the day of the old major motion picture studio, they had drawers and vaults filled with unsung or time-wasting scripts, which had come to them on deals, through agents. They'd say, "Well, if you want Cary Grant, then you've got to take these two scripts at $160,000 a line." [laughter] Now they have to somehow amortize them, so they turn around and put them on some mule like me. Every studio had its own donkey, and I was RKO's.

Schickel: You began your career, certainly, in the days when the major studios were indeed major studios. You've not only survived, but prospered after that. And nowadays we hear a great deal of talk about the "New Hollywood." From where I sit, as purely an observer of it, it doesn't seem to me all that new, at least, shall we say, in the spiritual qualities. Can you describe the differences, if any?

Mitchum: You're right back where you started. Back to the two-reelers. Now they extend a one-act play to two hours or 90 minutes. And it's still a one-line joke. And they hoke it up with camera work that's been discarded at UCLA in the cinematography department decades ago. And they all find it all new. It just comes full circle, full cycle.

Schickel: That's just a stylistic thing. One hears a great deal of talk about encouraging the new young filmmakers. Is anyone putting their money where their collective mouth is?

Mitchum: Not largely, no. Because there are lots of outside investors now, for instance, like successful farm combines. I think Kirk Douglas had a film [*A Gunfight*] that was financed by the Jicarilla Apache Indians. And these are outside interests. I think that banks are taking a much longer, much steadier, much more conservative look at film financing. Let's face it, most of the major motion picture companies were, in fact, land holding companies. They were real estate companies. If they had a new film in New Delhi, India, they'd buy the corner of Broadway and 42nd, and they'd erect a theater there. And it was very valuable real estate. And they'd charge the building of the edifice against the profits, if any. They would guarantee, as a matter of fact, that there would be no profit on the film. Meanwhile, they'd annexed a few more acres.

Schickel: In other words, the business of the business was business.

Mitchum: That's right. Exactly. They're not principally concerned with anyone's expression. Now, as always, you know, it's the only business that I've witnessed that faces up to crises with panic. They always react with panic. So, now, again, today, comes the heyday of the gilded amateur. The grab bag is open so all the amateurs are in. Beyond nudity and graphic copulation, I don't know what's next.

Schickel: Have you seen some of these trend-making films?

Mitchum: No, I haven't.

Schickel: Like *Easy Rider*?

Mitchum: I saw *Easy Rider*.

Schickel: What did you think of that?

Mitchum: Oh, I thought it had been made years ago. I always have that feeling about a lot of things. I remember when Scott Carpenter went up and spun around the Earth. I got to the studio, and everyone was grouped around one of the portable dressing rooms looking at a television set. And I thought, "That's odd." You know, you'd think that the efficiency department would root that out. I didn't know what it was all about—people were very cryptic all morning. I couldn't understand what they were talking about. My dressing room office was across the street, so finely I went up there and my secretary was sitting there. And she had the radio or television set on. And I said, "Reva, what the hell is happening?" She said, "He's in the water." I said, "Who is in the water?" She said, "Scott Carpenter." I said, "Who the hell is Scott Carpenter?" [laughter] I hadn't clue. I thought they had done it years ago. [laughter] That's how out of touch I am.

Schickel: I take it take you sort of stay out of touch by choice.

Mitchum: Either that or I'm just not equipped to participate, to keep up.

Schickel: Why you think that is? I mean, you're sort of a public figure.

Mitchum: I probably have inner perverted tastes, you know, that I choose not to share. I don't know.

Schickel: The thing that interests me is this enormous thing called fame or celebrity [Schickel later wrote *Intimate Strangers: The Culture of Celebrity*]. It crunches down on you, and I've wondered whether, through the years, in some way, it's easier to deal with or easier to handle. Of the actors I have talked to, so many of them seem to me to be really oppressed by it. And what happens, it seems, by necessity or some need for self-salvation really, is that they have to pull back from it, to sort of insulate themselves in some way.

Mitchum: I think, in the beginning, they rather emulate the image. They try to fill out the uniform, as it were. And they find that they have extended themselves beyond their identities, and they have to regroup. I have tried a contrary practice. Let's face it, there is no such thing as the recapture of anonymity. After all, your red eye is on the giant screen in glorious Technicolor. Everybody knows who you are. But you don't know who they are. You are as familiar to them as a Buick or pack of Chesterfields.

Schickel: Do you think, as an institution, movie stardom has a future? Do you think that people have some primeval need for these sort of archetypal figures?

Mitchum: Spiro Agnew proves that. [laughter] [The former

Maryland governor, who had been accused of taking bribes while in office, was elected vice president to Richard Nixon two years prior to this interview (and later resigned from office for taking further bribes).]

Schickel: One hears in the industry a lot of talk about how the day of the star is past and the day of the good story and the picture itself is now here.

Mitchum: That's sort of trendy and I really don't know that. I'm sure that somebody will come along with three eyes and five arms and they'll line up for blocks to see that. But, in this case, in the film we finished in Ireland, David Lean is really the star. And I should think that the combination of David Lean and Robert Bolt and Freddie Young, our cinematographer, is pretty heavy. It shouldn't make a great deal of difference who's in the film. You're sustaining fidelity to an illusion, like the manufactured identity of a person in popular published novels. There are always attractive protagonists or some memorable character in fiction. So, I suppose, there must be some focal point of identity in a film for people to examine at least, or with whom to associate. But I'm sure that it's not necessary that [he or she] dominate [the film] as it was created. You know, the star system was originally a French creation. But, on the other hand, in sports, there still are the Pelés and the Joe Namaths.

Schickel: Being a movie actor is a prosperous occupation. But one wonders if, conceivably, a salary of a million dollars to play in a picture is more than anybody is really worth. I think it overloads the person, indeed. In some ways, it's almost like putting too big a charge into his circuits—all that money for something that may be art, but also, at some level, is also a kind of play as well.

Mitchum: Yes, but that's really the product of the machinery, isn't it?—the deal. We go back to the agents and the producers and the deals.

Schickel: It seems to me that the English are not quite so deal conscious. The fine English actors have often worked in films and on stage for not so much money. It seems to me that some actors in this country, at least, have reached this point to where they don't look at things that they really should, because the price is below their price. And status quo would be lost.

Mitchum: That's right, but I don't know that it's a matter of status. I should think that somebody gets half a million dollars, or a million dollars, for a film, and then he goes off into something else, for less money, then the agent, I should think, fears that he won't be able to recapture that top figure. The professional weight—or worth or integrity or status or value—of a performer or actor doesn't enter into it very strongly, I think. The British allow themselves a great deal more variety. You can't see Cary Grant in a pair of overalls and chewing tobacco—no way. Because there's an establishment of style.

Schickel: On the other hand, an actor like John Mills, whom I admire greatly and who is in *Ryan's Daughter* . . .

Mitchum: Johnny is a very good journeyman actor.

Schickel: . . . he's done a lot of things, and he seems to have taken big parts and small parts, and this part and that part, and it seems to have added up to, possibly, a more interesting life, let's say, or more interesting career.

Mitchum: I'm sure it's far more fulfilling. There are actors and there are movie stars. Basically that's it. And the assumed rewards and returns and claims of a movie star are the goal of the actors.

Schickel: That's true, and rather human at least, isn't it?

Mitchum: They're encouraged to demand more, to desire more.

Schickel: Well, you also find that the devil theory of the movie industry—as I've heard it recently—is the agents. They're the guys, you know, who are screwing the studios to the wall with their demands. And they're screwing the actors to the wall.

Mitchum: Not anymore.

Schickel: Not anymore?

Mitchum: Oh, no. There's a pall of sadness over Beverly Hills.

Schickel: You just can't get those lovely deals?

Mitchum: I suppose I can. Or if you're Elizabeth Taylor, if you occupy some unique position. But, after all, the producer—it's not his money, is it? He's got to get it from somebody else. And that somebody else is really a board of stockholders, who have probably never seen a movie, and they just look at a graph.

Schickel: Some of the producers, I'm told, look more just at graphs.

Mitchum: Exactly. Sure.

Schickel: A friend of mine, who is kind of a well-known director and producer, went into, I think it was Universal, and the guy hauled out a huge sheet of graph paper. He's said, "Now what do you want? Something here? Here's one million? Two million? Three million?" He never talked a story, an idea, anything. He was merely asking what price range this fellow would like to work in. [laughter]

Mitchum: They used to do that in casting offices. They'd say, "For this part we need a $750 actor or a $250-a-day actor . . ." Honestly, that's how they cast it. I sat there and listened and watched them, in casting offices.

Schickel: Kind of demeaning isn't it, in a way?

Mitchum: Not if you're adjusted to it. When they told me what my position was—that I was a manure salesman at RKO—they paid me well and that was my job. I got out, eventually.

Schickel: We hear a good deal of talk nowadays about the famous youth market for movies. And yet, it seems to me, and I wonder if it does to you, that movies always have been—rather in terms of their audience—a youthful medium. If as a professional I weren't obliged to go to the movies a great deal, I don't suppose then that I would be going as much to the movies. It seems to me that there's some exaggeration of the force in the power of the youth market.

Mitchum: I'm sure it's always been a youth market, basically. During the Depression every kid whose mother kicked him out of the house to go out and look for a job wound up at a 15-cent movie—all-day movies in New York. I used to do that. I went to Haaren High School and we use to just take off and leave school. They used to have monitors on the door to keep you in. It was that kind of a school. [laughter] I used to come back and deliver reports to my English teacher and tell her of some fancy trip to the museum or to something educational—anything. And we would be at the movies. And the guy, my friend, Phil, and I were at Loew's 72nd Street, I think, and there was a fire in the theater. And so, as I was giving my pitch to the teacher—Mrs. Hollander her name was—she reached back in her desk and she took out *The Daily News* or *The Mirror*, I guess it was, and it showed a picture of Phil and me coming out of the theater. [laughter] You know, it was sort of a haven for the jobless. Of course, it was much cheaper then.

Schickel: We've talked some about David Lean. Are there other directors that you have worked with that you can talk about, that seem to you comparable in skill—people that have been particularly pleasurable to work with or particularly interesting to work with?

Mitchum: I found them all interesting to work with, from such widely diverse styles. For instance, I'm working with Raoul Walsh [on *Pursued*, 1947]. Raoul rolls cigarettes with one hand . . .

Schickel: A lovely man.

Mitchum: . . . and he rolls them on his blind side, and all of the tobacco falls out. He turns his back, he says "Action!" And he walks away. And all the tobacco falls out. And he lights it—and it goes *woosh*—the paper just goes up in flames. And he rolls another one. And he's walking around, he's not looking at the scene at all. And finally, if there is enough silence, he turns around, and he says, "Is it over? OK." And he rips the pages out, and he moves on. And Otto Preminger [who directed *Angel Face* and *River of No Return*]—I like Otto—he's one of the funniest men I know. And Otto gets so overwrought that he just becomes a pudding of inarticulation, frustration. I think that Otto is a very gifted producer. He has great taste. But I do not think that he is a very good director. The same with Stanley Kramer [who directed *Not as a Stranger*]. Stanley stands in his own way as a director.

Schickel: When you say "stands in his own way," what do you mean by that?

Mitchum: He impedes his function as a producer by directing. He's a far better producer. He's a very efficient, very good producer. But as a director, I'm afraid he's too earnest. And that's almost an epithet.

Schickel: In other words, the kind of earnest, hovering director who cuts you down, makes you feel constricted?

Mitchum: Not really.

Schickel: I kind of gather that you like maybe Raoul Walsh's style a little better.

Mitchum: Raoul's great. It's just a day's work. I remember one time riding a horse out of a little box canyon—and they had set up another camera around the corner. I didn't know about it, and the horse jumped, fell down, and rolled right over me. Of course, I was up over his withers—and I was riding bareback, so I didn't get hung up in the saddle or anything. But the horse rolled over me so quickly that it just knocked the wind out of me. And Raoul came over, and he didn't say, "Are your ribs broken?" Or, "Are you all right?" He said, "Listen, bring him out a little faster next time, will you?" Nothing to it. [laughter]

Schickel: He's a tough man. Of course, one of the things that interests me about Walsh—and maybe it's something that's getting lost a little bit in Hollywood—is that he was out there as [D.W.] Griffith's assistant in 1914. It was a much less pretentious business in those days, I should think. And he told me that he really liked directing in the silent days, because, you know, he could get up close to an actor, and say, "Come on, you S.O.B, start crying, we're getting late here." [laughter]

Mitchum: He still does that. Oh, Raoul still does that. He couldn't care less. You heard how he lost his eye? They were in Arizona, and they were making *In Old Arizona* . . .

Schickel: A pioneer talkie.

Mitchum: . . . and he was going to star in the film. So, they're driving to—or from—location, and they struck a jackrabbit, one of those big western jackies. And it spun up and hit the windshield and a shower of glass went through his eye. And they're about 50 or 60 miles from a hospital, so Raoul just took his handkerchief out, and held it to his eye while they drove him to the hospital. And they got there, and they had to put him face down, to make sure they got the glass straight out, so they didn't jiggle it around. He said, "I think it's in my brain." [laughter] So they finally pulled it out and, of course, he had a sympathetic blindness in the other eye. He said, "Jesus, I'm blind." And the doctor told him, "Well, that's just shock in the other." He said, "Well, in that case, get me a drink." [laughter] So, they got Warner Baxter, and Raoul directed him, instead. Never flinched.

Schickel: He's a lovely, tough man, I liked him very much indeed.

Mitchum: I should think that one of the unfortunately short-lived careers as directors was Charles Laughton's, because he would have made a brilliant and beautiful director.

Schickel: I imagine you're almost tired of everybody focusing on *The Night of the Hunter* as one of your terrific and memorable performances. But God knows, it was.

Mitchum: It was a good book. Really was. Frightening book.

Schickel: Yes, it was. And not a bad script. Why was Laughton so good?

Mitchum: He had great humor and, of course, an encompassing sensitivity. He was very gentle and, of course, he could be very caustic, too. He would kick Shelley Winters on the set and [Laugton imitation]: "None of that nonsense, you know." [laughter] And he wouldn't direct the children; he loathed the children. He made me direct the children. Couldn't stand them.

Schickel: Well, there is a point in his favor anyway.

Mitchum: So, I had to direct [them].

Schickel: Have you ever wanted to direct [an entire film]?

Mitchum: I'd like it, if I could get off the same time everybody else did. But having to get there before the actors, and then having to take your homework home with you, and then sitting there for at least three months in a cutting room, and going over and over and over copy and exploitation and stills—it's too much responsibility. And I just don't feel that, unless it were really ideal conditions, that I could justify trusting anyone else's future or anyone else's career or well-being to my hands. Because, I may not show up that day.

Schickel: Except you're famous for showing up, Mr. Mitchum.

Mitchum: Not as a director, though. [laughter]

Schickel: We talk and hear a great deal about the auteur theory of criticism, in which the director is the author of the film. Do you think he really is? My feeling is always that it's kind of a communal activity. It's also a very accidental business, that somehow all the right people get together at the right time and it works. You could put the same people together at another time and it isn't going to work.

Mitchum: That's true. I should think that the director is the consummate audience—the ultimate audience. Praise from Sir Hubert is praise indeed. I find it very difficult if they seem at all undecided. I know that David [Lean] found it difficult working with me, because I'd be over joshing with the grips, with the electricians, and he'd say, "Action!" And I'd go in, without explaining, and do it in one take—which would just, I'm sure, infuriate him. He'd be almost tearful and say [imitation], "Bob! That was *spot-on*! I can't tell you how lovely that once, how beautiful that was—simply marvelous." I would say, "You don't think it was a little too Jewish?" And he'd say [Lean imitation], "What's he *on-n-n* about?" It would just drive him crazy. I kept putting him on.

Schickel: You have taken a great deal of pride, I gather, in being "spot-on," to use the phrase. It's the kind of pride in professionalism which—if you don't mind a two-bit psychoanalysis— I think is a way of putting off any consideration that you might be committing this terrible act known as art.

Mitchum: Not really. [It is] the interpretation or translation or impression of an author's work—of a created situation. I should think that it would be generally or universally understood among the general group what you're doing. But, I'm sure, that given two different persons, that there are two entirely different interpretations of it, two different versions.

Schickel: You're saying, you only know your interpretation—and you know that pretty fast. I mean, as you read the script.

Mitchum: One time, I remember, in radio, I read the stage directions [on the air]. [laughter] But I find myself occasionally unsure, or find I have overlooked something—that's really the value of a good director, because I'm inclined to be lazy, just sail through it, get it done and get it out of the way. I don't subscribe to this sort of pretense of individual autocracy—you know, "It's your turn now." I'd like to just get it done and get away. I have a theory, you know. I pursue invisibility. It's my own private hack. And I suppose I just sharpen it up and do it as quickly as I can and as well as I can. But, I am inclined to overlook things. And I must say that David won't permit that.

Schickel: Is there a type of thing you overlook?

Mitchum: No, no. I just don't completely fulfill it. Lots of times I either stroll through or race through it.

Schickel: I think Laughton said you ought to do *King Lear*. [Richard] Burton said you would be the best Macbeth of your generation. I don't like to embarrass you, because I think it's sufficient to do what you want to do. But do you have any feeling of wanting to hack one of those things some time?

Mitchum: No, not at all.

Schickel: Why not?

Mitchum: Well, first of all, I'd be standing in someone else's place, breathing someone else's air, because it is valuable to many other people. And, I remember, pub conversations in England. And I'd say, "Why should I do Richard [*Richard III*] for $30 a week at Stratford?" And the Irish and English actors would say, "Do it for us, for us!" And I say, "I don't see that." I'm sure that my argument sounds very thin to them.

Schickel: Well, it sounds a little thin to me. I think it would be fun to try it once. I'd like to see you do it.

Mitchum: I'm not in it for fun. I enjoy working, but I enjoy the company of working. And mean, I practically grew up in it. I remember a lot of times when the day was over, I'd sit there on the stage. Wouldn't go home.

Schickel: In other words, you liked the camaraderie of it.

Mitchum: It works, really. And there's an exchange of respect. You respect the electricians for their jobs. And they are expert. And I think it's good. It's a good feeling. I suppose it's the same thing that any good team feels. And I enjoy that.

Schickel: It's been reported—I think I saw you on a television program talking about it—that you have done or do a great deal of writing, I guess for yourself, poetry and so forth. So, obviously, there's some juice in you that boils up occasionally.

Mitchum: I suppose that I've excused myself by coming to the conclusion—forcing the conclusion— that what I have to say or what I feel about it is really of very little importance to anyone else anyway. So, I just rationalize my own indolence.

Schickel: You lack the "writer's ego," for heaven's sake. [laughter] I think the two worst kind of egotists in the world are writers and actors. I'm one kind; actors strike me as the other kind.

Mitchum: Actors are involved too often in vanity.

Schickel: In narcissism, I think.

Mitchum: Of course. Yes. That's pretty scary because . . .

Schickel: Well, how do you avoid that? There's that image, that giant mirror up there, all the time.

Mitchum: Just embarrassment. If I caught myself acting, I'd go home and cry.

Schickel: Do you hold, then, with that little short adage that screen acting is behaving, really.

Mitchum: In an effective manner. I was just talking about that, in part with [Associated Press writer] Hal Boyle, and he said that [General] George Patton said that all men in positions of influence are, in part, actors. Well, they teach that, don't they? In officers school they teach the voice and attitude of command. That simple.

Schickel: In a sense, that's what being a movie actor of the kind you have been is. Much, it seems to me, of your effectiveness depends, very simply, on authority. Somebody—I think it was Raymond Chandler—said something about Humphrey Bogart, that when he enters a scene, it's like a knife cutting into it. It's seems to me that that's what good screen acting very often is.

Mitchum: Of course. There is the master of a unique presence. Even when he was awkward, he was unique.

Schickel: Do you fool around with your dialogue much?

Mitchum: Sometimes, yes. Some directors won't permit it. Every word is holy writ.

Schickel: I take it Lean would be such a person.

Mitchum: Not necessarily.

Schickel: Really?

Mitchum: No, no. Trevor Howard says that David has said that he regards actors as puppets. And I must say, he gets everything ready and he says, "OK, now you." He brings you on, and you better be ready. I'm sure that David would permit you to rehearse forever. I find, very often, rehearsals—as you go on and on and on—it just gets worse and worse and worse. It gets you bogged down.

Schickel: It dulls your energy.

Mitchum: Sometimes, yeah. You do lose sort of a spontaneous éclat. I mean, the purpose of rehearsal is tempo, timing, and to try to stay away from the furniture, so that you don't crash into things. But—I don't feel that he views actors as puppets at all. I think David has great respect for actors, because he allows them great leniency and leeway.

Schickel: He'll let you try things.

Mitchum: He would.

Schickel: Lean seems among some critics—not this critic—vastly underrated over the length of his career. He's won a lot of Academy Awards and honors, but I guess he seems too formal to some or, perhaps, too studied. This is one of my running critical fights because I think he's wonderful.

Mitchum: He's not too studied at all. He is really the complete director. He spent two years on *Ryan's Daughter* before they finally started shooting, then a year filming, and the better part of the year cutting it. And he supervises. He was instrumental in the choice of music and scoring—and he supervises the scoring. So he really is the complete director.

Schickel: He really does become a complete auteur, then.

Mitchum: He lives for nothing else, when he's involved.

Schickel: You like to live for some other events, I take it.

Mitchum: I'm not that involved. Were I he, I should be that involved. But I'm involved when I'm working. If I'm actually in operation, the walls could fall down and I wouldn't notice it. It doesn't bother me at all. They say, "Would you like us to clear the eye line?" There are people standing there, staring. Not at all. I don't care. I don't see them. I play straight to them—bystanders, visitors.

Schickel: You've done then, an odd thing through the years, because you've kind of cultivated the notion of being a lazy fellow. But obviously you're not. Because I don't think that anyone who concentrates that fiercely is a lazy person. And yet, you know, you've let it get abroad that you're a lazy good-for-nothing fellow. [laughter]

Mitchum: That's the development of facility. You can make it look easy.

Schickel: I think that's kind of important, don't you?

Mitchum: It infuriates a lot of actors, and infuriates a lot of directors. You know, "Well, it's nothing to him." No matter what you're playing, they say, "That's easy for him, because that's *him*." No matter what it is.

Schickel: Clearly you're not, for example, the psychotic preacher in *The Night of the Hunter*.

Mitchum: You know what people say? "Where there's smoke, there's fire." Or, "He's got it in him, because he couldn't do that [otherwise]."

Schickel: I think a lot of effective movie acting is not letting it all out, in the sense that you give the audience the sense that there is stuff smoldering there that isn't quite visible. But you know it's there.

Mitchum: There are actors like that who really approach greatness, like [Oscar] Homolka. And some of the French actors—

Raimu. Of course, his ego just overrode everything else. Harry Baur was marvelous. I used to go and watch him.

Schickel: Are there American film actors that you admire, or have noticed this quality in?

Mitchum: I've seen so few American films, and I'm ashamed of that. I think that the young Tony Quinn gave that impression, until he became Zorba the Italian, Zorba the Schoolteacher, Zorba the . . . you know. He keeps knocking his voice down another register between gleeful, bearish dancing.

Schickel: I saw a quote from you that made me laugh several times—saying something about Steve McQueen, like "Steve doesn't bring much to the party." I took this to be not only a criticism of him, but maybe of a kind of school of acting.

Mitchum: Unless it's there for him, Steve's not really going to come in and bring a lot to the party, unless it's something that requires a wrench and a quart of oil. He doesn't come in with a whole bagful of goodies and just enliven everything up. Steve needs a good director. I said that in association with his association with Bobby Wise [on *The Sand Pebbles*]. From my own experience and observation, that would not be the sort of ideal director for Steve McQueen. Steve needs to be reminded of his own potential. He should be kept alive at all times. Someone like David Lean would keep him on his toes. I'm very grateful for directors who keep me alive, remind me that I am capable of more. Otherwise, I just let it slide by.

Schickel: For you there's some kind of middle-ground director between the guy who paces out your footsteps for you, and tapes them on the studio set, and the guy who turns his back on the camera and wanders off.

Mitchum: [Wise] began directing as an editor, where it's all in footage and timing, and there's no spontaneity in that. Of course, I was working with a rather volatile young lady, Shirley MacLaine, when I was also with Bobby Wise [on *Two for the Seesaw*], so it was noticeable.

Schickel: It was not, I felt, in the end, one of your best pictures. Or her best pictures.

Mitchum: Not at all. I said, "Not me." In retreat, from the back, I looked like a Bulgarian wrestler. It's impossible. Visually, I can't make it. "Get Greg Peck," I said. "No, you!" For a year I went through this, and I finally said, "All right, you'll see." [laughter]

Schickel: Peter Ustinov said that he was under the impression that you were perhaps too intelligent a man to be an actor. And this squares with an impression that I have sometimes—not necessarily of you. But there is such a thing as being too intelligent. In a sense, intelligence leads to self-consciousness, which leads to . . .

Mitchum: Embarrassment. Yes, and I understand what he means. I can't have a practiced or controlled foolishness, which is necessary, I'm sure, for the complete actor. I just can't. It just embarrasses me.

Schickel: You mean, really let yourself loose—in the full sense of the word.

Mitchum: Yeah.

Schickel: Well, Ustinov would know all about this, because he's among the more intelligent people I've met. And I imagine he suffers somewhat the same problem.

Announcer [as Mitchum and Schickel continue to talk]: this has been *Sound on Film*, another in a series of broadcasts on films and the people who make them.

Schickel: Well, they're giving us all sorts of hand signals here, and we've gabbed on for an hour. So, I guess we're going to have to hang it up. I want to thank you very much for bearing with my questions and for talking with us. It's been a very great pleasure.

Mitchum: I thank you.

INTERVIEW WITH DICK LOCHTE

In 1973 Robert Mitchum agreed to do press interviews to promote *The Friends of Eddie Coyle* for Paramount Pictures at his offices at 9200 Sunset Boulevard. Dick Lochte of the *Los Angeles Free Press* interviewed the actor at length about his career, and the talk reflects the actor's free-form conversational style and personal opinions on a wide range of subjects. The interview appeared in the weekly in back-to-back installments as "Just One More Hangover" on June 29, 1973, and "Hell, I Look Like I've Changed Five Million Tires" on July 6.

DICK LOCHTE

Detective mystery novelist Dick Lochte was credited by *The New York Times Book Review* as having "a style of his own; giddy and gaudy on the outside, cynical and perverse under the skin." His New Orleans-set novel, *The Neon Smile*, was roundly acclaimed, and his other novels include *Laughing Dog, Sleeping Dog* and, in collaboration with former O.J. Simpson trial prosecutor Christopher Darden, the mystery novel *The Trials of Nikki Hill*. Lochte is also a screenwriter and a frequent contributor to the *Los Angeles Times Book Review*.

"Hello," Robert Mitchum says, showing my hand some mercy, "my name's George Peppard." Uh-huh. We're standing three flights up from Sunset Boulevard in the smartly subdued offices of Talbot Productions, the actor's film company. He's on what I suspect is a rare visit to the shop to talk to the press about his latest movie, *The Friends of Eddie Coyle*, a gritty gangster drama based on the best-selling novel by George V. Higgins.

Talbot, like all of Mitchum's business affairs, is watchdogged by an efficient, attractive, casually cordial lady named Reva

Frederick. Only moments before, she had led me into a section of the suite where two men were finishing a discussion. She introduced me to one of them, a departing journalist, and waited a few beats too long in getting around to the other guy, prompting the Peppard opening. Like most of Mitchum's one-liners, it can be read in a number of ways: a) as a good-natured chiding of his office manager for her momentary forgetfulness; b) as a mock-humble gesture, suggesting that anyone might fail to recognize that battered, world-weary countenance, or c) a simple, funny way of getting our meeting off to an easygoing start.

It could also be: d) none of the above; e) all of the above; or f) something else again. No matter. Mitchum is relaxed, loose as a goose, his chin tucked into his neck, eyes as sleepy as they used to be when Jane Russell sang to him, only now they're half hidden behind fancy-framed, tinted specs. He points to an empty section of couch, then reclaims his resting spot. His big hand goes over the coffee table, ignores a sandwich wrapped in wax paper and claims a frosted glass half-filled with a clear liquid. "Would you like something to drink?" Ms. Frederick asks. "Vodka for the heat?" I admit it sounds like a fine idea.

Mitchum leans back. I recall a quote of his: "I have to be able to drink, because the only way to get rid of people is to out-drink them. It takes 36 hours or more sometimes and it nearly kills me. But in the end, they go." Looking at the double shot of Kremlin Castor Oil in front of me, I get a flash of paranoia. He's got me pegged for a short-distance record. "Sometimes 36 hours," he'll be adapting the comment, "but then like that guy the other day, sometimes they kiss the coffee table after only 30 minutes."

I shoot him a suspicious look, but it's clear he couldn't care less about my drinking ability. He's at a point where he's already run through a couple of reporters, with others in the wings. And he's being very pleasant considering the savagery of two recent profiles. *Rolling Stone*'s Grover Lewis tried to cover him in "now" journalese and innuendo and Brad Darrach married Freud with *Confidential* for a gossipy little offspring in *Penthouse*. Oddly, both writers obviously admired the man they were poking at, which tells you much more about the writers than it does about Mitchum.

With a sip of vodka burning the back of my throat, I depress a few buttons on the tape machine. "I hope you don't mind if I use this?" I croak.

Cool as his shot glass, Mitchum replies: "Not at all. I hope you don't mind if I don't say anything." Is he smiling? Is the big guy smiling over there? Yeah. OK, then let's get the job done before the vodka starts working its way up the back of my head.

Lochte: I've been reading a lot about your, ah, private life. So, maybe we could go on to something else.

Mitchum [exaggerated surprise]: Really? I'd rather talk about *that*. I don't know much about that. Might be revealing.

Lochte: Well, if you think so . . .

Mitchum: No. You just go ahead with whatever you want. I will reply in kind. I think Reva's spent the whole morning on the phone talking to everybody at Paramount. The picture we saw last night [*The Friends of Eddie Coyle*] isn't the picture I thought we were making. There's the script. Read it. Tell me if that's the picture that was on the screen.

Lochte: Then you didn't like the movie.

Mitchum: I don't know, really. I think it's a matter of taste, like lime or wintergreen. What it is: These geniuses sit around having conferences and what they seek is a story. George Higgins is a rather narrative novelist and obviously quite successful at it. I don't think the day will come when Paul Monash [*Eddie Coyle*'s writer-producer] will be as good a writer as Higgins. Of course, he doesn't have the same access to materials, either. Higgins has certain advantages being a United States attorney. I assume much of his dialogue comes from what might be referred to as inadmissible tapes. But, anyway, we get the people who ask, "Where's the story?" The quote, "Hollywood screenwriter," unquote, has a tendency to look at the property and say, "I can fix it." Then he searches for a story. Mr. Higgins doesn't write that way—no beginning, middle and end. I thought we were there to celebrate the success of the book. Then they start with, "Do you realize that the computer says that music is 12 percent of the total success of a pic— . . ." Everybody chews on that one. It's a circle jerk. I'm not saying the picture is bad. It's probably good. I just think it would have been better except for the tampering of some not necessarily qualified people.

Lochte [as Reva refills glasses]: Isn't that just another problem that you always have to face—films being an industry rather than an art?

Mitchum: There *are* artists. But they have to work within the system. I don't see why it can't be a happy marriage. In the old days, the moguls had the good sense to engage innovators and artists. They recognized taste. But now they're not sure. I think Otto Preminger is a great producer, but a rather mediocre director. You find that pretty often. But they insist on directing. Stanley Kramer is another one. He's been bruised time after time, but he feels he has to keep doing it. I don't know why.

Lochte: Speaking of Preminger, I read a story about your first day on a set in which a director says, "I shout at actors, but it doesn't mean anything. The next morning I've forgotten that." Your answer was, "I punch people who shout at me, but it doesn't mean anything. The next morning I've forgotten it." Could the director have been Preminger?

Mitchum: Not at all. Those two other guys, as a matter of fact, Henry Hathaway and Dale Robertson [Mitchum worked for Hathaway on *White Witch Doctor* and *Five Card Stud*; Robertson was a B-western and television western star].

Lochte: Are there a lot of Hollywood stories that incorrectly get attributed to you?

Mitchum: I guess so.

Lochte: Did you ever hang a director upside down by his shoelaces?

Mitchum: No. It was a producer, Raymond Stross. I'd forbidden him from the set [in Ireland on *The Night Fighters*]. And he came on anyway. He tried to kick me privately. So, I think he warranted the treatment.

Lochte: Why did you decide to form your own company?

Mitchum: I wanted a white chair with my name on it. Actually, it was because of some of legal advice I got.

Lochte: Did you ever want to direct?

Mitchum: Sure.

Lochte: Why didn't you?

Mitchum: Nobody asked me. Any time the subject came up, somebody'd always say, "First we've got this script we'd like you to do." And I say, "I need an awful lot of money in front to do that one." And that never seems to be a problem. They pay it in yen, but they pay it.

Lochte: Do you up your price for a script you don't like?

Mitchum: Right. And they take me up on it. I don't want to sound like a complete whore. There *are* movies I won't do for any amount. Maybe I should go out and do *Patton* or *Dirty Harry* and piss on the world and its opinions.

Lochte: You're saying that the morality of the script is more important to you than anything else.

Mitchum: Of course.

Lochte: There are a lot of people who don't feel that way.

Mitchum: They need the job. I don't need the fucking money, daddy.

Lochte: Would you rather do a bad script?

Mitchum: No bad script. No way. I don't do bad scripts. I do things that I think have a chance—a chance of being useful or good. I present myself in good faith and expect everyone else to . . . Well, that's a fool's game. I know better than that. Still, I expect people to respond in kind with their efforts. Not so. They're just around to get the new convertible and pick up the new broads. They move on to the next caper. I'm confined in this business. I have great faith in it. I think the audio-visual medium is just now approaching its importance. I don't take kindly to the people who dismiss it and dismiss their responsibilities, to the clever pimps who employ it to their own advantage. We should add to it. We needn't all be millionaires. We needn't be all-powerful moguls. The word "producer" is a powerful word around here. You can hang it on your car door and drive down [Sunset] Strip and pick up women all night long. That doesn't appeal to me. How many can you use a night? Producers, that is. The movie industry is a togetherness group. You scratch my ass, I'll scratch yours—totally unmindful of what's going on out on the streets. Jesus Christ, you know the leaders of the communications fields should provide whatever can be provided. People have to be informed on everything. We can bounce signals off of satellites so that everybody in the world knows what's happening at exactly the same time. The most criminal form of slavery is the denial of intelligence, of information. The combined brainwashing system of the military and Madison Avenue is awesome. The least that can happen is that you know what's going on, that you know you're not being gulled. That you know you're not walking around with somebody's finger up your keister.

Lochte: Don't things like Watergate help to smarten us up?

Mitchum: All right. So?

Lochte: So, the problem is . . .

Mitchum: The problem is dumb people. Several years ago, I got back here from Vietnam [asked there by the U.S. State Department, the actor spent three months in the war zone and took part in 150 missions] and I tried to talk to people about it. I asked why people weren't being permitted to know what was going on over there. Bob Kennedy got up and walked out on me. His absence was excused by the statement that his advisers weren't present. Bullshit! Where were my advisers? I had just come from a place where something had happened and the newspapers were sending out the wrong information. I was there. I saw it. But he was gone, didn't want to discuss that. The implication was clear. Just sit there and keep on sucking. It's all so dumb, so very dumb. We're being manipulated. Take WASP, for example.

Lochte: WASP?

Mitchum: White Anglo-Saxon Protestant. Does that make any sense? How many GASPs do you know?—Green Anglo-Saxon Protestants. Or BASPs?—Black Anglo-Saxon Protestants. I mean, Anglo-Saxon means white, right? It's a fucking invention for a purpose.

Lochte: What's the purpose?

Mitchum: To provide an immediate label. To get a reaction, because you can't collect money from our reactive element. Sitting around, coining phrases like that is no different from sitting around in a boxcar trying to figure out how to rig a slot machine.

Lochte: If we could move rather abruptly back to your work in films, why do you think you've lasted as a motion picture star?

Mitchum: I endure because I work cheap.

Lochte: I thought you said you charge a lot.

Mitchum: That's true. But I'm a professional. And I produce more than I cost. I'm good at what I do. There aren't that many good people in any line, not many good newsboys, good pharmacists, good whores. Because we have a rising population, you might suspect we have an increase in the number of geniuses. But where are the Botticellis, the Shakespeares? Obviously, they have sold out for less, earlier on.

Lochte: It's not enough being a genius? You have to be a professional to know what to do with it?

Mitchum: Exactly. But it's an "R-A-T," like a rat-now style of performance. Get in, get out, and sell it. Rat now! I would hope that great art still struggles through all this and prevails. Maybe not. Maybe everything turns out like *Godzilla*.

Lochte: Speaking of great, do you think you've made a great film?

Mitchum: No. A couple of good ones, maybe. I had a chance with *Thunder Road*. That could have been a great film, I think, and it's my fault it wasn't. It was popular. But if it had been great, then at least I would have been indemnified.

Lochte: [What about the piece] by Grover Lewis in *Rolling Stone*?

Mitchum: I talked to that guy for about five minutes. He asked me about gun control, and I couldn't figure out what that had do with anything. This guy was accepted, wined and dined by everybody. Except me, because I didn't really know what he was doing there. *Rolling Stone*? I never heard of *Rolling Stone*. I was called away while I was talking to him, and he *resents* this. At least, I assume he does. And he writes the piece. The first thing I see is that he's got Tim going to Africa [Tim Wallace, Mitchum's stand-in], which is wrong. Then I find more and more wrong-o's and I realize that this cat is just writing a piece for himself, to extol his own mission and virtues. Also, I note that he has stepped on people—not me, incidentally—but people who don't like to be stepped on and who might make it very difficult for him. If he's going to take on the Teamsters and the longshoremen and a few other groups and he doesn't know what the hell he's talking about, well . . . That's not being exactly cautious. If he really wanted to be bold and brave, he should have taken on the fuzz. The fuzz were around the whole time, and they're merciless, right?

Lochte: I heard somewhere that you were going to make a film version of John Updike's *The Centaur*.

Mitchum: I read it. I liked it. And that was the end of it. The minute I said I liked it, it became poison. I thought it was a good story. . . . Getting back to that *Rolling Stone* thing, I wonder what makes writ[ers] . . . ? Probably it's the old story. Frank Sinatra once explained it to me: "They jerk off, and we buy yachts," is the way he put it.

Lochte: That's pretty cynical.

Mitchum: Well, I'm a cynical-style girl. I'm a true believer that a certain amount of cynicism is inherent in the beast. I know it's all bullshit. But it's also a pretty good ride.

Lochte: Of all the people who have put down [your] acting ability, [you've] done the best job.

Mitchum: I've got a baritone voice, a broken nose, stand six feet high and can change a tire without using a stand-in. Hell, I look like I've changed five million tires. So men say, "That bum's just a goddamn mechanic. If he can get to be a movie star, I can be a king."

Lochte: You made 19 movies that were released in 1943—your first year in pictures.

Mitchum: Nineteen easy. All under my own name, too. I got the work because I was good at it. I was reliable. Whenever I wasn't doing anything else, I could always do a Hopalong Cassidy.

Lochte: What the hell was *Doughboys in Ireland*?

Mitchum: That was with Kenny Baker and—wait minute now—a nice girl who was under contract to Columbia. What was her name? [Jeff Donnell]. It was about American soldiers being accepted in Ireland.

Lochte: A serious movie?

Mitchum: *Serious?* You've got to be joking. The director—I forget his name [Lew Landers]—tells me that I arrive at this party with a baseball bat up my pants leg. Looking for trouble, you know. Then a girl comes over and charms me and when she's not looking, I remove the baseball bat and toss it out the window. She said, "I'm glad y'all like me." That was supposed to end the scene, but the cameras kept going so I ad-libbed, "Like ya?? You should have seen that old bat that I just got rid of." I don't know if it made it into the movie. But it broke up the joint.

Lochte: There's a movie titled *We've Never Been Licked* that was supposed to have been a turning point.

Mitchum: At the time, we called it *Hardly Ever Been Licked*. Dick Quine and Ted Beery [Noah, Jr.] were in it, too. I guess I had more to do in that one. But I had things to do in the Hopalongs, also.

Lochte: You made a movie with Laurel and Hardy.

Mitchum: Yes. *Dancing Masters*.

Lochte: You were a hood in it?

Mitchum: I don't remember what the hell I was. Remember going over to Columbia Studios on Sunset, checking in. There was Doug Fowley and me and Laurel and Hardy.

Lochte: Is it true you appeared in drag in a movie?

Mitchum: Yeah. Ah, *The Girl Rush*.

Lochte: Anything more about it?

Mitchum: Not that I can recall.

Lochte: What do you remember about *The Story of G.I. Joe*?

Mitchum: I was at RKO. I'd been drafted in the Army when I went to see Bill [Wellman]. He's always twitching and grabbing himself in his bad arm that's full of steel and arthritis and nastiness. He said, "How come you never changed your name?" I told him I'd just learned how to spell it. "How tall are you?" "Six feet," I answered. He said, "Come on—every actor who comes in here is at least six-feet-three. Alan Ladd is six-feet-five." I said, "My police department measurements say six feet, and they're good at that sort of thing." He said, "How come you never had that nose fixed?" And it was a question I got a lot. I said, "I can breathe through it. Look, I didn't come down here to be insulted. The hell with this." And he said, "Sit down!" So we shot a test. I got my hair cut twice on the way. I didn't know there were guys to do that for you. When I first went to work, I didn't know. I shot the test with Buzz [Burgess] Meredith. At the end of the scene there was a long silence. I kept waiting for somebody to say "Cut." Finally, I looked over and they were all standing behind the camera weeping. And that was it. I think they were flabbergasted, because I remembered all the lines. That's been my great charm ever since.

Lochte: Did Katharine Hepburn make her comments about your acting ability directly to you when you were making *Undercurrent*?

Mitchum: Which comments?

Lochte: Something about, "They keep sending me these good-looking men instead of actors."

Mitchum: I never heard that one. But I remember several from the movie. For one scene, she was sitting in a wheelchair and I was at the piano playing Brahms's Fourth. There was a light behind me, a bright light, and I asked her, "Can you see me, Miss Hepburn?" And she replied, "Nah-ht for dust." Another time, she turned to me and said, "Mr. Mitchum, darling, don't let them fuck you around," which I thought was pretty juicy. She also went to my stand-in [Boyd Cabeen], who was hanging around, stripped to the waist, sketching on an easel. She watched him for a while. It was tea time. She had this tea ceremony. She told him, "You look like a rather attractive young man. With obvious aspirations and talent. I should think you could find something bet-*tah* to do with your time than stand-in for a cheap flash actor like our friend, Mr. Mitchum." He said, "Thank you, Miss Hepburn. I have a compliment for you that I'd like to make in the nature of a request. Should I survive you, would you please leave me that lovely collection of bones?" She went across the set and just sat there for 30 minutes as if hypnotized. Those are about the only Hepburn insults I can recall.

Lochte: You made a film [*Pursued*] for Raoul Walsh. Today, he seems to be considered the number two American director, after John Ford.

Mitchum: It's not a question of being number two. I don't think Raoul had the upbringing that Jack Ford had. First of all, he ran away from home when he was 11 years old. Came out west to be a cowboy and wound up riding with Pancho Villa. So he was pretty well-grounded. Never lost his New York accent, though. He's a double-tough mother and a great man. I have great respect for him.

Lochte: You never worked with him again.

Mitchum: No.

Lochte: Nor did you work for Ford. Or Hitchcock, for that matter.

Mitchum: They probably didn't want me. I remember one time George Stevens told me, "I suppose I'll wind up having to use you one of these days." I said, "Oh no. Listen, don't lose any sleep over that possibility."

Lochte: What about *Out of the Past*? I really like that film.

Mitchum: They treated it like any cheap picture and I was a cheap actor, so what the hell? We just did the best we could. Had good people involved. Jacques [Tourneur] was a very sympathetic fellow. I remember one scene where Bettejane Greer [the actress's real name] was supposed to enter her bedroom suite to answer the telephone. It rings. She walks in. Only there's no phone there. The cameras are rolling. A hand comes through the drapes and places a phone on the table. There was a prop man who was in more pictures than John Wayne. He was always scuttling around in the background, sticking his hand in where it shouldn't have been. Never got out of the way in time. Anyway, Jacques says, "Print it." We tell him about the hand. Jacques said [elegant French accent], "Oh, really? This hand was where?" He looked at the spot, shrugged. "Oh," he said. "that could be anyone's hand." You probably can see it in the film, if they haven't trimmed it out by now.

Lochte: How did *Desire Me* wind up with two directors?

Mitchum: I think there were five directors on the film. That was really a mess. You wouldn't believe the dialogue in that script. George Cukor and Mervyn LeRoy are both exemplary directors in their own right. But together, they don't spell mother.

Lochte: You made two pictures with Robert Wise.

Mitchum: Yes. *Blood on the Moon*, and later, *Two for the Seesaw*.

Lochte: Had he changed much over that period of time?

Mitchum: No. He still took four straight ahead, three to the left and two forward, working on what they call German Absolutes in the ballet. He times a kiss with a stopwatch. In the morning he gets there before anyone else and walks it all out. He does your part for you.

Lochte: Don Siegel is very hot today. What was he like to work with in 1949 [on *The Big Steal*]?

Mitchum: All right. But he had Thrifty Drug Store taste.

Lochte: Think he still does?

Mitchum: I know he does. He exhibits it. He does *Dirty Harry*, which I sent back immediately. [Siegel imitation]: "There's a big market for it. Big sales. A-hem."

Lochte: Tell me about *Macao* and [Josef] von Sternberg.

Mitchum: Things got so bad on that one, I would have no more of it. But as I was walking off the lot, the crew came to me and said, "[If] you don't work, we don't work." So I said I'd be back. "On Monday?" they asked. "On Tuesday," I said with a last gasp of integrity. I got drunk in a bar Monday night, slept under the table, got to work by 10 the next morning, an hour late. Joe was standing on his box—he was, like, a four-feet-eight-er—and he was hollering at Tommy Gomez, who was walking down a ship's gangplank. I wandered in and asked, "To whom should I apologize?" "No one," Joe answered. "We're delighted at your presence." So we did the picture and they couldn't figure out how to release it. I was meeting myself coming through doors. A directive came from Howard Hughes to re-shoot. Jerry Wald [the producer] told me this. They got Nick Ray to rework it. When I walked in that first day of re-shooting, Jane Russell handed me pencil and paper. My dressing room was being re-painted, so I used Vic Mature's and wrote the day's work and gave it to the secretary to type up. We shot it in the afternoons. Did that for almost 10 days. At least they could release it. Before that it was a flat impossibility.

Joe was really something. He told me, "We both know this is a piece of shit and we're saddled with Jane Russell. You and I know she has as much talent as this cigarette case." I replied, "Mr. von Sternberg, Miss Russell survives, so she must have something. Lots of ladies have big tits." He had a lectern he permitted no one to use. I made my lunch on it most of the time, fixed it up with some nice greasy delicatessen items. And that apple box. A director of photography [Harry J. Wild] got mad once and kicked it out from under Joe. He'd tell me, "Bob, if you have any questions in matters of art, feel free to ask me. I am an expert in matters of art." I thought this was rather presumptuous. He had a junk shop over in Jersey or something. He wanted me to buy some paintings from him. What presumption—the way he acted. It was like we were right back in 1910 or whenever. He was autocratic towards the crew, really laboring people. I used to tell the crew, "Why don't you quit? Fuck him and the boat that brought him. Let's all go home." Joe would go, "No, no, no." And that was supposed to settle everything. I took him aside and said, "Don't make assholes out of the electricians and grips. They're hacking away at it. They do what they can." He'd be nice when I was there, and when I was away, not so nice. What was I going to do, bat him around? He only came up to here.

Lochte: Did your association with Nick Ray on that film lead to *The Lusty Men*?

Mitchum: Not really. I'd known him quite awhile. Nick had never gotten off my back, because I refused to do a picture for him, *Thieves Like Us*, which later became *They Live by Night*. I told the producers I'd cut off my hair and play the Indian bank robber, but they said, "You can't play the Indian—you're the hero." I went to Nick and said, "I tried." But he went around patiently sorrowful and I figured I'd better do a picture with him. Jerry Wald and [Norman Krasna] would call me at the office and ask for good ideas. I gave them one. A modern Western. They reached in the drawer and came up with the title. They had a title for any kind of picture. One would walk up and down and cry while the other sat down to talk to you. Then they'd reverse. I always thought that the producer was *The Producer*. I didn't know I was making more money than him. I didn't know that if I sneak-talked to the boss, he'd be out, too. I didn't know that—no shit. Howard Hughes called me and said [imitation], "Bob, would you for godsakes tell me you don't want to do this goddamned picture, so I can get this son of a bitch off my back?" I said, "No. I'll do the picture." He said, "Is it a good script?" I said, "We don't even have a script, but we'll whip one up. Don't worry about that. Let him [Wald] have Ed Killy as production manager and give him a bonus action and let me have Nick Ray as director." The next day, Wald called and said [confidential whisper], "Hey, guess what? Howard's OKed the story and guess who we have as director?" I said, "Don't tell me." But he told me, "Nick Ray." Now he hires these writers, Niven Busch and the guy who wrote *They Shoot Horses, Don't They?*, Horace McCoy. They were at opposite ends of the lot and they kept walking right through each other. They passed each other going out of the gate. So Nick and I, both stoned, worked out the script. We finally got the picture finished. Wald had designed an ending that was impossible. I got Reva

[Frederick] to go among her friends and we stole that section of the film and put it in the incinerator. The production number was still active, so we just went out and shot another ending, bang-bang-bang, like that. And Jerry Wald went to colleges across the country, lecturing on the art of motion picture making.

Lochte: Stanley Kramer described the making of *Not as a Stranger* as "ten weeks of hell." There were stories about you and Sinatra . . .

Mitchum: No stories about me. I didn't do anything.

Lochte: About you breaking up the sets.

Mitchum: No. None of that happened.

Lochte: What about *The Night of the Hunter*?

Mitchum: I tore up all of the sets of *Night of the Hunter*.

Lochte: Killed the rabbits?

Mitchum: The rabbits, the frogs, the kids, Shelley Winters and Charlie Laughton, by slow poison. Actually, the picture was a novelty exercise. They worked on it for five months after I was finished and Charles put in all of those owls and pussycats. Said he thought I was too horrific. He didn't want people to drag their children off the streets every time I passed. The character was too strong for him, but that was what he asked me to begin with. [Laughton imitation]: "It's the story of a shit, you know." "Present," I said. "Well, I'm not with you in that," he said. "I make my living reading *The Bible*, you know." I told him to leave the character to me. We were very good friends and he didn't want to make it too uncomfortable for me, so he reduced the effectiveness of the film, I think. It should have been right down the fucking line. Read the book. If it had been like that, it would have been for true.

Lochte: You were still pretty terrifying.

Mitchum: Yeah. That's because between Charlie and me, we were good. But he still put in a lot of root beer floats and lacy laundry.

Lochte: What about *Thunder Road*?

Mitchum: It could have been a great film. That's my fault. I didn't realize I owned it. Honestly. It was popular. You can't believe how popular. But it wasn't great and I'm sorry about that. It was my own design. My shots.

Lochte: Did you like *Home From the Hill*?

Mitchum: It was a good picture,

Lochte: Very rugged film for [Vincente] Minnelli.

Mitchum: Well, he relied a little on us for that. He mounted the film well. Got a lot of fan letters for the interior of the house. Things like that.

Lochte: The Jack Webb movie [*The Last Time I Saw Archie*, an Army comedy] seems a strange choice for you.

Mitchum: I was living in Maryland then. I tried to talk him out of it. But I couldn't. People ask me my favorite picture, I always say that one. I got paid a hundred grand a week, the first time that ever happened, and I went home for Christmas and New Year's. So, I couldn't give less of a fuck who saw it. It's my fay-vo-rite.

Lochte: What about *Cape Fear*?

Mitchum: *Cape Fear* was one of those things where I told them I'd prefer it if they got someone else. Meanwhile, I demonstrated that I knew more about the behavior of the functional criminal than anyone they can get. I told them if they wanted to do it as a play in Arizona—and my wife wanted to be in Arizona for a couple of weeks—I'd do it for free, as a demonstration. As a movie, try someone else. [But] no mother way would they try someone else. After I agreed, the story was drawn through a suck hole, you know, given the Hollywood treatment. There had to be a heavy and a hero. So, they made a hero of a crooked lawyer, who had committed God knows how many trifling felonies.

Lochte: You went a year without making a movie before *El Dorado*. Were you in retirement?

Mitchum: I'm always in retirement. I said, "Swell." You know, after the *Blood Alley* thing [Mitchum was replaced by John Wayne in a film made by Wayne's company], Duke felt culpable. I told him, "I understand, Duke. It was either that or lose

11 million bucks. So, fuck me, what the hell." [Howard] Hawks is a beautiful, consummate, all around writer-director. He has a habit of standing there, staring out into space. "Don't bug him," people say, "he's writing." I watched him one day [Mitchum stands tall, stares off, a faraway look in his eyes, then he pauses to glance at his watch]. He's just checking to see if it's time to break. That's precisely all he's doing.

Lochte: How did you get involved in *The Way West*?

Mitchum: The script was around for 11 years. I'd come back from Vietnam and I called my old lady and she told me she'd sold the farm. I felt I had to get back to work, so I called Reva and asked what scripts were around. She mentioned *The Way West*. "Is that still floating?" I asked. "Who did they finally con into it?" She said, "Kirk Douglas." I said, "Good, that's the one." Vietnam wasn't exactly a rest cure, those three months. So, I figured I'd go out there and get a little outdoor exercise and relaxation while those clowns would be talking to each other with all that dialogue. I told them I'd play the part of the scout, so they got Dick Widmark for the other part, the one who had all that dialogue with Kirk. I go off giving it that hand over the eyebrow, looking for Indians, right? I was off trout fishing and fooling around.

Kirk was sort of running the company, which was all right with me. Except, every now and then, some guy'd show up with yellow or pink pages and say [imitation], "*Koik* wrote these last night." I'd drop 'em on the floor. "I already learned the dialogue and the hell with this stuff," I would say. I mean, I could have done the same thing to Kirk, right? What was that? First day I went to work, I was going around goosing the grips and trying to head down to shore, when I hear a voice saying, "There'll be no levity in this company." A big lecture. I thought to myself, I wonder who's putting up with this shit? I turned around and Kirk was smiling. I went back, continuing my way through the rocks. I hear Kirk giving out with another tirade. And when I turn around, he's smiling again. About a month or two later, I was talking with some guys and I said, "I'd like to know who the asshole in the company is who was putting up with that kind of bullshit." And they answered, "It was *you*. He was talking to *you*." I couldn't believe it. It was very dumb of him to try and provoke a confrontation with me. He alienated the crew, which is never a good thing. So many guys wear balls in their pockets. Tightening their guts, shouting, "Look at me; I'm a wrestling champion." As far is Douglas is concerned, all I have to do is whack him one between the horns and it'd be all over. And he knows it. No levity on the set. Right.

Lochte: *Secret Ceremony* seems like a strange film for you to be in.

Mitchum: Elizabeth [Taylor] called here and we talked about it for a while. Then I went down to Mexico, and Joe Losey called me on the beach at Mazatlán. After about ten minutes of telephone conversation, I asked, "Where are you calling from?" I was very impressed when he answered "London," figured he must have a healthy company. Then, Roddy McDowall told me, "You must do it for Liz." And I said, "OK."

Lochte: Roddy McDowall?

Mitchum: He's a good friend of hers. He'd read the script.

Lochte: He sold you?

Mitchum: I figured, what the hell? My old lady wanted to go to England. I think I had a parenthetical 21 days and only had to work 11 of them. So why not? Pick up my $65 and go home. I like it when it works out like that. Even the weather worked.

Lochte: I read stories about you and Trevor Howard hoisting a few during *Ryan's Daughter*.

Mitchum: Trevor lived two miles away at one end of town and I was at the other. When I first met him, he hit me in the head— whap! Then he'd say, "You sweet thing," and then he'd kiss you. Then—whap! Again. There was this bartender in the club who started moving forward, but I waved him back. I was reeling. We got along fine.

Lochte: There is a story about your impressing David Lean.

Mitchum: I guess you mean that the time I was fooling around on the set. He thought that nobody could be a sincere *ack*-tor and behave like that. So, he shouted, "Roll 'em!" or whatever they say, "Act-*shun*!" And I went through the whole thing in one take. He was decimated. What did he expect at those prices?

Lochte: What about the film itself?

Mitchum: It's good enough. But at half the cost, it might have been great. That would have improved the product. If it hadn't been so overloaded.

Lochte: What about *Going Home*?

Mitchum: That was a case of the director concentrating on long, static closeups of Jan-Michael Vincent and not allowing him to show what he could do. Herbert Leonard was the producer-director. He'd done *Route 66* on TV.

Lochte: I thought *The Wrath of God* was pretty entertaining.

Mitchum: I don't know what happened with that one. MGM had to release *Shaft* and they pulled that picture out of theaters. Probably for business reasons.

Lochte: That brings us to *The Friends of Eddie Coyle*.

Mitchum: Yeah. I hope we get paid in front. Actually, I think it's a pretty good movie. I liked the book, the script. They asked if I'd play Dillon [the second lead played by Peter Boyle]. Reva relayed the request. I asked, "How long will it take?" "Three weeks." That sounded OK. It meant that I could leave here, get to London to pick up my laundry. I couldn't have done that, otherwise I'd wind up with the most expensive wardrobe this side of Liberace. So, I'd go by way of Boston. Three weeks later, I'd be free—head down to the Caribbean and fool around. Then be home for the holidays. So, I said OK. Then, hesitatingly, they asked, "Ah-h, would he play Eddie Coyle?" "I don't know," Reva said. "You mean he'd rather play a relatively supporting role than a title role?" She asked how long it would take and they said six weeks. So, they said, "We'll cut the part so that he gets off earlier than six weeks." And I did it. I'd do the scenes in one take. I forgot some lines, but, what the hell, they printed it anyway. Everybody's good in the picture. It's a good picture, but it doesn't happen to be the one I made. I think it'll be successful. I don't know how much it cost, but let 'em take their best shot. If they'd put it back together the way it was in the script, they'd have a better picture.

Lochte: They have the footage then?

Mitchum: Maybe they burned it. I don't know. Maybe they had this meeting and decided, "Let's burn this shit." You should read the script and see what it could have been. But there's not much I can do about it, really. Oh, maybe I could go out and do *Dirty Harry* or *Patton*. But that means pissing on my opinions and pissing on myself. And I don't find that truly necessary. Do you?

INTERVIEWS WITH
CHARLES CHAMPLIN

Robert Mitchum was interviewed by Charles Champlin in the journalist's Bel Air backyard for an installment of *Champlin on Film* for the Z Channel. It was taped in the late spring of 1988 and first aired on June 8, 1988. Mitchum reciprocated the hospitality in a second videotaped interview at his Santa Barbara County home in 1994. The actor was scheduled to be an honored guest at the Lone Pine Film Festival in Central California later that year, but backed out to make the film *The Sunset Boys* in Europe. That second interview was shown to the Lone Pine audience in lieu of Mitchum's presence.

CHARLES CHAMPLIN

Charles Champlin was the principal film critic for the *Los Angeles Times* from 1967 to 1980 and served as the paper's arts editor for 26 years until his retirement in 1991. He was host for *Champlin on Film* on the Z Channel and later on Bravo in the 1980s and '90s. He is the author of *George Lucas: The Creative Impulse*; *The Movies Grow Up, 1940–1980*; *Hollywood's Revolutionary Decade: Charles Champlin Reviews the Movies of the 1970s*; *John Frankenheimer: A Conversation With Charles Champlin*, and *Back There Where the Past Was*.

Charles Champlin: Robert Mitchum has always been one of those distinctive personalities, one of those rugged individualists that the movies can't get along without, and haven't been able to get along without for 40 years. Some of the titles we all remember are *The Story of G.I. Joe, The Friends of Eddie Coyle* and

Farewell, My Lovely, and for television, *The Winds of War* and the sequel coming up early next year, *War and Remembrance*. I'm really struck by the fact that you made 19 films in 1943. You must have been going someplace different every day.

Robert Mitchum: Bicycling back and forth, yeah.

Champlin: Were you ever under contract at one point to any studio?

Mitchum: At one point I was. For ten years I was under contract to RKO from, I believe, 1944 to '54.

Champlin: Were you independent by choice?

Mitchum: You go to work. At that time, under a regular star contract, they put you to work for $250 to $300 a week as against a free-lance salary of $500 a week.

Champlin: So, for security reasons . . .

Mitchum: It was steady work—40 weeks a year.

Champlin: You have worked a lot of places. You've had an adventurous life, I take it. You were born in Connecticut, but lived all over, didn't you?

Mitchum: We had to stay ahead of the rent. My father was killed when I was two years old. My mother went to the work for the *Bridgeport Post-Telegram*. Before then she worked in a photographer's studio. We were just kids and were farmed out to relatives mostly. We just went from place to place. My father was from South Carolina, so I lived in South Carolina a while. I lived up in the country in Connecticut, and in Philadelphia and down in Delaware—my grandmother had a farm in Delaware. And I went to school in Connecticut, Delaware, Philadelphia and New York.

Champlin: I read somewhere that you worked on a freighter once.

Mitchum: Yeah. Seems to me I was about 14. Worked on a salvage ship out of Fall River, Massachusetts. Those Howard Line coal barges would just suddenly sink without any warning. And we would go out and suck up the coal and salvage it. We had two divers aboard and a big suction hose—not a very glamorous job [laughs].

Champlin: How did you come to California?

Mitchum: On a freight train. We were in Delaware and the temperature went down to 18 below zero, which was the coldest on record at that time. The outdoor plumbing froze up, and I said, "That's it for me." My sister was out here. She was married to a Navy man. So, I just crawled onto a freight train and came out to California. It wasn't too bad. It wasn't very comfortable. As a matter of fact, I remember the first time I ever rode the cushions on a train. I couldn't sleep, because I was so accustomed to that jar when they stop to pick up cars again.

Champlin: [laughs] That's funny. Your sister was involved with theatre down in Long Beach, wasn't she?

Mitchum: Well, she had been involved in vaudeville since she was 14. She married this fellow in the Navy. And he was transferred out to Long Beach and she came out to Long Beach, and they had the Long Beach Players Guild there. And she became involved in it. And I was working at the American-Hawaiian docks. We got 14 hours a week—I was a longshoreman. I had my evenings free, so I went down and I started writing children's plays and they cast me in, I think, *Rebound* and *The Petrified Forest*, things like that.

Champlin: How did the break to movies come about?

Mitchum: I worked down there in radio, and when I came up to L.A., I was writing radio continuity, largely, and somebody said, "If you ever want to step on the other side of the microphone to do a bit now and then . . ." And I was doing, I guess it was, *The Lower Depths* with an old Russian emigré named Michael Marks down on La Cienega Boulevard. And Paul Wilkins, an agent who had been a casting director, said, "If you ever want to do something professionally, let me know." I was working at Lockheed. I worked the graveyard shift. And I went blind. And they put me in Physicians & Surgeons Hospital for three days. When I came out, I went to see the doctor. And he said, "There's nothing wrong with you." I said, "You don't go blind for 'nothing wrong.'" "Your problem is," he said, "is that that you just don't like the job. When you wake up, you know you have to go to work, so you don't sleep." So I said, "What's the answer?" He said, "Quit." So, I probably slept four hours in maybe a year. I'd go to work on 15 or 20 minutes sleep. So I said, "By the time I quit and cash in my two checks, I've got $18." He said, "Things will have come to a dire pass when a clown like you has to walk out on the street and starve to death. It's up to you. Either blow your mind or quit your job." I went to work in a shoe store, working on commission. And, it was two weeks, I guess, Paul Wilkins took me out to see people and on probably the second or third interview, I went over and saw Pop Sherman and Bill Boyd. And they nodded in agreement and, I thought, "Good." I had borrowed a suit from a fellow named Jack Shea, who was a working actor. I thought, "Boy, I'm going to be the juvenile." Bill says, "He looks a little mean around the eyes. Listen, don't shave or cut your hair until you hear from us." I went up to Kernville, California, and started falling off horses.

Champlin: Had you done any riding before that?

Mitchum: No. Well, they asked me, "Can you ride?" I said, "Oh, yeah"—anybody then who had long hair they used to call a New York actor, and I had hair that I could tuck into my shorts just to save the price of a haircut. But I said, "Oh, yeah, I used to break horses on my daddy's ranch." They said, "Where was that?" I said, "Texas"—just made it up. So, I got on the first horse and he threw me 40 feet. I got up. And he threw me three or four times and I managed to get him under control. There was a cowboy, one of the first all-around champions, guy named Cliff Parkinson, and he came up to me and said [sarcastic imitation], "Just look like you can ride, kid."

Champlin: [laughs] You did several of those Hopalong Cassidy pictures . . .

Mitchum: I did six of them, I think. It was kind of my road game. Whenever I had nothing else to do, I could always get a job on a Hoppy.

Champlin: I guess the turning point for you was *The Story of G.I. Joe.*

Mitchum: It sure was.

Champlin: You were working for William Wellman, a real character. Where did you shoot it, by the way?

Mitchum: On the 40 acres, the backlot at Pathé. And we went out to Victorville, I guess it was, on a dry riverbed out there. Bill was great, really.

Champlin: I got to meet him at the end of his life. He was a real original, a really salty character.

Mitchum: He was a funny guy. As you know, they called him "Wild Bill." But he was a really tender-hearted, sympathetic man. He hated producers, wouldn't let the producer on the set. If he saw the producer on the set, that was it—all osmosis ceases. He was a great man.

Champlin: He was married quite a few times, then settled on Dottie, but there, for a while, he said, he thought the whole world was populated exclusively by mothers-in-law . . . . One of the films that people always associate with you is *Out of the Past*, a film noir. I don't know if you had any idea while you were making it that it would become such a classic. But it had a hard plot to keep track of.

Mitchum: I'm sure it was. I don't remember it. But it was originally called *Build My Gallows High*. And I was working on *Pursued* just prior to that and Dame Judith Anderson and Teresa Wright both said, "You're not going to go off after this and do a picture called *Build My Gallows High*? We did it though. We were sort of the B-faction at RKO.

Champlin: Jacques Tourneur directed it. He was doing a lot of stuff that still holds up, the horror films such as *Cat People* . . .

Mitchum: I believe so. He spoke French and he had Simone Simon. I remember one time in the picture there's a scene in which I'm hiding behind the drapes in the bedroom and the telephone rings and Janie Greer comes in and picks it up. So, we shot it, cut, print. They said, "Wait, wait a minute, Mr. Tourneur." He said, "What's the matter?" And they said, "There was no telephone on the set, and a hand came right through the wall and put it down there"—on film. Jacques just looked through the viewfinder and said, "It could have been anyone's hand. Print it."

Champlin: [laughing] We've got a clip from *Out of the Past*. Let's take a look at that and come back and talk more with Robert Mitchum.[clip] That was good to see again. It reminds me of a line that Bobby Clark said of a revival of *Sweethearts*—"Never was a thin plot so complicated." But on the other hand, that was really an interesting study of good and evil and the corruption of a good man by an evil lady.

Mitchum: I kind of enjoyed seeing it again.

Champlin: That reading was so natural. Did Tourneur talk much about performance?

Mitchum: No. He didn't talk about performance at all. Paul Valentine, who plays Joe—he had to keep Paul Valentine on track, because he thought the whole thing was just silly. "We're just kidding, right? We're just making believe"—that sort of thing. And in a moment of horror, he'd be giggling, and that took up a little of Jacques's time. And we had just seen Kirk [Douglas] in *The Secret Love of Martha Ivers* . . .

Champlin: Yeah, his first film.

Mitchum: . . . and he was very good, so we were very pleased that he was working with us.

Champlin: You worked with Howard Hawks on *El Dorado*. He must have been an interesting guy, another original.

Mitchum: Well, I had known Howard slightly, more or less socially. At one point they wanted to do *The Big Sky*. And the script had been so changed [from the original story], that I just didn't want to do it. I was a good friend of Bud Guthrie's [A.B. Guthrie Jr., the author of the novel on which the movie was based, and also of the Pulitzer Prize-winning *The Way West*, which was made into a film with Mitchum and Kirk Douglas in 1967]. And Eddie Lasker [associate producer] sort of dismissed Bud Guthrie and I was a bit offended by that. So, I opted out. Ed Lasker was furious—"How *dare* you turn down a picture with Howard Hawks!?" I said, "Just that simply" [Kirk Douglas replaced him]. Finally, Howard called me [in 1966]. I was in Chicago visiting someone. Howard said [slow, sonorous Hawks imitation], "*Bo-h-h-b*, how about a Western with Duke Wayne?" I said, "Fine. Sounds great. Where are you going to shoot it?" He said, "I thought we'd do it in Old Tucson." I said, "Good—I like that, too. What's the story?" "Oh, no story, Bob. Just character. Stories bore people. No story, just character." I said, "OK," and that was it, too [Champlin laughs]. When we were on location in Tucson, I'm shot in the right leg. And so I would assume that the crutch was under my right arm. He and Duke both argued against it. Duke said, "I used to break my leg every Saturday afternoon playing football." Howard said, "Besides, it keeps your gun hand free, *Bo-h-h-b*."

So, I have a crutch under this arm and I hippity-hopped around on the bad leg—the crutch under the wrong arm. We went back to the studio and had to reshoot the shooting scene, because of the light. And we went on from there directly into the sheriff's office and there we are and I've got my finger in the hole in my leg, and it's established that it's the right leg, certainly. The fellow playing the doctor was a young Canadian physician, a surgeon. He said, "Oh yes, the crutch substitutes for the injured member." So, the crutch is now under my right arm. So they came back from lunch one day—the dailies—and [Hawks' associate] Paul Helmick says, "Oh God . . ." They had just seen the rough cut. "What Is it?" He said, "Every time you come in through a door the crutch switches, from exteriors to interiors and vice versa—the crutch goes" . . . *ph-ph-t, ph-ph-t!* [gestures indicating a switcheroo]. [Champlin's laughter] I said, "What are we going to do?" He says, "Oh God!" So, Howard came in and they said, "Mr. Hawks, we've got a big problem." Howard says, "Oh, what's that?" Paul explained it to him and Howard said, "*Oh-h-h*, they'd never notice that—they'll never notice that."

So, finally, we cut to last sequence in the picture and I'm sitting behind the sheriff's desk. And we have just arbitrarily sprayed Duke in the leg with shotgun pellets, you know, they had just picked them out, nothing really serious. But he's on crutches. And he's taking off to go across town to visit the madam. So, he picked up a crutch. And Howard had come to me and said, "All right, Bob, you were a writer. How do we solve the this? How do we get out of this?" This is the *last day*. So, when Duke picked up the crutch, I said, "That's my crutch." He says, "Where's mine?" I said, "Right under your nose." So he picks it up and starts out and I said, "You've got it under the wrong arm." He said, "How the hell would you know? You've been switching back and forth ever since . . ." And that was it.

Champlin: Really? [laughing] Ah, reality. That's funny.

Mitchum: And nobody paid much attention to it. I asked the continuity girl, I said, "Charlsie [Bryant], when the girl runs out to stop the wagon, was that the same night [as] . . . ?" She said, "Wait a minute. If you're talking continuity, forget it. I gave it up last November." We sat down at a table one time. There are five guys there. I said, "Howard, this guy's already dead"—[interruptive imitation] "Might want to use him again, *Bo-h-h-b*."

Champlin: I didn't realize he had such a carefree attitude.

Mitchum: He knew what he was doing. He had all the material and he would juxtapose when he cut it—put this scene there and this one back there. They would run it at sneak previews and the one that worked the best, that was it.

Champlin: Someone I wanted to talk about, who is quite removed from Howard Hawks, is David Lean and *Ryan's Daughter*. It was a long shoot, wasn't it?

Mitchum: Eleven months. That was due really to David's introspection. He would stare into space for long periods of time. But I had seen him in Rome, I believe, and they were talking about the desert picture . . .

Champlin: *Lawrence of Arabia.*

Mitchum: . . . and he said [Lean imitation], "No, Bob, I want to do a quiet little love story." And *Ryan's Daughter* was it, $10 million later.

Champlin: We have a scene from it in which Sarah Miles confesses her love for you. Let's take a look at that. [clip] That must have been pleasing for you to do, because it's a stretch.

Mitchum: It's my job, isn't it?

Champlin: It is indeed. That must give you some satisfaction to look at that.

Mitchum: Yeah. It's a matter of being accepted, really, by David. I'm not sure that David might have had second thoughts. Trevor Howard had insisted that David hates actors.

Champlin: [laughs] Listen, thanks for this talk and so much good work through the years.

Mitchum: Thank you.

[music up]

[Following is the second taped interview conducted by Charles Champlin in the backyard of the Mitchum home.]

Champlin: Well, Bob Mitchum, here we are in sunny Santa Barbara, not in Lone Pine, but I'm willing to talk to you anywhere, anytime.

Mitchum: Before we get into this thing, there's been a bit of a change. I planned, really and seriously, to be in Lone Pine for the festival, but I signed to do a film that will take me to Norway and to Germany, then back to Norway, and I cannot be in Lone Pine. I'm very, very sorry, and I'm sure you can forgive me.

Champlin: Bob, talk a little about the picture in Europe. It's called *The Sunset Boys*.

Mitchum: It involves four ancient physicians who have a burial pact. As each one expires, the others get together and sing the old songs and put him in the ground. There is sort of a subplot about one of them who was madly in love with a singer during the Third Reich eminence and he keeps looking for her and they collectively keep looking for her during the period in Germany.

Champlin: Our demon historian, Dave Holland, calculated that you made six films up in Lone Pine, going back to *Hoppy Serves a Writ* in 1943. I was wondering if you have any particular memories of your exposure to Lone Pine.

Mitchum: Not really, I just remember the Dow Hotel and the Sierra Cafe and one more place up the road that they called "The Bucket of Blood." I'm usure as to the true name of it. We sallied forth every day and went to the Alabama Hills or, on one occasion, out to the alkali desert, east of Lone Pine. And I remember that the cowboys, when it used to get really overbearing out there, would gallop by the camera and throw a handful of sand in it. Well, that's about a four-hour delay. And they'd go fall into the shade of a cactus.

Champlin: You had done your first starring role up there. That was in *Nevada*, 50 years ago. Do you have memories of that one? Did you get treated differently now that you had the starring role?

Mitchum: No. Tim Holt had gone into the Air Force and he had done those Zane Grey westerns prior to my emergence. They grabbed me and pulled me up there. There's not really much difference. I think I got better wardrobe.

Champlin: I'm always amazed to talk about your early days. You had been on a chain gang, I guess. Talk about that, because you were just a kid, weren't you?

Mitchum: I was just 15, and they nailed me down in Savannah, Georgia, [. . . on a] common charge of vagrancy. And they gave me 180 days on the chain gang. It cost them 16 or 30 cents a day to feed you and they hired you out to the highway department for $2 a day.

Champlin: But you found your way west riding the rails into Los Angeles into the yards out there.

Mitchum: The rest of the bums on the train said, "Don't ride into the yard in L.A., because they grab you and put you in Lincoln Heights [Jail] and de-louse you and keep you for three days. But I was so exhausted by the time I got in there—they said, "Go and hitchhike from an earlier stop"—but I just rode right into the old Alameda Street Yards and there were four Mexicans sitting under the water tank and they had a guitar and a big jug of wine. And they called me over, gave me some wine and played a few numbers and they showed me how to get out of the place. They gave me directions to the Midnight Mission. And I thought, this must be it, the promised land, because they have a reception committee even for the bums, the hobos.

Champlin: How did you decide that acting was something that you wanted to do?

Mitchum: While I was at Lockheed, I did *The Lower Depths* in a theatre on La Cienega Boulevard and I had done some work with the Long Beach Players Guild—*Rebound*, *The Petrified Forest*. And this agent said that, "If you ever want to work professionally, please call." So, I called.

Champlin: And I gather that at one time at RKO that they wanted you to change your name, that Robert Mitchum would never go as a screen name

Mitchum: Well, I would go through the same routine everywhere. They'd say, "Did you ever think of getting your nose fixed?" And I'd say, "I had it fixed several times with a straight left." And "Mitchum" [shakes head] . . . So, RKO wanted to change my name to Robert Marshall. So I went home and talked to the wife and she said, "No way, Mr. Mitchum." So, my wife and I are having lunch with Jill Esmond, who was married to Laurence Olivier, and we were discussing this, and she said that when Larry had first come out here and was talking to RKO, they had wanted to change his name, that Olivier—they'd never be able to pronounce it much less it be a draw. And she said, "We insisted on keeping our own names and I think we've done rather well." So, just then a man comes up and says, "Hello, Bob. Hello, Mrs. Marshall." She said, "No, it's Mitchum." And he kept this up. And, finally he left and said, "I'll see you later, Bob. Goodbye, Mrs. Marshall." So, Jill Esmond says [imitation], "Is that the chap who tried to change your name?" I said, "Yes." She said, "What's his name?" I said, "Herman Schlom" [longtime RKO producer]. And she said [imitation, rolling eyes], "Re-e-eally? Re-e-eally?"

Champlin: When ever anybody talks about you as an actor, they say that you have this really direct relationship with the camera, that you don't appear to be acting. Is that instinctive or what? Do directors help you with that or what?

Mitchum: I have no idea where the camera is or what it's doing, honestly. I remember one time, I was working with Loretta

Young [on *Rachel and the Stranger*] and she started changing the lights. She said, "Put an inkie on this one and put a kicker on number two . . . ." And she said, "I don't know why I'm worried about him, he's been working in nothing but Klieg light all his life and here he is, he doesn't even know what we're talking about." I said, "I know, Loretta, I just don't care." And she says, "I'm sure you don't. But *I* do. So, put a half- . . ."

Champlin: It's a wonderful quality, because you do communicate with the camera, so I assume that you must be a dream for directors to work with.

Mitchum: I assume that they know their jobs. As a matter of fact, a long time ago, there was an article in *Esquire* magazine on "Why a director?" Because, with a good cameraman, which is the very same thing in a lot of cases, you don't need a director.

Champlin: People remember you so specifically for some parts. In the original *Cape Fear*, you played one of the most menacing characters that you've ever played. You had quite a scene where you had a fight—who was the actress in *Cape Fear*?

Mitchum: Polly Bergen. It wasn't a fight, really. I just manhandled her. The door was not fixed, so I had to use her body to open the door. And we had to do three takes, because a lamp fell down and I forget what happened on the second one. So, finally, she subsides in the bulkhead, sobbing. And the director said, "Cut." And I picked her up and said, "I'm sorry we had to go through three takes and in all this roughness, I hope I haven't hurt you." And she dug her fingernails into me and said, "Are you kidding? I dig that." And I said, "Now you tell me"—this was her last day on the picture.

Champlin: In the remake of *Cape Fear*, you played a good guy, the lawman in a little town.

Mitchum: The first one was in Savannah, Georgia. And for the second one, we were in Fort Lauderdale. And Bobby De Niro had all these tattoos on. And I said, "God, you've got to go in there in the morning and have the makeup department put all those tattoos on you . . ." He said, "If you don't use soap, it doesn't wash off."

Champlin: [laughs] Well, I think the first one is the scarier of the two pictures. There's something about black and white. Another picture people always remember you for is *The Night of the Hunter* with Mr. Laughton. He was no doubt a great person to be around I should think.

Mitchum: Well, he was a great appreciator. I wanted so much to please him. He was a total audience.

Champlin: You worked with a man I knew slightly, but whom I worship as a filmmaker, and that was David Lean, on *Ryan's Daughter*.

Mitchum: A very complex man, a very dear man.

Champlin: More recently, you did a voiceover thing on *Tombstone*, which I liked a lot.

Mitchum: Well, they sent me the script to play Old Man Clanton. In the first shot, I come helter-skelter out of a rocky canyon four miles up into that canyon, which I figured I could manage. Then the second scene, I'm lying there with a dead horse on top of me. So, the doctor said, "Uh-uh. No way." I had to bow out of that and they cut the scene out of the picture.

Champlin: All kinds of stories have become attached to you that have become kind of legendary over the years, such as the one about you getting a better dressing room.

Mitchum: I guess that was on *Nevada*. At the studio, I was upstairs in the locker room where all the extras change, and I couldn't get my big western hat in the locker. And there was no place to shower or anything like that. So, I just went out into the park in the center of the studio, took off my clothes, took a garden hose and took a shower. Had a bar of soap. And Ed Killy, the director, came up and said, "What the hell are you doing?" I told him. He said, "Put your pants on." He took me to the producer's office and said, "This is the star of my picture, for crissake! He's gotta have a dressing room." So, I got a dressing room.

Champlin: [laughing] You've got to take matters into your own hands sometimes. That's funny. It's amazing how much you worked in those days. I remember Raoul Walsh once telling me that he would finish shooting a picture on Thursday and on Friday morning there would be a new script on the porch right along with the *L.A.Times*.

Mitchum: At one period when I was at RKO, they loaned me to Metro to do *Undercurrent* with Bob Taylor and Kate Hepburn. And while I was in the office somebody came in the office from Arthur Hornblow and I ended up doing the thing with Greer Garson [*Desire Me*]. And I was working on a picture with Laraine Day [*The Locket*], and we were working nights out on the 40 acres. I'd finish up at dawn, go into makeup at Metro at 7 A.M. and at noon, they shipped me to Monterey and I worked all afternoon with Greer Garson. I worked something like 21 days and nights. Never got a chance to sleep. Completely lost my mind.

Champlin: You worked with Darryl Zanuck, because he was very close to *The Longest Day*. Did you see much of him on that picture?

Mitchum: No. He was very much like the general, you know, flying all over the place. He had three or four companies going at once when we were in France. Zanuck would show up, then take off again, overseeing the whole project.

Champlin: That film saved Twentieth Century Fox, because it was on the verge of bankruptcy from all of the cost overruns on *Cleopatra*. *The Longest Day* was such a big hit that it kept Fox from rolling over.

Mitchum: He had sent me the script. For that sort of venture, it was a very good script. And so I said, "Sure. Fine." So Duke Wayne called me and asked me if I was going to do it. And I said yes. And Duke says, "Well, OK." And Hank Fonda called me. Darryl credited me with bringing them into the fold, which was the reason they presented me with *Patton*. But I didn't feel up to that. I had been under contract for so long, I felt that they had all of that World War II hardware in Spain, where they were going to shoot the film, that they would just march that stuff back and forth in front of the camera—clank, clank, clank!—and then back-charge $14 million and then back away from the story of Patton. Patton was really a strange and complex character. I knew his nephew, and he suggested me for the thing. So, I went in for wardrobe and I then begged off. I said, "Please, I suggest you get somebody who's really going to fight for the character." And I suggested George Scott, and I'm glad I did.

Champlin: People will remember him forever for that. It's one of those completely indelible roles. It seems to me that you love to work.

Mitchum: Yeah, I do—my vacation.

Champlin: First-cabin treatment and a decent wage, I suspect. I wish we were going to be at Lone Pine. I expect to be there. Listen, it's been really terrific.

Mitchum: Thank you.

INTERVIEW WITH JERRY ROBERTS

This interview was conducted on June 12, 1991, at Robert Mitchum's home in Monecito, California, and was primarily used as the final word to correct and clarify points of confusion about the actor's life and career for a research book entitled *Robert Mitchum: A Bio-Bibliography*, published in 1992 by Greenwood Press. Part of the purpose of the interview was to discuss aspects of Mitchum's life that weren't publicly known. Most of the yes/no clarifications have been edited out. This informal talk took place over coffee for much of the morning and afternoon in Mitchum's study, a spacious room with floor-to-ceiling bookshelves.

JERRY ROBERTS

Jerry Roberts's books include *Robert Mitchum: A Bio-Bibliography; Movie Talk From the Front Lines: Filmmakers Discuss Their Works with the Los Angeles Film Critics Association* (co-edited with Steven Gaydos); *An Annotated Guide to Over 1600 Nonfiction Books About Central and South American Jungles;* and *Rain Forest Bibliography.* A frequent contributor to *Daily Variety* and *DGA Magazine* and other periodicals, Roberts was a columnist and critic for the *Cinemania* World Wide Web site and San Diego-based Copley News Service, and a news reporter for the *Pittsburgh Post-Gazette.*

Jerry Roberts: You told me on the telephone that Durman is your real other middle name, following Charles, not "Duran," as it appears most places. And that name came from a friend of your father's. Is that the friend's first name or his last name?
Robert Mitchum: First name.
Roberts: Do you know what his last name was?
Mitchum: I have no idea.

Roberts: Did you ever live in Florida?

Mitchum: At one point, maybe, before my father was killed, we may have lived in Florida for a time.

Roberts: So that would have been in your first year.

Mitchum: Yes.

Roberts: Have you ever investigated your Blackfoot Indian heritage?

Mitchum: I was going to do some of that when I was down in Charleston, but I didn't have the time. I ran across a [Works Progress Administration] book that investigated the rivers, the Indian tribes, in a rather cursory manner. They gave some explanation for the presence of the Blackfoot Indians in the Carolinas. [Native American features] are quite apparent in some of the Mitchums.

Roberts: Is there any indication how far back it goes in the family?

Mitchum: My father was half-Indian. His mother was half-Indian and his father was half-Indian. I vaguely remember the grandmother, or somebody's grandmother, called Alice Pat, and she was a full-blooded Indian in South Carolina.

Roberts: Were you ever in a reform school in New Haven?

Mitchum: No. I was in a juvenile detention hall. A kid named Manuel Barque and I took off and we got as far as New Haven. They picked us up and put us in this place, a detention hall, and eventually turned us loose. We were about 11, I guess.

Roberts: Where were you living at that time?

Mitchum: Delaware.

Roberts: How old were you when you attended Haaren High School in New York City?

Mitchum: Fifteen.

Roberts: And 1933 was the year when you were arrested in Savannah, Georgia, and put on the chain gang . . .

Mitchum: That was the same year.

Roberts: You eventually got your high-school diploma from Felton High School [in Delaware] . . .

Mitchum: Yes.

Roberts: That wasn't too long ago, was it?

Mitchum: A few years ago.

Roberts: They just sent it to you, right? There was no explanation with it, was there?

Mitchum: No. I was a graduate of Felton. I was 14, I think. And I got to New York and was 15 years old. And you couldn't be on the street in New York if you are under 16, unless you had a work permit or a high school diploma. So, I went to Haaren High School.

Roberts: You graduated at 14?

Mitchum: I had gone through school fairly rapidly.

Roberts: I read somewhere where you were expelled for life from Felton High.

Mitchum: Yes. That was retracted, too. There's a very funny story. There was a girls' basketball game, and the girls all run into the showers. Someone had shit in a shower cap. And when we heard about it, I was the one who laughed the loudest. Everybody else froze, and I fell out laughing.

Roberts: You had to be the one then?

Mitchum: Had to be the one. There was a guy named Francis Murphy, who played tuba in the high school band, who confessed to it.

Roberts: And they still threw you out, too?

Mitchum: Because I laughed. Manuel Barque was the salutatorian and I was the valedictorian. On the night before graduation, Barque set fire to the school, started a fire in a closet. And we took off on an excursion. I never got my diploma until they mailed it to me a few years ago. [Lake Forest School District, which encompasses the area once served by long-defunct Felton High, conferred Mitchum with a diploma in 1976, 44 years after he completed his studies.]

Roberts: There's a story that you worked as an engine wiper. What exactly is that? I guess that was on a boat of some sort.

Mitchum: It was on a salvage ship called the Sagamore out of Fall River, Massachusetts. I was the only one on board, as a matter of fact. My uncle got me the job and I was only there for a very short time.

Roberts: How old were you?

Mitchum: Fourteen, I think.

Roberts: Your aborted career as a prizefighter—was that totally in Sparks, Nevada?

Mitchum: No. Redding, California, too, here, there, off and on. I used to be what they called a "bum fighter." Somebody doesn't show up, you've got a job.

Roberts: You mean guys just wait around for an opportunity . . .

Mitchum: More or less, yes. You got about $25.

Roberts: So, you had about 17 fights?

Mitchum: I don't remember, really. I think it was 17 that I counted.

Roberts: Outside of Redding and Sparks, are there any other cities where you did that?

Mitchum: Actually, no. I was about 18 years old—18 or 19—and I was traveling a lot.

Roberts: There's the story that your brother tells about getting held at gunpoint in Alabama on your first cross-country freight hop. Could you tell the details of that?

Mitchum: We weren't held at gunpoint. We were hitchhiking and we were picked up by a bunch guys in a car who had been carousing around the countryside. We wound up sleeping under a tree at one of their homes and we thought this was a walnut tree. But come morning, we found out that these were pig turds, not walnuts. Their mother gave us breakfast. But these were just some wild kids careening around through the backwoods, down along the Black Warrior River in Alabama. We had just left Bessemer, Alabama.

Roberts: Some bit of information in the press clippings have you spending time during the Depression Era as a dognapper, ransoming the pooches of the rich.

Mitchum: [laughs] It was a funny thing. There was an empty house in Washington, D.C., when I was en route from one place to another. And there was another guy, this tall skinny kid, and another guy, a little Cajun Indian or Creole. I was there three days and in that time he had two dogs. I asked him, "What do you do?" He used to go to Georgetown or someplace and spirit away a dog, and he was marvelous with them, too. And they'd check it out in the paper, a $50 reward or whatever and he'd go, "No, lady, you like the dog so much, you take it for just $25." I couldn't believe it. That's what he did. He was a dognapper.

Roberts: So, someone construed your telling of that story by making you the dognapper.

Mitchum: I guess. I'm sure it's practiced by itinerants. He was very good at it and he loved those dogs. He could spot whether one was a well-bred dog or just a mongrel. And he used to go to affluent neighborhoods. I don't know how he hypnotized those creatures, but he could get them to come around.

Roberts: Are there any towns other than what you've confirmed where you stayed for any time, a month or so? [The towns included Savannah, Georgia; Libertyville, Pennsylvania; Toledo, Ohio; Long Beach and Chico, California.]

Mitchum: No. I just kept moving. Next train out. I think that's why I'm shy in crowds. I remember one time in some town in North Carolina, the whole town was out with pick handles. They could get two bucks a head for you and turn you over to the sheriff. We would scurry around. Slept in a barn. A crowd like that, all of them headed in your direction, they look like a lynch mob to me. They don't mean you well.

Roberts: Your play, *Fellow Traveler*, sort of has the theme of a man without a country, about West Coast labor organizer Harry Bridges . . .

Mitchum: They couldn't deport him from the United states. He was in San Francisco. They tried to deport him to Australia. Australia wouldn't have him. He got as far as Hawaii, which was an American territory then [1930s]. And he tried to organize a union in Hawaii.

Roberts: Since you wrote a play on this and you had been a longshoreman at the American-Hawaiian docks in Long Beach, this was obviously something that meant something to you.

Mitchum: Not really. [In the play] he winds up on a godforsaken island in the South Pacific and there's a little cockney castaway there. And it was a Russian shipping stopover. If you're accepted [by the local native island society], then you must be married, and a criterion for beauty is weight. So they match him up with a great big woman—the cockney also had a great big fat wife. And the cockney says that the preacher had been a missionary. So [the Bridges character] says, "What happened to him?" Cockney says [accent], "Et 'im. I 'ad a bit of 'im, too." He said, "Why didn't they eat you?" Says, "The truth now: You'll eat me." [laughs] He's a little snaggle-toothed, dirty cockney.

Roberts: Have you ever thought about resurrecting the play?

Mitchum: Yes, I thought about it when I saw that they were making a film called *Fellow Traveler* [released, 1989]. I dug it out to look at my registration. But that had long since passed. I was about 18 when I wrote it.

Roberts: Considering that the deportation attempts into the 1950s were based on the fact that the United States accused Bridges of Communism, it might seem that the play and its title—and you have the Russians in there, too—would have been ripe for an investigation of you by the House Un-American Activities Committee, which ruined many Hollywood lives.

Mitchum: The HUAC never had any interest in me, as the play itself remains unknown.

Roberts: Was that about the time you got involved with the Long Beach Players Guild?

Mitchum: Around that time.

Roberts: I understand that you would go to the Players Guild to walk your sister home at night. So what happened? Did you start hanging around a little bit?

Mitchum: Well, that and the people—[guild administrators] Elias Day and Oranne Truitt Day. They asked me to fill in on something and I became involved with them.

Roberts: Do you think you would have become an actor if that never happened?

Mitchum: I have no idea. It was kind of a hole card. Because agents would come down and say, "If you ever want to do anything, let me know." Laraine Day was there. Hugh Beaumont was there.

Roberts: Did you ever write revue material or stand-up material for a man named Pat Rooney? It would have been in the 1940s.

Mitchum: I don't think so.

Roberts: He claims you did.

Mitchum: I used to do that. I used to write material for nightclub performers.

Roberts: Nan Blackstone, Peggy Fears . . .

Mitchum: I wrote a radio show, called *Calling All Girls*. Peggy Fears, Patsy Kelly, I forget who all. I didn't know you were supposed to take a long time. I was writing three scripts a week.

Roberts: Was that for CBS?

Mitchum: I have no idea. I just wrote it, handed it in. Peggy was handling the thing. Alan "Cupid" Ainsworth was the agent.

Roberts: Was that in the 1930s?

Mitchum: It must have been, yeah. I stayed at Peggy Fears's house part of the time and my sister was working in a joint called the Mad Russian, and I stayed in her apartment part of the time.

Roberts: That was before you were married.

Mitchum: Mm-hmm. When I got married I figured I couldn't be coming home at two o'clock in the morning, three o'clock, after I had spent all night with some girl singer and a piano player and arranger. I figured a guy gets married, he gets a lunchbox and goes to work. I went to work at Lockheed. But I had a standing deal with, I believe, MCA, for $500 a week to write for their clients.

Roberts: You wrote me that, with some recording artists, you had a deal whereby you wrote them songs without attribution, without getting credit . . .

Mitchum: Sometimes, I'd write a lyric and sell it for $25.

Roberts: Were any hits made out of them? Can you say?

Mitchum: No. Not really. I sold all rights—$25. Sometimes $50.

Roberts: When you were working for astrologist Carroll Righter [as an advance man and assistant on an Eastern Seaboard tour in 1939], you never did any writing for him did you? It appears several places that you helped ghostwrite his syndicated news-paper column.

Mitchum: No. Do you know what that involves? High mathematics, logarithms . . .

Roberts: You mean astrology?

Mitchum: Yes. Fixing positions, and degrees, my God. He was a summa cum laude graduate of Dickinson College in Pennsylvania. And one of his first essays after he graduated was going to be a legal debunking of astrology. And he got so involved in it that he became an astrologer.

Roberts: He credits you with saving his life when the car you were driving slid off a bridge during a tropical storm into a Louisiana bayou. His door jammed, and the car was sinking and you got up the girders and managed to flag down a car and convince the driver to help you go back and get Righter and pull him out of the car up the girder to safety.

Mitchum: Three days later they pulled the Ford out of the bayou. They hosed it off and it started. And we continued on our merry way.

Roberts: In almost every reference to your first year in movies, they say that you played in 17 pictures in 1943. It was actually 19. A lot of the sources fail to mention *Minesweeper* and *Aerial Gunner*, the two pictures you did for William Pine and William Thomas—the "Two-Dollar Bills."

Mitchum: That's not very unusual, you know—the number of jobs. You work two days on this, five days on that, going back and forth.

Roberts: When you started in westerns in June 1942, what sort of bits did you do?

Mitchum: I played the heavy.

Roberts: I mean particularly the stunts. Did you fall off horses?

Mitchum: I was on top of a rock and I got shot, and I guess I over-acted, because I fell off the rock and came down about 30 feet. And of course, the chaps sort of just kind of dragged me down the side of the rock, and they kept rolling. In time I heard a couple of the other heavies hiding in the rocks, back in the crannies, saying, "He broke his neck." "Yeah, I heard it pop." So I was afraid to move. So, they finally said "Cut!" And they came over and said, "Now just take it easy, move your hands, move your feet . . ." And I was all right. So then they raised hell. They said, "You should have let us known that you're going to do that. We could have gotten a lower shot—that's a hell of a shot."

Roberts: You were just another body to them?

Mitchum: Actually, it was very pleasant company, the old Pop Sherman/Bill Boyd Hopalong Cassidy group. A guy called me just the other day from Orange, [California]; the guy who went up with me on that first job, a guy named Pierce Lyden. We took a Greyhound bus up to Bakersfield, then we took what they called "The Stage" over to Kernville, along the Kern River. The guy was driving like a bat out of hell and there was a young sailor and his bride who were the only other passengers. And Pierce had a crashing hangover, and he grabbed the driver and said, "Either you slow down, or I'm driving." He reminded me of that when he called me the other day.

Roberts: The actor who has played in the most pictures with you was Earl Hodgins, who was in the Hopalong Cassidy pictures with you, but also cast in some of your other movies as well—seven in all. Were you buddies with him?

Mitchum: No. They used to call him "Meatball." He had played snake-oil salesmen, was just a character actor. He was a fixture in a lot of the old westerns.

Roberts: The story has been told by William Boyd that when you started in the Hopalong Cassidy westerns, you were given a contrary horse. And that this stunt man named Charlie Murphy had been killed earlier by the same horse.

Mitchum: No, no. That day we arrived in Kernville, the sun was shining brightly and everybody was sitting around on hotel porches. So Pierce and I got off and were greeting everybody, and they were very somber. And I learned that Charlie Murphy, or Murray, I forget which it was, was driving what they call a four-up. And against all the rules, he had the reins around his wrists. He bounced out of the wagon, went under the wagon, and the wagon went over and over him, just cut him to ribbons. That's why they had taken the afternoon off. So I went in to be fitted for wardrobe. Earl Mosier was the wardrobe man. And he gave me the shirt and the chaps and the pants and so forth. He reached for a hat and said, "What size?" I said, "Seven and a quarter." And he took the hat, took a knife, and scraped the blood from the inside of the hat. I wore the hat during the picture.

Robert: The same hat? You didn't keep it did you?

Mitchum: I wore it in the picture. You don't get to keep the wardrobe. The girls go home at six, you know.

Roberts: There is another story concerning *Thirty Seconds Over Tokyo* about [the director] Mervyn LeRoy calling the cast and crew in on a sound stage and saying, "Nobody's going to make a phone call from here anymore." And you had necessary calls to make to your agent or whomever. And he said specifically that "Bob Mitchum isn't going to make any more phone calls." And the phone rang in the middle of this, as the story goes, and you went over and pulled it right off the wall and took the phone over to LeRoy and said, "Here, Mervyn, I think this is for you."

Mitchum: Sounds good.

Roberts: There's the story that when the cast and crew for *Thirty Seconds Over Tokyo* went to Pensacola, Florida, that you got into a heck of a fight with somebody—with a sergeant when the soldiers were making fun of the Hollywood cast and crew. I think it was Steve Brodie who told some writer the story.

Mitchum: I think it was some guy who was browbeating Bobby Walker. And I just stuck up for Bobby Walker. We were living in a barracks out at Eglin Field, near Fort Walton Beach. Mervyn and all those guys were staying in Pensacola. We were living on the base in the barracks with these guys.

Roberts: You were pretty well established as a movie star around 1946 when you decided to do *The Gentle Approach*, another stage production. Why did you decide to do that?

Mitchum: I honestly don't remember. They were just a group that

I knew. And they were looking for a title. I gave them the title, and I wound up involved, you know.

Roberts: I searched everywhere to find the name of the playwright who wrote that. It's not on the books in New York, because it never played New York.

Mitchum: It played Catalina.

Roberts: That's where I ended up going, to the Santa Catalina Historical Society.

Mitchum: John something-or-other . . . [John O'Dea]

Roberts: That was around the time you were working simultaneously on films starring Katharine Hepburn and Greer Garson.

Mitchum: I remember working once with Kate Hepburn and—the script—and [Hepburn imitation]: "'The world is too much with us; late now soon, spending . . .'—who said that?" I said, "Nobody ever said that." I go to the director and say, "What's this mean?" We sent down to the studio library and I said, "I think you'll find out that Mr. Wordsworth said,

> The world is too much with us; late and soon,
> Getting and spending, we lay waste our powers: . . ."

She was pissed off . . . . She used to come on the set and she knew everybody's first name. The crew would tell you that this was a thing of hers. She couldn't care less about those people. And she would climb up into the gantlines in a pair of jeans with the crotch ripped and a little red muff peeking out there [laughs]. When I was sitting at the piano she comes up in a wheelchair, directing the changing of lights all around. I haven't got a clue. I don't know one side of the camera from the other. She turns to me and says, [Hepburn imitation], "Mr. Mitchum, darling, don't let them muck you about like that." She was changing all the lights on my behalf. I haven't got a clue. That's their department, isn't it?

Roberts: Director Josef von Sternberg, on *Macao*, was pretty autocratic from what I've heard and read. In a story that Jane

Russell told, he didn't allow any food on the set and the next day you walked in with a picnic basket.

Mitchum: He had an altar piece, something they could put the script on. So I was making a sandwich on it.

Roberts: He didn't like that?

Mitchum: No. He got apoplectic at that.

Roberts: Did the "Pounded to Death by Gorillas" thing come from *White Witch Doctor*? Was it because of the scene in which you wrestled with a gorilla?

Mitchum: I don't know. I never saw it.

Roberts: I just thought that that's maybe where it came from.

Mitchum: I just said that that's what I do. The picture opens, I walk out onto the stage, no directions, no plan of action, and a huge gorilla looms up behind me and pounds me on the top of the head, keeps hammering and hammering and hammering until I'm down to the bottom of the floor. And then the gorilla collapses, exhausted, on top of me. And a little girl enters, stage left, and says, "Where is he?" And she peels the gorilla back. She says, "I know he's around here someplace, I can smell him," because I haven't bathed or shaved through the whole thing—in any of these pictures. She peels the gorilla back and drags me up to my feet, puts her arm around me, and looks straight into the camera and says, "I don't care what you say, I like him." I said that that was a Mitchum picture—"Pounded to Death by Gorillas." Every time the writers run short of dialogue or action, they get somebody to beat the bejesus out of Mitchum.

Roberts: On *River of No Return* you and Marilyn Monroe got into a fairly perilous situation. Something happened to the raft you were on in the Banff River . . .

Mitchum: That's right.

Roberts: What happened?

Mitchum: It was anchored to a rock. And the cable just—[snaps fingers]—and we were headed down the river, five sets of falls. Next stop was Calgary. The kid [Tommy Rettig] was tied down. I told Marilyn to lie down because the sweep was going back and forth and I couldn't control it. I knew I could make it to shore, but on the other side of the river. The rescue boat finally came out. So we got the kid into the boat. I told Marilyn to get in. I had the flu. She wouldn't get in until I got in. I said, "Look, it may be a matter of life or death—just get into the boat." She wouldn't do it. So I got in. And then she got in—worried about my flu. So after I got in I realized what the problem was with the rescue boat. Coming out they had hit a rock and there was a hole in the side of the skiff. I just plugged that up with my elbow. And we finally made it back to shore. But she just wouldn't get in there until I did.

Roberts: She was worried about you with the flu, and she could have drowned.

Mitchum: And five sets of rapids ahead.

Roberts: How far off were they?

Mitchum: We were in them.

Roberts: While we're on the subject, you've been in some fairly perilous situations making movies: strapped to the sea turtle in *Heaven Knows, Mr. Allison*, dodging explosion points in *The Longest Day*, getting thrown off horses. There's a quote that's attributable to you, that "Victor Mature wouldn't step off a high curb without a stunt man."

Mitchum: That's right. For good reason.

Roberts: And yet you have done many of your own stunts through the years. Were you told to? Did you do them for authenticity?

Mitchum: On that one, Otto [Preminger, the director] said [gruff Viennese imitation], "You aren't going out on that raft, are you? Are you crazy?!" I said, "Marilyn is there." He said, "She's crazy!" I said, "The kid is there." He said, "His mother vants to send him over Niagara Falls vhile she's vaving ze check dry like zhis! She says, 'Don't forget [to know where] the camera [is]!'"

Roberts: Were you in a plane crash in 1946? This was the crash of a small plane near Bridgeport, Connecticut. I found a couple of small items clipped from newspapers in the library at the Academy of Motion Picture Arts and Sciences that were datelined Bridgeport. You and your stand-in, at that time Mel Sternlight, and another guy were in the plane.

Mitchum: Bridgeport, California. On the way to locations on *Out of the Past*.

Roberts: What happened there?

Mitchum: Crashed [shrugs].

Roberts: Well, I mean, was it an emergency landing or what?

Mitchum: Well, we were coming in. The pilot had no L's or R's. He said [imitation], "Weww, it's not an aiwpowt exactwy. It's a fiewd, a fiewd." As we approached, you could see the wind indicator sticking out straight in front of us, and I said, "Aren't they kind of breathing down our necks?" And he said, "Weww, thewe's some powew wines at the othew end, and the FAA won't awow you to wand at that end, so we have to take hew as she comes." And that was it. We hopped and skipped our way down the field. And there are cars waiting for us at the end and I said, "Just don't hit the Cadillac." At the same time we both jammed down the throttle—I was in the co-pilot's seat. And we shot off this-a-way, jumped a ditch, took down a couple of barbed-wire fences and there was an old lady, an Indian woman, hanging out clothes. We bumped on by. We hit an Indian outhouse and scattered Indian shit all over Mono County. We finally came to a stop and the pilot turned to me and said, "No bwakes." And Leonard Shannon and Mel Sternlight—one of them had fainted. And we got into the car to drive to Bridgeport to the motel. We passed a sign that just said, "Bar." Leonard just tapped the driver on the shoulder. As he got out of the car, he said, "Leave the bags." And then the FAA came up to investigate it and they crashed and landed in the hospital. These power lines were not working, but they hadn't taken them down. They were just a hazard.

Roberts: In 1944 or '45 you had a business manager who embezzled all of your funds. Was his name Behrmann?

Mitchum: That was the second one. Well, he went to San Quentin on several counts of grand theft. He had cleaned out a number of people.

Roberts: How much did he get away with from you?

Mitchum: Whatever I had. I had to go down and testify in court [against him] and he said that anybody who did that, well . . . When they busted into the place up in Laurel Canyon [the marijuana arrest, 1948], I said, "Look, I'll go quietly, but he's got to go—state and federal." I said, "OK, take your best shot." Howard Hughes went crazy. I said, "It's in the papers, Howard, therefore it's true. If I fight it, beat it, they'll say, 'Bought off.' I'll do it up to six months. I'll do it on this ear. Beyond that, we'll talk."

Roberts: There's always this fuzzy connection between the two events—the embezzlement and the marijuana raid. But you're saying that there's a direct link.

Mitchum: According to Mr. Hughes's investigation, there was a very direct link. According to [Mitchum's attorney] Jerry Giesler's investigation, there was a very direct link.

Roberts: That never came out at the time, though.

Mitchum: No. That need never come out.

Roberts: He did go, though.

Mitchum: He did two and a bit in San Quentin. I asked a couple of fellows to bid him welcome when he got to San Quentin. They said, "He'll never see the light of day."

Roberts: Were you worried when he got out?

Mitchum: Why? He was harmless as long as he didn't have your power of attorney or access to your pocketbook. I ran into his rabbi in England and he said that he had gone back to Philadelphia to settle down and become a model citizen.

Roberts: So, if both Hughes and Giesler came up with the same information, then I have to ask you if you think he, Behrmann, instigated or had something to do with the marijuana raid? This whole episode has been rehashed to death, but wasn't Robin Ford the guy who tipped off the police that you were going to be at that cottage on Ridpath Drive in Laurel Canyon?

Mitchum: Danny Ford? They called him "The Moat." It's a long story. He was going to become a real estate man. So we were trying to help him out. We were going out to some chili joint out in the [San Fernando] Valley. He wanted to stop. I said, "No, man let's go." I didn't want to stop. He wanted to stop in Laurel Canyon and make a telephone call. I'm taking him out to dinner. So, I stopped. Seven minutes later [laughs] . . .

Roberts: The police came through the door.

Mitchum: You better believe it. And they knew him.

Roberts: They what?

Mitchum: They knew him. "Robin the golfer," they said.

Roberts: You seem to have rolled with the punches over the years.

Mitchum: What are you gonna do?

Roberts: Did you ever do any rewriting on *Where Danger Lives*?

Mitchum: Was that that thing with Faith Domergue?

Roberts: Yeah. Claude Rains and Maureen O'Sullivan, too. That appeared somewhere, that you rewrote some of the dialogues.

Mitchum: No. The director had a sadistic streak.

Roberts: John Farrow [O'Sullivan's husband and Mia Farrow's father]?

Mitchum: He treated [Domergue] terribly. He had me falling down a set of outside stairs wrapped around a four-story building, with only a railing preventing me from toppling down over the side. [RKO executive] Sid Rogell came on the set, saw what was going on, and practically tried to strangle him [Farrow]. When she's gunned down, he was the guy off-camera shooting the pellets at her—had her do a lot of takes.

Roberts: There's a story about when they had you tied up on a ship during *His Kind of Woman*, that Raymond Burr accidentally bumped your head so hard that it actually knocked you out for a time. And John Farrow, said, "That doesn't look real. Let's do it again."

Mitchum: That's right.

Roberts: There's another story on *Second Chance*, with Jack Palance, that you guys were boxing, and that he also knocked you out. Did that happen?

Mitchum: No. He hit me. We were up in this little conveyance—a cable car. You usually work those things out beforehand. I dropped down and caught him in the gut, because I knew he had a weak gizzard.

Roberts: You nailed him?

Mitchum: I had to. He puked over my shoulder. It took a little while for him to get his breath back. But it worked out all right. The stunt man had already warned me. He said, "Look out."

Roberts: There was also a story from that production that one night in a nightclub, you guys were there with a Mexican general, who was drunk. And he went up to embrace Palance and slipped and just bumped into Palance, who just threw him off . . .

Mitchum: No. I introduced Palance to the Mexican general, who stuck out his hand and Palance just slapped it away.

Roberts: That doesn't sound like a very smart thing to do to a Mexican general.

Mitchum: No. Emilio Fernandez was with us, and Emilio came over and spoke to the general. There were two guys sitting there with violin cases. They thought Emilio was Mexican and Emilio said, "I'm no goddamn Mexican; I'm an American!" And—wham!—the general hit him right between the horns with the butt end of a .45. So, I said, "Let me get the ladies out of here." I went to the side door and tried to talk them into letting Emilio out. And the two guys with the violin cases opened them up and came out with machine guns. So, our driver said, "Don't go back in there. They may think you went out to get a piece. You would be the first one to get it if you went back in." Anyway, Emilio finally came out and then collapsed. It was a delayed knockout. And Palance vanished, switched hotels, registered under another name. This general was head of the National Guard, which in those days was really the security police. He could order a whole village demolished and go home and go to sleep, and not bat an eye. Do you think some actor is going to stop him? Jesus—really, this was one of the most powerful men in Mexico, and not known for his good humor.

Roberts: Palance isn't really known for that, either. They say that you don't even want to have to deal with him.

Mitchum: He's eccentric, to say the very least [laughs]. We lost Palance for a couple of days. We finally had to track him down.

Roberts: Toward the end of your RKO contract, the studio tried to get you to do a couple of movies that you didn't want to do, one with Debbie Reynolds that . . .

Mitchum: The one with Debbie Reynolds was *Susan Slept Here.* I would have had to have taken a summer to learn how to dance. So I said, "What about Dick Powell?" Howard [Hughes] said, "Bob, he's my executive producer." So I said, "He's got a pair of tap shoes up on the shelf somewhere, too." So, Powell, on his way down to the set, stopped at my dressing room with a pair of tapping shoes over his shoulder, and said, [clowning imitation] "Thanks, honey."

Roberts: Trouble seems to happen to some people. Over your career, you've had recurring episodes of trouble with the law, in the press with controversy over things you've said in public. Have you developed any philosophy about it? When you got fired off *Blood Alley,* it was front-page news. When you knocked out Bernie Reynolds in that bar in Colorado, it was front-page news [On November 8, 1951, in a booze-fueled altercation in the Red Fox Bar of the Alamo Hotel in Colorado Springs, where Mitchum had gone to make *One Minute to Zero,* he got into a tangle with Bernard Reynolds].

Mitchum: That's because he was the No. 5-ranked heavyweight in the country. Bernie Reynolds. He had backhanded a colonel and shoved a major away. I said, "Man, you're in trouble." He said, "*I'm* in trouble?" He cocked his hand back like this [demonstrates] and I shifted over and he hit the wall. He said, "You broke my hand!" I said, "*I* broke your hand?" His first contest after he came out of the Army was, unfortunately, with Rocky Marciano. And Rocky came up to see me one time at RKO. He said, "Yeah, we had the same opponent—Bernie Reynolds." I said, "Yeah, you took him out in five heats." He said, "Three."

Roberts: Did you connect one with him?

Mitchum: I had my back against the wall and I had hold of him all the time, digging in, like that. Yeah, I finally—that's how I dislocated this thumb. They finally had five guys on me, one here, one here, one here, one there and one there. He got up and took a roundhouse swing at me. I figured, no way, and I sucked back and he hit the guy on this end. Took a piece of meat out of him. I thought that was not too sporting to try to hit me when I'm standing there crucified. So, I got all of this weight on me, got an arm free, and I hit him with the right hand and—bam!—and that was it. And it jerked my thumb loose. They were going to court-martial him and I really tried to help, and I don't remember if I was really successful there. The brig or the street were his only two options, because they had reprimanded him. But he was beyond control. I heard that they said to him, "Would you like to try him again?" And he said [laughs], "Sure, but not under those circumstances."

Roberts: We have to talk about *Blood Alley*. Basically, you were dismissed by William Wellman . . .

Mitchum: No. Bill called me in and said, "Bob, I want you to know that I had absolutely nothing to do with this."

Roberts: Who, then? Was it Wayne? [John Wayne replaced Mitchum in the film after it was widely reported in the press that Mitchum had gotten involved in an altercation and was fired.]

Mitchum: No. The tax laws had changed and Duke was in New York with Jack Warner. They wanted one more picture [made at a cheaper rate by Wayne's Batjac outfit] on the old format. Duke said, "I don't have another picture." They said, *Blood Alley*." *Blood Alley* was a Batjac production. Duke said, "No, Bob Mitchum is doing that." They said, "Was." The next morning, to save a few million, that was it.

Roberts: Didn't you feel a little framed by that?

Mitchum: I knew what was happening. The true story was never published here in L.A., but it was published in San Francisco. The story goes that I threw [Batjac transportation manager] George Coleman into the water. George Coleman weighed more than 300 pounds. And he had a sheepskin jacket on. I woke up in the morning and the place was full of reporters. And there's

George Coleman in the same sheepskin jacket. It would have been wet, wouldn't it? They said, "Mitchum denies throwing Coleman in the water; Coleman denies being thrown into the water. Obviously, someone's covering up." So, that was it. I came back and they offered me another job with a raise. And I said, "What?" And they said, "Just pick something." I did *Man With the Gun* instead, with young Sam Goldwyn.

Roberts: Didn't that infuriate you?

Mitchum: It was disappointing, because Bill initially would not explain everything to me. They made a gesture toward getting Bogart, but Bogart said no. And Betty Bacall was going to leave the film. He said, "No, dear, stay with it."

Roberts: You once said that the toughest location shoot you had to do was for Wellman on *Track of the Cat*. Is that accurate?

Mitchum: Yes. Mount Rainier. They'd call lunch. And by the time we got up the hill, lunch was over. We had 30 feet of snow. People kept disappearing. We'd hear cries for help. There were pine trees with no snow underneath and someone would be walking and hit a weak spot and fall down in there into these spaces beneath the boughs and we would have to go and pull him out. It was physically exhausting, just rough.

Roberts: Did you direct the children in *The Night of the Hunter*?

Mitchum: At times, yes. Because Charles [Laughton] got so fed up with them. In the scene where the kid comes in the house calling for his mother, suddenly the preacher steps out from behind the doorway. And I said to the kid, "Do you think John is afraid of the preacher?" He said, "Not at all." I said, "Well, you don't know John very well and you certainly don't know the preacher very well." So, he said, "That's possibly why I got the critics' award for *Three Wishes for Jamie* in New York." Laughton just blew up. [Laughton imitation]: "Despicable little snot!" After that I had to go in and direct the scenes. The little girl was all right, a little monosyllabic Kewpie doll. She used to come in with her grandmother and grandfather, in overalls. The grandmother said [imitation]: "Go kiss Mr. Mitchum. Sing him your French song. . . . Give Mr. Mitchum a bi-i-ig kiss. Mr. Mitchum's a producer, you know." She went [slurp] like this. Laughton just threw up. He didn't mind kids, but he didn't like precociousness, presumption.

Roberts: There were also stories that said you immobilized producer Paul Gregory's Cadillac. Shelley Winters tells that in her book [*Shelley*, 1981] and it has also appeared in several magazine stories.

Mitchum: That's not so.

Roberts: Does Frank Sinatra still send you Mother's Day cards?

Mitchum: I have the latest one right here. A telegram.

Roberts: How did that come about? Something to do with your association on *Not as a Stranger* . . .

Mitchum: He went, I believe, to the premiere of *A Star Is Born*. Anyway, I came in in the morning, and he's lying in the dressing room, still in his dinner jacket. So I went over to the refrigerator and mixed up a bloody mary. It was a hospital picture, so we had one of those hospital sippers. I just put it between his lips and put a cold cloth on his head. The bloody mary level went down, he opened his eyes and said, "Mother." Brod Crawford had made one room out of the three adjoining dressing rooms. He just walked through all the doors, picked up the doors and threw them over the side.

Roberts: [Director/producer] Stanley Kramer at the time made the comment that with you and Sinatra and Crawford and Lee Marvin together, it was quite a potent crew. He eventually said that the making of that picture was "ten weeks of hell." And he had wanted to head off any trouble that might dawn by hiring Myron McCormick not only for his acting talent, but also as a sort of stabilizing force. But then he found out that no sooner did McCormick show up from New York that he joined you guys.

Mitchum: Myron McCormick arrived and he had a suitcase with three dirty shirts and the rest of it was filled with Scotch. Tim Wallace [Mitchum's stand-in] said, "Jesus Christ, didn't you think they had any in California?" He put the thing down and "Clank!" We were working at the Beverly Hills Courthouse and he went out when he arrived there before shooting began in the morning, and he was in a state of shock because there were no bars open at 8:00 in the morning . . .

Roberts: As if it were New York.

Mitchum: Exactly. So some cop directed him to the Copper Kettle and he went down and nourished himself. And he came back and he was ready. At the operating table, I said something like "Steady this." He said [jittery imitation], "M-m-maybe you should say, 'J-j-jiggle it around a little bit'—change that line." And Brod Crawford drank Sinatra's wig . . .

Roberts: He *what*?

Mitchum: He drank Sinatra's piece. We were trying to pull it away from him. He's got this hairpiece halfway down, and he takes a glass of vodka and downs the goddamn thing. So, I called Frank—Frank was in Palm Springs—I said, "Guess what? The Crawdad just drank your wig." He said, "Good, I don't have to show up Monday."

Roberts: [laughing] I'll bet that was a sight. Good lord. Ahh . . . Deborah Kerr tells the story about your fight with some sailors. I don't know whether that was in Australia on *The Sundowners* or in Tobago on *Heaven Knows, Mr. Allison*.

Mitchum: Tobago. Our associate producer had a very pregnant wife there, and these three sailors came in. And they were abusing her pretty badly. I went over to speak with them. They weren't supposed to be there. They had orders from the ship that the place was off-limits.

Roberts: They were U.S. sailors?

Mitchum: Yes. They went through what I didn't realize at first was sort of a mock situation—they all jumped on one little guy. So I went over to pull them all off, and that was it. I was in it. Everything worked out very well. So I bought them all a drink, you know, sitting in this little bar. And the largest one of them said, "I don't believe it. I don't believe it. How the hell did that happen?"—working himself up again. I said, "It happened like this." I stepped up, and he went out the door, and I was really afraid I'd broken his neck or something. So then the rest of them came, and everything worked out very well. It was like Errol Flynn. And finally the last sailor—who had been the victim, the patsy in this whole setup—came in and I got him over the edge of the parapet and there's a child's pool down there and I figured that I could just spot him in that. But someone hit me in the kidney. It was my wife. I said, "You're supposed to be on my side." She said, "You're beginning to enjoy it." So, I apologized to everybody, and the Shore Patrol came in and rounded them up. And I tried to plead in their behalf. The Shore Patrol said, "No, this is the only group of troublemakers we've had. We will deal with it." The place was off-limits.

Roberts: Did those guys know who you were?

Mitchum: That's why they came there.

Roberts: You've used a couple of phrases over the years to describe aspects of celebrity. One is "flak fat" and the other is "freak finders." Could you offer your own definitions of those terms?

Mitchum: People contrive or invent stories and put them down and then it becomes gospel and the people eat it up, puke it out and then the next one comes along and repeats the process. Then it's been in print so many times that it becomes true. I told Roger [Ebert], "Print whatever you want. Why waste your time with me? Just go home and write whatever you want. It's got to be true." It's in the papers. Dewey is president.

Roberts: How would you handle the autograph hounds?

Mitchum: All the children want to pet the giraffe, don't they? You don't see a giraffe every day. We were working in Ireland, a little town called Lough Drum. It's market day, Monday. Between the setups, the crew is over in the pub. All these Irishmen say [imitation], "Put your signature on there." They have all of these tiny slips of paper, matchbook covers and things like that. At 5 P.M. they all go home to tea, don't they? And down there are all of these tiny slips of paper in the sawdust, in the spit.

Roberts: Weren't you also involved with John Huston in trying to make a very large man into a prizefighter while you were down in Tobago making *Heaven Knows, Mr. Allison*?

Mitchum: Yeah. John was his babysitter.

Roberts: Irving something . . .

Mitchum: That was just the name that they gave him. We had just been down there on *Fire Down Below*, which was produced by [Albert R. "Cubby"] Broccoli and [Irving] Allen. That's how he got the name—I don't know what his real name was. So, John was going to make a heavyweight out of him. I was just getting over dengue fever and John said, "Go ahead, Bob, put the gloves on." The guy couldn't get out of his own way. And I just reached out and touched him with a left hand and he fell over. And they had a guy there, one of the crew, who had, like 110 fights, a welterweight. And he worked with him. John took him to London. He had his first fight at Wight Stadium. He had to crawl out of the ring after the third round. Coming back from the fight—he had a cousin who was a very good light heavyweight and he was in the car with him, the four of us—and he said, "Did I do anything right?" And John said [imitation], "Not a thing, kid. Not a goddamn thing."

Roberts: You got on well with John Huston. And he has said that *Heaven Knows, Mr. Allison* is one of the best things he ever did. He says no one hardly mentions it within the scope of his career, but it's one of his personal favorites.

Mitchum: Only one time he spoke direction to me. I looked over, past the camera and he said [imitation], "Even more, kid. Even more." I said, "Do you really think so, John?" We did it even more and that was it.

Roberts: Well, that stunt with you roped to the sea turtle was a pretty dangerous deal, wasn't it? Didn't it take off and nearly drag you along a coral reef?

Mitchum: Yeah, but I got myself loose. We had to have a lot of them, you know. They're very large and very strong. But after they dragged my weight through the water, they'd tire and we'd have to bring in a fresh one. They could disembowel you with one claw. We had them all tethered over at Poku Reef and had this giant, Cecil Anton, and he's talking to our secretary one morning and she says, "Good morning, Cecil," and he says [imitation] "Good morning, mistress." She said, "How are you,

Cecil?" He said, "Just keeping body and soul together, mistress." And he comes to report the death of the sea turtles. He says, "They die from the homesickness. They are very far from home." Meanwhile, there's a pile of shells building up on the beach and there have been bonfires going every night. They were eating these 400-pound monsters. But John—the thing with Johnny Huston was that you always knew, no matter what the situation is, he's been there.

Roberts: Well, had he been strapped to a sea turtle?

Mitchum: He'd offered to try it. He'd line up a shot and say, "What do you think, kid? Will it kill you?" I'd say, "Let's try it, John. See if it works." Did you read his book [*An Open Book*, 1980]?

Roberts: Yeah.

Mitchum: There are a lot of things in there that I didn't think he'd put in. Like the time he went to the girl's house during the London blitz, the wartime bombardment [and a medical condition hastened a bodily function]. He told me [Huston imitation]: "Funny thing about shit, kid, it just goes everywhere. It goes in her powder box. It goes behind the mirror. Shit's all over the place. I often wonder what that girl thought."

Roberts: He made five pictures with Bogart and worked with Burton and George C. Scott, but he says that you were his favorite actor.

Mitchum: I didn't hold up production. That's it. Roll it. Cue it. Print it.

Roberts: Only that.

Mitchum: Looks good on the camera report.

Roberts: Which movie did you break your back on?

Mitchum: What the hell was it?—a picture with Dick Powell.

Roberts: *The Enemy Below*?

Mitchum: *The Enemy Below*. I was running across the deck and then down a ladder, which ended below the horizon. I fell about 20 feet down to the next level. Then I had about a week off while they did the submarine stuff. After the third day, I couldn't get out of bed. Well, they said I should go down and have some pictures taken. So I'm walking down Wilshire Boulevard like this Quasimodo imitation strapped to a chair— and a woman asks me for an autograph. I went into the office and the nurse said, "Could you hop up on that table?" I said, "*Hop* up on what?!" The doctor took all the pictures and said, "This is this and that's that"—meaning what? He said, "You have a broken back. Tough shit. You can't nail it together." So I wore a brace for a few days until it started digging into my skin. I got rid of that. The doctor said, "Just don't forget that you're hurt." I said, "It reminds me."

Roberts: So you just had to wait for it to heal?

Mitchum: Yes—well, it never really has. It calcified over. First shot I had to do when I got back to work was lifting Theo Bikel over the rail. He was about a 260-er. I had to figure out a way to roll him onto my hips so I wouldn't strain my back. I don't think the doctor will OK me for any more bronc riding.

Roberts: Did you ever want Elvis Presley to play the lead in *Thunder Road*?

Mitchum: No. He wanted to do it. He wanted to do something in which he didn't sing. And I was talking to United Artists and I told them that Elvis wanted to do it. "Fine," they said, "OK." And he was getting around $150,000 a picture. And that would have been, like, a big chunk of our whole budget. So they said, "If he doesn't do it, will you?" And I said, "Sure, I'll do it." And I don't think Tom [Colonel Tom Parker, Presley's agent] wanted him to do it, because he was progressing him through musicals at Paramount and 20th.

Roberts: What was the final budget on that movie?

Mitchum: $630,000.

Roberts: And wasn't that filmed in North Carolina?

Mitchum: Asheville. I went to the meeting with nine pages. They asked me if this all could be authenticated. And I said, "Oh, yes." And I have the cooperation of Alcohol Tobacco and Firearms and the North Carolina ABC—Alcohol and Beverage Control. And I had access to what they called "closed files." So, I had a lot more material than I could possibly use. They said,

"What's the budget?" I think I said, "It will be between $350,000 and $750,000." They said, "Why the discrepancy?" I said, "The more we screw up, the more it will cost."

Roberts: You were responsible for hiring practically everybody on that picture, right?

Mitchum: Well, pretty much.

Roberts: Why did you choose Arthur Ripley to direct?

Mitchum: Arthur had written an adaptation of *Look Homeward, Angel* and there were a number of us who were impressed—Van Heflin and a few others—who would donate our services. We said we would do it for nothing. Arthur had done a film called *Voice in the Wind*, which was shot in four days or something like that. So, I thought he'd be useful. He said, "Fine." He was lecturing at UCLA, so we furloughed him out of UCLA, pulled him out and down to North Carolina.

Roberts: Although your son, Jim, is in the picture playing your younger brother, another casting decision that seemed unique was using Trevor Bardette to play the old moonshiner. He'd been in westerns for years, through the '40s in small roles. But this might be the biggest role he ever had in movies. He certainly looks the part.

Mitchum: Probably. I had seen him in something and thought he would be very useful. There's a road out of North Carolina up through Virginia called the Skyline Drive. So, I detailed a guy to shoot from it. We took the back seat out of a sedan and strapped a camera in there. In the morning, I wanted him to drive up through there and turn the camera on where it's lighted from the morning sun. It's quite spectacular . . .

Roberts: I've been through there. My brother lives in the area.

Mitchum: . . . then drive back down in the afternoon. Just turn the camera on. That's all. Catch the shadows back down—all the houses look like miniatures from that point of view. And it would've been very useful footage. This guy Johnny Burke went up there, files the camera reports and everything. Then we got back [to Los Angeles] and all they had was one shot of a hog and one shot of Peter Hornsby completely gassed, leaning against the fender. That was it. I went to Disney, went to the National Park Service, looking for footage that I could use for that, because on the run it would have been spectacular. But they never got it.

Roberts: What were spectacular were the bookending funerals with those grainy shots with the far-off torches.

Mitchum: Yes, but the picture did a great disservice to the whole industry, because you can't film a baptism without a car crash anymore. It set up a great career for Burt Reynolds.

Roberts: Robert Aldrich, who was assistant director on *The Story of G.I. Joe*, once wrote an article that has been anthologized that said basically that it was his fault that he really couldn't connect with you to make you really function as an actor on *The Angry Hills*, that you were unwilling to create the kind of character that he wanted.

Mitchum: His problem—wasn't it?

Roberts: I guess it was.

Mitchum: Usually, they just say, "Roll it." I remember George Cukor one time saying [fey imitation], "Now, look, Bob, I want to see a tear at the end of the scene, Bob." I said, "OK, roll it." "N-n-no, no, Bob, a tear, a tear . . ." I said, "*Roll* it!" So we did it. At the end of the scene, there are tears streaming down my face. He says, "Cut! Get you!"

Roberts: That was on what?—*Desire Me*? That's the one where they had the two or three directors, wasn't it?—Mervyn LeRoy, George Cukor, and Jack Conway, who wasn't credited.

Mitchum: And Victor Saville.

Roberts: Four?

Mitchum: I don't remember Jack Conway.

Roberts: Chuck Roberson wrote a book [*The Fall Guy*] mostly about his experiences as John Wayne's stunt double, and one of the chapters is entitled "Wonderful Durango," about when you and he went down to Mexico to make *The Wonderful Country*. He says you guys saw a murder committed in a bar.

Mitchum: That's right.

Roberts: Somebody came in and just shot someone?

Mitchum: That was almost a nightly occurrence. We had just arrived, and we were staying at the Casablanca Hotel and my wife and I came downstairs. I heard gunfire. So I told her to stay back and I peeked around the corner. And there's a guy staggering through the lobby. He's got a blue hole right here [points to his forehead]. So, I reached out, but he just brushed by me and went out. And the cops were backing him up and told him, "Come on, don't die here in front of everybody, for Christ's sake." The guy, very obediently, turns around and walks into the empty lobby—and the cantina's at the other end of the lobby—and I looked out. There was a guy going over backwards in the cantina. He fired one round into the ceiling and collapsed. So this first guy walks all the way through the lobby, down the three steps into the cantina, steps over the victim, up the three steps on the other side, outside, and drops dead obligingly. So, we had a standby director named Raoul, and he's sitting, back against the wall with a Panama hat on, drinking mescal. People were coming out from under ashtrays and doilies. So, he said, "Sure, I'm OK." I said, "Jesus, you had to be scared." He said [Mexican accent], "Jeez, I thought it was a rehearsal."

Roberts: Why didn't you produce a movie after *The Wonderful Country*? Your company had production responsibility on *Bandido*, *Thunder Road* and *Wonderful Country*. Your company went in with Brando's company, Pennebacker, on *Man in the Middle*. But you never again produced one of your own movies.

Mitchum: It was simply a tax device, actually, a co-production. I had a co-production on *Cape Fear*, too. The only film I ever really produced was *Thunder Road*.

Roberts: So, your company was just involved on the other ones. You were never really key behind-the-scenes force, were you?

Mitchum: No way.

Roberts: You mentioned you did some rewriting on *Macao*, and, of course, you wrote *Thunder Road*. Are there any others that you wrote?

Mitchum: Earl Felton and I worked on *Bandido* [the actor received no writing credit]. That's all.

Roberts: Of all of your pictures, I think *Home From the Hill* is my favorite. I think it's an extraordinary film. There was one point, though, where they were going to shut the picture down. What was that all about?

Mitchum: I don't know what it was. The production manager or whomever [snaps fingers] and that was it. And Vincent [director Vincente Minnelli] was in tears, very upset. They said, "That's the end of location." And they called him back to Metro. And he thought he was going to get a gold watch or medal or something for 30 years of diligent service to MGM. It was to get a pink slip instead. That happened to us one time at RKO. They began a picture with Jack Buetel called *The Half Breed* . . .

Roberts: With Robert Young, too.

Mitchum: . . . the production manager shut it down. It ran 40 minutes. We called it *The Quarter Breed*.

Roberts: I read somewhere that you once met William Faulkner and you and he had an evening's discussion.

Mitchum: Yes. We were down there working on *Home From the Hill*.

Roberts: In Oxford, Mississippi?

Mitchum: Yes.

Roberts: Did he make any impression on you?

Mitchum: I so admired him. Well, he had fallen off his horse. I said, "How did you do that?" He said, "Drunk." He was supposed to pick up some award and he said, "What time?" They told him and he said that no, he couldn't do it, and they said, "Why?" He said he planned to be drunk. I met him earlier, when he was out here as a screenwriter, the time he left and went back home . . .

Roberts: To Mississippi.

Mitchum: They thought he was going back to the Beverly Hills Hotel. But he went back to Mississippi.

Roberts: Do you want to talk about Vietnam for a while? I know that you toured for the troops. I know there was no big splash about it here. But these were two big chunks of time, the springs of 1966 and 1967. Did you get up to the front lines?

Mitchum: You're at the front lines the moment you get there. When you're at Saigon you're in the front lines.

Roberts: I mean, were there battles going on while you were there?

Mitchum: Yes. Certainly.

Roberts: Was it frightening?

Mitchum: Not after the first day.

Roberts: Why not?

Mitchum: I had a lot of professionals surrounding me. I was classified as an observer, whatever that means. I had a simulated rank of full colonel. I had an escort officer with me most of the time. And I made 152 missions, pretty well covered the whole territory.

Roberts: That's on both trips you took there?

Mitchum: Mmm-hmm.

Roberts: Battles were going on?

Mitchum: Yeah. But I was concerned mostly with sniper fire. They had signs on the beach that said, "Beware of snipers, watch out for sea snakes." If you were bitten by a sea snake, you've had it. You couldn't tell the players from the spectators, could you? You couldn't shoot back in a lot of places.

Roberts: What about your own personal feelings about the war, now, at this late date?

Mitchum: I was just the general, average cynic. I thought there were no heroes left. But I saw guys there—volunteers, jump-troop volunteers, Ranger volunteers, green-beanie [Green Berets or Special Forces] volunteers, four-, five-time volunteers—working on a degree out of Boston College, had a wife and two kids back in Framingham, Massachusetts, walking through rice paddies with an old lady on their backs, hauling babies under their arms. They were honest-to-God trying to help those people preserve themselves. They were wasted. I spent my time with professionals, Special Forces. We came from Camp Carroll and the Rockpile one time, we took a Huey [helicopter] and went down to the coordinates. You have to follow a map like you would a road map, because Hueys didn't have much instrumentation—altimeter, speed indicator, compass—that's about it. So, we were looking on the map, and nothing matches. The pilot said, "I think we're in the wrong country." He's trying to find somebody on the radio and we were looking for smoke to come in. Green smoke, come in; red smoke, stay out. We got green smoke and we come in there. We dust the joint off to reduce local fire visibility, and hop me out. They take off, because if the bird hangs around too long, it draws fire. So a guy comes in through the dust. He said, "What the hell are you doing out here?" I said, "Anything to get out of the house." He said, "You're out, man. You're out about as far as you're going to make it." So we get inside and he says, "Here, how about a drink?" Special Forces—that's it—first thing after you get inside, it's "Here, how about a drink?" I'm sitting there, bantering with these guys, and a major comes in. And he walks up to the bar and he's taking off a grenade harness, meaning he's been out on foot patrol. So he says, "Look who we have with us. Did you come to share our excitement?" I said, "Just color me Walter Mitty." So I said, "Here, have a drink," and he sits down. So I tell him where I've been, what's happening east of us. And I said, "Look, I don't want to be a tattletale, but there are a lot of people over there." He said, "Yes, that's the Ho Chi Minh Trail. That's why we're here, to keep an eye on it, monitor the movements." I said, "Well, there's a lot of shiny stuff over there." He said, "Yes, that's materiel that they're shipping down the line." I said, "No, man, they're all in position, pointing in this direction." He said, "Well, we have 250 of South Vietnam's finest between us." I said, "They'll go through that like shit through a tin horn." He said, "I know. How about a nother drink?" So a runner comes in and talks to him. He said, "Well, I guess we better call a chopper in. It's going to get hot around here." So they call the chopper in, and I take off. Eleven minutes later, they got hit—six survivors. He got out—Major Fisher. Somehow they got a fixed-wing aircraft down there for him to broadside a jump in. I was telling this story when we were working on something down in L.A. And this one guy listening says, "That's exactly how it was." His name was John Paul Jones and he was a captain in the same outfit. This was the beginning of the end of the Assau Valley Massacre. They overran this place.

But there were a lot of great men and real heroes and they really worked for those people. I overnighted one time to some fixed BOQ. And there was a huge fighter pilot, about six-foot-seven, big grizzled guy. He's got a .44 Magnum Smith & Wesson. He lays it down. And he didn't want to have anything to do with me, because he thought I was some itinerant actress. So, he found out what I was up to, and he said, "The whole thing can be over in two days." I said, "How?" He said, "Take strategic weapons up the Black River and the Red River on both sides, blow out those dams and wash everything down through Hanoi to Haiphong Harbor and out." I said, "Yes, kill all those people, cause epidemic conditions, then it becomes a black mark in history attributable to the Americans." He looked at me and said, "I think it's time the United States of America quit trying to win an international popularity contest. When surgery is indicated—cut!" How can I argue with him? He's huge, he's got that .44 Magnum in front of him. I said, "What is that?" He said, "My escape kit. There's no room for me in anything around here if I get caught."

Roberts: Why did you leave the farm in Maryland? The family had been there since 1959.

Mitchum: Dottie said, "Well, it's all very well for you, off on those glamorous locations"—you know, Wilkes-Barre, Pennsylvania, places like that. She says, "Here I am. It's hot and humid in the summertime, freezing cold in winter, snowed in." I said, "Well, when it gets hot and humid, have Bob Gurlock bring the car around, flip on the air conditioning and go someplace where it's cooler. In the wintertime, get the tractor out, plow it out to the road, bring the car around with the heater on, and four hours later, you're in the Bahamas. If you don't like it, sell the joint.

Don't bug me about it. Please yourself." I came back from Vietnam and we landed in Honolulu. I called [Dorothy] up, expecting tears of rejoicing that I have been spared the destruction of the great conflict, and she said, "I sold the joint." And I know the meaning of the word "nonplussed." Nothing was forthcoming. So, I said, "What about the cows?" She said, "They were the first to go." I said, "What about Bob Gurlock?" She said, "I sold the farm, farmers, farmhands and all." I decided that that was the time I would go to work, so I went up to Oregon and made *The Way West*. I didn't want to be around when the moving van came. My wife rented a house and moved everything out to California.

Roberts: On *The Way West*, you were offered the Richard Widmark part, but said, "Give me the other guy's part," because there were less days you had to work. Isn't that right?

Mitchum: Yes. Well, I had just come back from Vietnam. That's not exactly a health cure. So I figured I could get outdoors and cool off. My wife had sold the farm in Maryland. I was homeless and decided the best thing to do was to go to work. I asked Reva to read off the list of scripts that were around, and one of the scripts was *The Way West*. I said, "Who did they get to go for that?" They said, "Kirk Douglas." I said, "Great." So I talk to the producer and director at the Beverly Wilshire Hotel, and I said, "What about the Indian scout?" I figured while Richard [Widmark] and Kirk were upstaging each other, I can go fishing.

Roberts: In John Mitchum's book [John was in the cast] he makes mention that Douglas made Widmark mad because he began directing the picture. And [Widmark] pointed to Andy McLaglen and said, "There's our director." And John said that he came to you and said that Douglas was up there trying to run the company. The upshot was, that you then had a talk with Douglas and the cast and crew.

Mitchum: No. If he wants to run the company, good luck to him.

Roberts: Well, that's John's story.

Mitchum: I never read John's book [*Them Ornery Mitchum Boys*,

1989]. Every time I have to sign a copy, I say, "Brother John was never one to let the facts stand in the way of a good story."

Roberts: How did you get along with Douglas? Here was a man who seemed to be competitive no matter what.

Mitchum: Oh, yeah, yeah. He's not very social, you know. He takes the role quite seriously.

Roberts: Jane Greer talks about him trying to underplay you in *Out of the Past*. But that no one could underplay Mitchum. She says that, after a while, he quit that and he seized the role and went about it the way he normally operates. Did you feel any of that, like here's this guy who all he wants to do is compete with me?

Mitchum: Hell no. We had just seen him in *The Strange Love of Martha Ivers* and were all delighted that he was in the picture.

Roberts: You spent almost a year in Dingle, Ireland, making *Ryan's Daughter* . . .

Mitchum: Eleven months.

Roberts: This was no quick in and out. You lived there. What did you do while you were there?

Mitchum: Worked.

Roberts: Well, there's a lot of down time on a Lean picture.

Mitchum: By the time I got there, all of the accommodations were pretty much taken up. I don't know where David was living. Bobby and Sarah [screenwriter Robert Bolt and his wife, actress Sarah Miles] had a place. Johnny and Mary Mills had a pleasant little cottage. So, they gave me a hotel. It had nine rooms numbered one to ten—I never could figure that out. Upstairs, at one end of the hall, the sign said "Bath," and "T-I-L-E-T"— at the other. It was $450 a month. Furnished it with a bunch of directors chairs. All the stand-ins would stay there. Visitors would stay there. In Ireland it doesn't get dark in the summertime until 10:00 P.M. By the time crew would come back, when I wasn't working, I'd be cooking. There was no place to eat around there. I had a dozen people for dinner every night.

Roberts: Sounds idyllic.

Mitchum: It wasn't bad. That's when the Bronfman family that owned Seagrams had possession of MGM at the time. They also distributed Chivas Regal. Used to send me a case of whiskey and a case of Chivas Regal a week, which my stand-in, Harold Sanderson, promptly drank. I suppose that I would have had the script for *Nostromo* and I suppose I would be over in France working on that now, but the bum died on me. [David Lean was preparing an adaptation of Joseph Conrad's epic novel *Nostromo* when he died in 1991.]

Roberts: I had a long chat with him a couple of years ago when he was over here before the release of the director's cut of *Lawrence of Arabia*. Delightful guy.

Mitchum: Whenever they gave him the [American Film Institute's] Lifetime Achievement Award, they came and asked me to make the presentation. And I said, "You had better check with David and ask him if I'm acceptable or not." Instead, they told David that I had refused. And he cried.

Roberts: Well, he told me that his favorite picture of his own films is *Ryan's Daughter*. He had nothing but praise for you. Here he's made all these great films with all of these great British actors—Trevor Howard, Alec Guinness five times, Ralph Richardson, John Mills, O'Toole—and yet his two favorite actors are you and William Holden.

Mitchum: You could never catch Bill acting, either. In *The Bridge on the River Kwai* all Guinness did was purse his lips. But Bill Holden gave one of the most remarkable performances in that picture that anyone has ever seen. Perfectly, totally natural. I think Bill's first picture was *Golden Boy*. Bill was never flirtatious with a camera. You talk about all these other guys flirting with the camera—combing their hair and wetting their lips. Bill never did that. I never did it.

Roberts: Were you responsible for suggesting some of the casting on *Midway*?

Mitchum: No. Walter Mirisch called me up and wanted to know if I'd play whomever. I said, "How long is that?" He said, "Ten weeks." And it was five weeks aboard a carrier. And I had just spent three days aboard the Kitty Hawk in the South China Sea on a trip to Vietnam. Then he called back and asked if I'd play Admiral Fletcher. And I said, "How long?" He said, "Five weeks and one week on a carrier out of Pensacola." And that was in May and I thought, what if by a miracle we have an early summer, which occasionally does happen in California. There I'll be, stuck on this bloody aircraft carrier, tied up for a week. I said, "No, I can't handle that." And he called back asked me if I'd play Admiral Halsey. I said, "How long is that?" He said, "One day—in bed." I said, "You got it. Make the check out to Motion Picture Relief and I'll be there." And that was it.

Roberts: You mention that charity, but are there any charities that you like to contribute to?

Mitchum: My family mostly.

Roberts: Roger Ebert has pointed out around the time of *The Winds of War* that a sort of Mitchum cult has accumulated through the years, a re-interest in your career.

Mitchum: I'm rediscovered every five or six years. But it's a matter of survival, I think. I remember coming out of the Paramount Theater with Sinatra one time and the jam-up was big. They all seemed to be fairly volatile people. And one girl kept trying to get to him and she couldn't, so she finally [gestures a jab]. He's still got the mark where she tried to take his eye out with a pen. Some years later, I was coming out under the same circumstances. There they were, 3,000 people—all warts and wens and terminal dandruff—typical Mitchum fans, you know.

Roberts: Those are "typical Mitchum fans?"

Mitchum: Christ, they think if that bum can make it, I can be queen of the May Day.

Roberts: There are about seven different versions of the *Rosebud* imbroglio [In 1975 Mitchum was fired off Corsican locations for the movie *Rosebud* by producer/director Otto Preminger, who accused the actor of being drunk]. In fact, a book was written about that production called *Soon to Be a Major Motion Picture*. Was it as complicated as the versions sound or you just had one argument that morning or what?

Mitchum: Yeah. He was over-acting, that's all.

Roberts: Preminger was?

Mitchum: Yeah, he was in a state of shock when he said [imitation], "You're through!" and I just said, "Taxi," and I'm gone. He looked like he just messed his pants. And that was it. The next time I saw him, I saw him at a restaurant in Beverly Hills. He said [imitation], "Bobby, Bobby, vhere haff you been?!" Even at that time you had to kind of help him off the curb. I think that the bug had begun to affect him already then [Preminger died in 1986]. We had only been shooting for a week to ten days. I had only worked three days and I was the thirty-something person he had fired.

Roberts: The star of the picture no less.

Mitchum: I was recently with someone who was there at the time and they told me it got much worse after that. It was a funny thing, I got back here and Victor Buono called me. He said, "Who did they find to replace you?" And I said, "Peter O'Toole." And I thought he was going to die. When he finally got his breath back, he said [imitation], "That's like replacing Ray Charles with Helen Keller."

Roberts [laughing]: There's a parallel for you. A lot has been made over the years about you being a carouser and a heavy drinker.

Mitchum: I wouldn't say a carouser. I used to astonish people with my capacity. And I was with a group of fairly good drinkers, guys like Nick Ray and the guy who worked with us on *Not as a Stranger*—Crawford . . .

Roberts: Lee Marvin?

Mitchum: I've seen Lee Marvin coming out of the Cock 'N Bull feeling his way along the walls. He'd get out, jump on his motorcycle and take off.

Roberts: I interviewed him not long before he died.

Mitchum: How was he?

Roberts: Just wonderful.

Mitchum: A very bright fellow, you know.

Roberts: This was after he quit drinking. He said, "You know, I had a lot of fun at it for a long time—you take a lot out of it, but it takes a lot out of you." He said that he just didn't have fun at it anymore. The mornings didn't work for him.

Mitchum: Dick Boone was living in Hawaii and you can't keep up with those Kanakas. And he thought, "If I hang around here, it's going to kill me." So he tried to think of a place to move to that'd be accessible and at the same time isolated. He settled on Tucson. He watched the sun set, the cacti, very peaceful. He woke up the next day and found out that his closest neighbor was Lee Marvin. That wouldn't do. Then he moved to Florida. He figured at least in Florida he wouldn't be able to fall into a canyon. So, he broke his leg stepping off a curb. That's when he showed up in England with us on *The Big Sleep*.

Roberts: Right—with a cane.

Mitchum: And a cast.

Roberts: He was Kinino—"the brown man"—a big rough mobster. And he was limping around.

Mitchum: We were working in London one morning and Brian Owen Smith, the wardrobe master, came in and said, "Oh, God, he's been going on the Scotch, he's had six Guinnesses and now he's starting on the Irish." This is nine o'clock in the morning. Nine in the morning! Six beers, a bottle of Scotch and a bottle of Irish whiskey.

Roberts: Sheesh. But quite an actor.

Mitchum: Oh yeah.

Roberts: Having gone through hundreds of articles and clippings and read about your life and career down through the years, one thing that seems to crop up constantly is your sense of humor, a real appreciation for amusement.

Mitchum: It's my whole life, really.

Roberts: And yet you have all of these bewildered people—co-workers, journalists, whatever—and they say that Mitchum, well, "He's an enigmatic character." It seems to me that having fun is a pretty big priority for you. Am I assuming too much?

Mitchum: No, not at all. If you can't enjoy it, well . . . I think they get a little upset about being put on. Bogart used to do that all the time. He was a funny guy. Really a funny guy. He told me that one time. He said, "You know, Mitch, the difference between us and the rest of those guys is that we're funny."

Roberts: And what are your reputations? The two tough guys.

Mitchum: There is an inner comedian.

Roberts: You made a comedy or two early on and there was the occasional *She Couldn't Say No* and *What a Way to Go!*. And *El Dorado* can be described in many ways—but it's certainly a comedy, especially with regard to your performance. But why didn't you do more comedies?

Mitchum: I never saw it.

Roberts: You never saw *El Dorado*?

Mitchum: I don't think so.

Roberts: I was trying to find relationships between films. You have done several fairly outstanding films about orphans—*Pursued*, *Home From the Hill*, *River of No Return*, also *Holiday Affair*. And *The Night of the Hunter* is certainly about orphans. Allison talks about being raised an orphan in *Heaven Knows, Mr. Allison*. In *Going Home*, Harry Graham orphans his own child by killing the boy's mother. Is orphanhood something that you paid attention to?

Mitchum: It never occurred to me.

Roberts: Your mother passed away recently, didn't she? [Ann Harriet Gunderson Mitchum Morris died on February 2, 1990, at the age of 96].

Mitchum: Every now and then I still pick up the phone to call my mother.

Roberts: You do?

Mitchum: Yes.

Roberts: Do you think that you got your performing talent from her?

Mitchum: I have no idea. She was a very bright lady. And she came to this country [from Norway] and didn't speak English. And she graduated high school in New London, Connecticut, at age 17 with the highest honors that any girl had ever received at that school.

Roberts: She encouraged you to write, didn't she?

Mitchum: Yes. She also discouraged me. Because I would throw things away and they would fish them out of the wastebasket and treasure them. I met this guy, a radio guy, Robert Kennedy, in Boston, and he suddenly read a poem on the air that I had thrown away. And I don't know where the hell he ever got it. He started: "Consider now this child of April . . ." [about his daughter, Petrine]. I couldn't believe it.

Roberts: Do you still write?

Mitchum: I broke my pencil.

Roberts: You broke your pencil?

Mitchum: I used to wait until everybody had gone to bed and then I'd be up to two or three in the morning. I didn't want anybody to see it. Probably still have it all around here somewhere.

Roberts: Why did you stop?

Mitchum: I didn't.

Roberts: Ever think about publishing it?

Mitchum: No.

Roberts: Would you want to?

Mitchum: No.

Roberts: Maybe people would be delighted by it.

Mitchum: Oh, I'm sure [laughs sarcastically].

Roberts: You once said, "Rin Tin Tin was a big star, and that was a mother dog, so there can't be too much of a trick to it." You always seem to deflect any deeper analysis of what you do. Could you talk a little bit about your resources as an actor? There are dozens of newspaper clippings about filmmakers trying to talk about how you work—Sydney Pollack, Peter Yates, Paul Monash, Robert Parrish. The upshot, usually, is that they have no idea what you do—just that, in the final analysis, it works, often ends up great.

Mitchum: You simply animate the character, that's all. That's your function. Try to breathe some life into the character. One time, it was on *Five Card Stud*, I guess, and I had to clean the joint out with the butt end of a rifle. One of the heavies shit his pants. He said, "He couldn't do that unless he has it in him." I scared him so bad that he shat himself [laughs].

Roberts: I have to ask a few standards here. What's your favorite film? Favorite director?

Mitchum: I have none. I judge what I'll do by the most comfortable locations, like the island of Tobago. The directors, a lot of those, really, primarily Johnny Huston, Raoul Walsh, Nick Ray, Bob Parrish and David Lean, of course.

Roberts: You mentioned in one documentary about directors that tell you how to think, directors who don't leave the actor to his devices. Are there any filmmakers who were overly domineering on pictures with which you were involved?

Mitchum: Not with me.

Roberts: You're known as a practical joker.

Mitchum: No.

Roberts: Several of the actresses you've acted with—Susan Hayward, Greer Garson, Myrna Loy, Theresa Russell—have attested to you as such.

Mitchum: No.

Roberts: Getting back to this trouble-follows-me thing. Any thoughts on that?

Mitchum: No. I'm just reminded of the little guy in the L'il Abner cartoons, you know, with the cloud over his head [Joe Bftsplk].

Roberts: What comes across in a lot of the press clippings is that people go in with preconceived notions about you. A lot of people have been intimidated by you.

Mitchum: People tell me that.

Roberts: Helen Lawrensen interviewed you for *Esquire* in the 1960s and she asked you about movies and why you didn't have more aspirations for your career and acting. And you said that you can make these movies without taking any overall responsibility for them, that you can get in and get out, just do your job.

Mitchum: That's right.

Roberts: Yet there's also the perception by some fellow actors and filmmakers that you care deeply about the movies you make. Others just see you in the get-in and get-out mode. Very black and white perceptions.

Mitchum: I do it as well as I can, that's all. I don't want to hang around after that. My job's finished.

Roberts: You have consistently played fringe types, people detached from society, detectives, mercenaries, outcasts—not your normal star-actor career in the 1950s.

Mitchum: That's what was offered to me. I just take it as it comes.

Roberts: Very few people of your standing in the business ever played heavies in the decades when you were playing them. They didn't want to see their stars diminished or tarnished. You didn't seem to have any sort of care about that. Could you talk about that?

Mitchum: If it's a decent script and it makes sense and the location is pleasant enough and the terms are acceptable—yeah.

Roberts: Do you ever regret not taking a certain role?

Mitchum: No.

Roberts: Is there anything about making movies, since you've done it most of your life, that you really enjoy, aside from the actual acting?

Mitchum: That's about it. And just the interacting with people. It's the most communal enterprise that I can think of, because, when somebody walks onto a motion picture set, they see everything and say, "What are all those people doing there?" They're there because when their time comes, that's it—they're indispensable in that moment. And it is a complete community effort. I like that part.

Roberts: Well, I think that'll tear it for now.

Mitchum: Jesus Christ, you didn't even call lunch.

Quotes from Mitchum

" . . . I have never mortgaged my tongue to hold a job. . . . I don't believe in making plans. It has been my experience that nothing I planned far in advance and with what I considered intelligent care, ever panned out. . . . I have seen entirely too many thin slices of integrity, sincerity and competence, wrapped in cellophane and passed out as the total product, to have any confidence in fancy verbal packages. . . . In the last analysis, I presume that one of my least popular attributes is my inverted sense of dignity. Many of my statements have been smoke screen, designed to allow me to follow my own course without exposing it. I learned early in life that by telling a story far more colorful than the truth . . . one's truth is let alone. I like to be let alone. I know what I am: I am a patient cynic."

—Writing in *Movieland*, 1948

On an Autobiography:

"What for? Who needs it? The Los Angeles police station has it all."

—To Helen Lawrensen in *Esquire*, 1964

On a Broadway Offer:

"I went to the studio [RKO] with the *Streetcar* [*Named Desire*] offer and they said, 'Bob, look. Every time we make a deal with someone, it comes with another script we've got to buy for fifty grand, so we have a whole drawer full of horseshit. Every studio has a horseshit salesman. Paramount has Alan Ladd. Warners has Bogart. You want more money, let us know. But you're our horseshit salesman.'"

—To Barry Rehfeld in *Esquire*, 1983

ON HIS FAVORITE MOVIE:

"Listen, Charlie, as the man just said, I never see my junk. That's right, j-u-n-k. So how can I have a favorite? . . . Of course I've got pride. I'm no slob. I've got pride in the ass in *The Last Time I Saw Archie*. There, that's my favorite film . . . . four weeks to shoot . . . paid me $100,000 [a week], which ain't bad bananas for a few days work . . . . I like getting up at 5 A.M. and having my head painted for the cameras. What real man doesn't?"

—To Alan Ebert in *In the Know*, 1975

ACCEPTING CAREER ACHIEVEMENT AWARD
FROM THE LOS ANGELES FILM CRITICS ASSOCIATION:

"When I was a child, I wanted to be invisible. Looks like I chose the wrong profession."

—Reported by Charles Champlin in the *Los Angeles Times*, 1980

ON PUBLICITY TOUR FOR 'THE BIG SLEEP':

"When I first went to work, I'd go into casting offices and they'd say, 'What's he do?' Or, 'Did you ever think about getting your nose fixed or changing your name?' Then later, not too much later, they'd say, 'We need a Mitchum type.' I'd say, 'What exactly is that?' I turned out to be the only one, which insured my longevity."

—To Kirk Honeycutt in *The New York Times*, 1978

ON BEING CAST:

"Gordon Douglas wanted me for *The Girl Rush* with Frances Langford. He took me to the producer, and I could hear them whispering in another room. 'He looks like a monster,' said the producer. Gordon insisted. I came on like a tall dog . . . . In those days, Frank Ross was thinking about doing *The Robe* at RKO; so a director took me to his office to see about me playing Demetrius. Ross was sitting at his desk and in the center was a big bowl of oranges, walnuts, avocados. I sat down by the centerpiece. Ross looks me over and says, 'He's a clean-cut American youth.' Yeah, the livin' end. I cracked a walnut and began eating the centerpiece. I used to tell David Selznick I wasn't his type of actor, but he kept insisting I was. After many trials and errors, he decided I wasn't."

—To Hedda Hopper in the *Los Angeles Times*, 1953

"I gave up being serious about making pictures years ago—around the time I made a film with Greer Garson [*Desire Me*, 1947] and she took 125 takes to say 'No.' . . . I'm a fool and don't make enough fuss. Look at *The Angry Hills* which I was making in Greece when we last met. Originally, they wanted Alan Ladd for that. But when they drove out to his desert home to see him he'd just crawled out of his swimming pool and he was all shrunken up like a dishwasher's hand. They decided he wouldn't do for the big war correspondent. So, what happened? Some idiot said, 'Ask Mitchum to play it. That bum will do anything if he has five minutes free.' Well, I had five minutes free, so I did it . . . . I never take any notice of reviews—unless a critic thought up some new way of describing me. That old one about my lizard eyes and anteater nose and the way I sleep my way through pictures is so hackneyed now."

—To Roderick Mann in the New York *World Telegram and Sun*, 1959

"Ralph Nelson has this script he wrote, *The Wrath of God*, about a priest with a machine gun, and he's talking about casting and I'm suggesting Victor Buono and after a while Ralph says, 'What the hell do you think I've been talking to you about for three weeks, dummy? I want you to play the priest.' Well, I'll do anything to get out of the house. I'd prefer no work, but the others, the producers, directors, the entrepreneurs who gather all of this nonsense together, keep saying, 'Hey, what about us?' They have to feel they're doing something worthwhile. [Between movies, I] try hard to avoid the next one."

—To Sidney Fields in the *New York Daily News*, 1972

ON JAIL:

"It's like Palm Springs—without the riffraff."

—In *The Tough Guys* by James Robert Parish, 1976

ON RESPONSIBILITY:

"That's just the point. These pictures—I can do them and then walk away from them and forget about them. It's all finished and I never have to see them—I usually never do see them—and I'm not *involved*. Furthermore, I don't let anyone down. I don't want that responsibility. I don't want that deep involvement."

—To Helen Lawrensen in *Esquire*, 1964

ON FAME:

"Had I written seriously, I would have become a total recluse. When I came into this business, I found it was no longer necessary to bare my soul for a loaf of bread. I don't bare my soul acting.

"I wouldn't mind being a recluse but it would have meant a different life for the people around me. They might like it better. After all, it's not easy living with a public freak—and what else is fame but that? It is like being a talking bar of soap. You're like the Mercedes Benz emblem, known all over the world. But *this* one talks and eats and breathes and—look!—it is going to the john!

"Everyone knows you—and you don't know anyone."

—To David Lewin in *Photoplay*, 1978

OPENING REMARKS TO THE YALE LAW SCHOOL FILM SOCIETY:

"Gentlemen, shall we get it on? . . . I have been asked what it is like to be a personage of the cinema. [long pause] It's like being trampled to death by geese."

—Reported by Brad Darrach in *Penthouse*, 1972

ON FILM SETS:

"Actually, I'm most at home with the grips—you know, the old-timers who have been working behind the scenes since Wallace Beery was a juvenile. They like me. Even in Europe, the grips pitched in to buy me this [a $2,000 watch] after we finished *Foreign Intrigue*. They know I talk a stream of consciousness and sometimes I fall flat on my face."

—To Ed Meyerson in *Photoplay*, 1956

Home from the Hill, 1960, below, from left to right, with George Hamilton, George Peppard, Dub Taylor and Guinn "Big Boy" Williams

Cape Fear, 1962, with Polly Bergen and, below, from left to right, with Martin Balsam and Gregory Peck

El Dorado, 1967

Ryan's Daughter, 1970

The Friends of Eddie Coyle, 1972, with Steven Keats

Farewell, My Lovely, 1972

The Yakuza, 1975

The Last Tycoon, 1976

The Amsterdam Kill, 1977

The Big Sleep, 1978

The Winds of War (television miniseries), 1983

Promises to Keep (television movie), 1985, with son
Christopher Dopler Mitchum, left, and grandson Bentley Mitchum

ON JOHN WAYNE:

"Duke was six-four, but he wore four-inch lifts and a ten-gallon hat. He had a station wagon modified to fit all that paraphernalia. He even had the overheads raised on his boats so that he could walk through the doorways with the lifts on. And he was bigger than them all. I was with him one time and he was cussin' everybody out. 'You goddamn assholes,' Duke was saying. Then he turns to me and says, 'Come on.' So we walk into his office, he pours out a drink and says, 'You gotta keep 'em *Wayne-conscious.*'" That's what he had to sell. It was his business."

—To Barry Rehfeld in *Esquire*, 1983

"Sure I was glad to see John Wayne win [the Oscar], if it made him happy. I'm always glad to see the fat lady win the Cadillac on TV, too."

—To Burt Prelutsky in the *Los Angeles Times' West Magazine*, 1970

AFTER REFUSING TO STAR IN RKO'S 'SUSAN SLEPT HERE':

"People are always telling me, 'Watch it, boy. Play it safe. Be careful.' But that chokes me off. What for? Being careful's not living—that's for the cemetery. If I ever get out of pictures, I'll open a factory selling fancy celluloid buttons marked 'Genius.' I'll bet I sell one to every producer in town."

—To James Hunt in *Photoplay*, 1954

ON GAY RIGHTS:

"I don't see why you've gotta join something to be somebody. I won't join a political party—I'm registered as a Druid . . . . It's contrary to the whole concept of individualism—self-defeating. All you gotta do is get people together, and you can march 'em over a cliff."

—To Steve Warren in *In Touch For Men Magazine*, 1978

ON BEING AN ACTOR:

"I'm an actor only because I don't know any other job at which I can make so much dough. Let's face it, being a movie star doesn't call for skill. . . . I'm ashamed of being an actor because people accord you the respect and fame and attention you don't merit. The other month I was on a plane flying back to Maryland where I've got my home, raise horses and keep away from the crowds. And some guy sits down next to me. He's an executive with some steel company. He says, 'My wife and I were discussing you only the other night.' 'Well, sir,' I said. 'All I can tell you is that my wife and I weren't discussing you, and you're a bigger man than I am.'

". . . A lady who teaches blind children wrote me . . . 'My pupils believe that when you say something on the screen, whatever it is, it must be true. Your voice has the ring of honesty and sincerity in it.' Stuff like that bothers the hell out of me. It's embarrassing, because I'm only a survivor of the Stone Age of American middle class culture. I'm no hero or paragon.

". . . The reason I'm in demand is that I work fast and cheap . . . . I'm the luckiest son of a gun ever born."

—To Lloyd Shearer in *Parade*, 1961

"They pay me and I have to get up early in the morning to work for them, so it's all the same to me. The only difference between me and other actors is that I've spent more time in jail than any of them."

—To Bill Davidson in *The Saturday Evening Post*, 1962

"I think I'm lucky to get away with what I have—honest to Christ, I've been faking it now for 25 years. That's a pretty good score. I'm happy as a clam I skipped by this far."

—To Joseph Haas in the *Chicago Daily News*, 1970

"What counts is peace of mind and laughter—especially laughter. I am more than a happy man—I am delighted and astonished at the way things have gone. I don't regret a damn thing. If I had more comfortable shoes on, I'd jump up and down. Had I known acting is as easy as it is, I'd have started sooner. It is really just like being a plumber. You pack your bag, check your tools and do it. I did it at the time because I wanted a square meal. Today it is basically the same."

—To David Lewin, *Sunday People* (London), 1983

ON RUSHES:

"I've made it a practice of never looking at the rushes of my films. In fact, I haven't seen half the movies I've made. But in *Ryan's Daughter*, the director [David Lean] insisted that I examine some footage. I agreed just to keep him quiet. The first thing that comes on the screen was Leo McKern completely gassed in a pub. Then the scene shifted to a shot of Trevor Howard staggering up the beach, absolutely stoned. And then Lean cut to a shot of me on the beach—wiped out. All I could say was: 'The camera never lies.'"

—To Bob Lardine in the *New York Sunday News*, 1970

ON FAME AND FANS:

"Yeah, I take off sometimes. I just float off like I used to when I was a kid. Dorothy? She understands. She'd better by now. She's had enough of it. I've been in a constant motion of escape my entire life. I've just never found the right corner to hide in. And now I've sold my anonymity to become a chromium-plated geek . . . . You know what the average Robert Mitchum fan is? He's full of warts and dandruff and he's probably got a hernia, too. But he sees me up there on the screen and thinks, 'If that bum can make it, I can become president.' I bring a ray of hope to the great unwashed."

—To Roderick Gilchrist in the *Daily Mail* (London), 1974

"Somebody asked my wife once, 'What's your idea of your husband?' And she answered: 'He's a masturbation image.' Well, that's what we all are. Up there on the screen our goddamn eyeball is six feet high. The poor bastards who buy tickets think you really amount to something."

—To Roger Ebert in the *Chicago Sun-Times*, 1969

ABOUT A PUB SCUFFLE IN IRELAND:

"Hell, that was no fight. Some guy thought I was Kirk Douglas and kept pestering me for my autograph in a pub. He grabbed me by the arm and got nasty. So, I wrote, 'Up your nose' and signed it 'Kirk Douglas per Robert Mitchum.' And the next thing I know, he swings a right and hits me—whap—in the eye. Then he ran away and hid behind some people in the corner. Why that fellow couldn't break an egg. It didn't worry me."

—To the Daily Telegraph (Sydney), 1959

ON MAKING BAD MOVIES:

"After you've lost your girlish laughter and become a disappointed virgin, you're not going to recapture the starry-eyed belief that it's for real. They sit you down and say, 'We don't make pictures. We make money.' It's a matter of exploitation. But the alternative is to go to work and get the hives. I have the same feeling that Johnny Huston has. He says, 'You can make bad pictures, too. If they want bad pictures, we can do it. But it'll cost them more.' . . . The trouble with movies is that they're so damn dumb. I'm just a guy making a living, the only way I know."

—To Sid Adilman in The Toronto Star, 1979

ON SCRIPT SELECTION:

"I've always turned down a lot of scripts. I turned down *Wild Rovers*. It sounded like Blake Edwards wrote it as a compilation of old *Street and Smith* western magazines . . . . I turned down *The Wild Bunch*, too. What do I need with crazy Sam Peckinpah? I was down in Durango the same time he was. I was doing *Five Card Stud* with Dean Martin, and we lived much better. Peckinpah's company was living in tents in the desert, with reptiles and spiders and cheap whores crawling around. Who needs that? I turned down *Patton*, too . . . . They get very offended when you turn down their scripts. 'What do you mean, you don't want to do it?' they ask. 'Get somebody else,' I say. 'Who would you suggest?' What the hell do I care . . ."

—To George Anderson in the Pittsburgh Post-Gazette, 1971

"I never take much notice of scripts. Dick Powell once sent me 30 pages of a script [*The Hunters*], saying how good it was. And it seemed fine to me. I got to fly a fighter plane and spend a lot of time in the officers club in Japan. 'And you can go to Japan and scout it out for a couple of weeks,' he said. That sounded good. So I said, 'Yes.' Then he sent me page 31. And I found out my plane crashed and I spent the rest of the film carrying some fellow through Korea on my back. 'You ought to cast that part by the pound,' I said. 'Find some wisp. What's Sinatra doing?' But of course they saddled me with some hulk [Lee Philips] who got heavier by the minute and we did the whole thing on the Fox ranch and I never got near Japan."

—To Roderick Mann in *The Sunday Express* (London), 1978

ON MENTORING:

"Why shouldn't they be? They were impressed because I was very impressive [on *Home From the Hill*]. I was like someone an old cameraman used to describe when I was at RKO. He was an Argentine-Italian, and I think illiterate. He probably started out as Bessie Love's gardener or something. To him, a woman artist was anyone who made over $1,000 a week. If she got less, she had to be a whore. Why else would she hang out with foul-mouthed guys and juicers? I was an artist to Peppard and Hamilton in the same way. But I'll tell you something. George Peppard has caught up to me. Next time around, he has to play *my* father."

—In *I Remember It Well* by Vincente Minnelli with Hector Arce, 1974

ON PRODUCERS:

"I can't imagine what caused it [*The Night Fighters* producer Raymond Stross's ulcer], unless it was the time I slipped that noose around his ankles and hoisted him over a lamppost and let him hang head-down for a few minutes. I do that to all my producers. It's kind of playful, I think. A playful set makes for a good picture."

—To James Bacon of the Associated Press, 1960

"The best producer is the absent one."

—To Joseph McBride in *Daily Variety*, 1977

ON THE CANNES FILM FESTIVAL:

"How did I know it was going to cost me $500 a day? I've got to get out of here. I am a shuddering wreck. Everyone pushes you around. You come down in the morning at eight o'clock and one of the wounded tennis players says, 'Mr. Mitchum, you're late.' I say, 'Late for what?' And they've got you visiting some old broken-down maharajah who has a villa overlooking 7,000 other villas overlooking the sea. You get pushed around from dawn till dawn and the only time the photographers and journalists leave you alone is when someone yells, 'Free lunch.' Not only is this thing rough on the nerves, it's rough on the bank account . . . . They promised me all my expenses were paid . . . . Every time I speak to somebody about it, he waves his hand, it's love-forty and he's off to the garden party."

—To Art Buchwald in the *New York Herald-Tribune*, 1954

ON ACTING:

"I had a role with Loretta Young [*Rachel and the Stranger*]. She rehearses in front of mirrors the night before and is letter-perfect in every action and reaction. I didn't even know what I was going to do. There was a mirror behind us and Loretta kept looking at herself in it. I rubbed soap over the mirror and said, 'Let's pay attention to each other, not the way we look.' I have to feel my way in a part. No one has ever directed me except once. That was with Greer Garson in what I think was called *Desire Me*, with George Cukor directing, and it was disastrous. I couldn't be myself or handle the lines by Zoe Akins, which were pretty formal. Usually they let me be myself. For instance, when I did *Heaven Knows, Mr. Allison* with Deborah Kerr, John Huston would say after a take, 'Fine, Bob, but more of it. More.' I . . . would just throw everything I had into it. I never read my lines until I got on the set . . . . Lines that seem unnatural throw an actor. Once, when I worked on *Blood on the Moon*, a western with Robert Preston and Barbara Bel Geddes, Bob had a line, 'Confound you, woman, and your tongue!' He couldn't say it so it didn't sound stilted, so he just recited it. I had to break up—things weren't helped by the fact that every time he uttered the line, Walter Brennan would emit a rude noise."

—To Myles Standish in the *St. Louis Post-Dispatch*, 1959

"When they asked whom they could get to play the part [in *Man in the Middle*], I told them Trevor Howard. Trevor always said he'd never work with me, but the part was written so well, he couldn't turn it down. Every scene he played with me he stole from under my nose. But that's OK with me when it's right for the picture; and in my opinion, it's right. If there's one thing I'd like to teach young actors, it's this: Worry only about whether the picture as a whole is good and whether or not your performance in any small way is contributing to its being good. Only the amateur worries about whether he looks right and is getting a big enough share of the lens."

—To Hedda Hopper in the *Chicago Tribune*, 1963

"Some English writer asked, 'Do you follow the Stanislavski method?' I said, 'I follow the Smirnoff method.'"

—To Don Alpert, *Los Angeles Times*, 1965

"Brando can spend three minutes saying hello . . . . I learned from Spencer Tracy that your basic effectiveness onscreen comes from the way you work in close-ups . . . . If you swing a dead cat and knock over eight producers, five of them will turn out to be babbling idiots."

—To Lewis MacAdams, *Los Angeles Weekly*, 1982

"I have two acting styles—with and without a horse."

—Reported by Geoff Brown in *The Times of London*, 1984

ON THE DAY HE GOT OUT OF JAIL, 1949:

"They'll always remember. Ten years from now if [co-defendant] Vicki Evans' second cousin gives birth to a baby the papers will get 'Mitchum' in the headlines . . . . Who says an actor can't have privacy? I'll have it. No more interviews about my personal life. I'm shutting out my so-called pals. I'm not going anyplace or see anybody except my wife and kids and a couple of understanding friends that I'll choose very carefully. I never liked parties anyway. I stand out like a monster . . . . Everyone in Hollywood is demanding. It's 'Gimme, gimme.' In jail I can trust anybody. No element of profit or loss. My jail term has been one of the happiest periods of my life. [I'm] disillusioned about life and not enthusiastic about anything. I just hope people leave me alone. I don't want anything from anybody. I never have, except independence."

—To Aline Mosby of the United Press, 1949

On Ronald Reagan:

"I used to go to dinner on occasion with Ronnie when he was a great friend of Bob Taylor's. And it was always like we were being monitored by an eagle scout. He didn't want to tell the bad joke. You always felt a little constricted with Dutch, at least I did."

—To Barry Rehfeld, *Esquire*, 1983

On His RKO Contract Years:

"RKO made the same film with me in it for ten years. They were so alike I wore the same suit in six of them and the same Burberry trench coat. They made a male Jane Russell out of me. I was the staff hero. They got so they wanted me to take some of my clothes off in the pictures. I objected to this, so I put on some weight and looked like a Bulgarian wrestler when I took my shirt off. Only two pictures I made in that time made any sense whatever. I complained and they told me frankly that they had a certain amount of baloney to sell and I was the boy to do it."

—To Don Ross in the *New York Herald-Tribune*, 1955

On His Wife Dorothy:

"We've had our moments and she's come through a lot. But I guess after all the years we've been together she knows what to expect and how to handle me. Not as though there has been anyone else in my life except Dorothy. There's not one of 'em—and I've met the best of 'em—worth lighting a candle for alongside her. You know something? My old lady knows more about the business than I do. It beats the hell out of me. I can never understand how anyone ever gets around to hiring me."

—To Don Short in *People*, England, 1977

ON MARIJUANA:

"When I was a kid hoboing around America, it grew on every countryside track and railway. All the bums I moved with rolled it—not much sense in picking up cigarette butts when this stuff grew free all over the South. Throughout the Prohibition days it became the poor man's whiskey. You could buy a gunnysack full of it for 25 cents. Then came the repeal of Prohibition. Marijuana became illegal in America in the 1930s. Naturally, the big boys moved in on it. Then came the protection rackets, the undercover organizations, and it suddenly became big business with all kinds of cross-effects and illegal organizations, runners, fixers and so forth. The big setup. It's become big business, and of course the law had to step in. But today the Indians still use it just as they always did—west of the Mississippi and on across. Hell, they use it in their peace pipes. It's like Louis Armstrong said, 'The last time they passed the peace pipe around, no one inhaled.'"

—To Mike Tomkies in *The Robert Mitchum Story:*
'It Sure Beats Working,' 1972

ON HOLLYWOOD SOCIETY:

"I was never very social in this business. The people I knew and liked, such as Noel Coward and some of the French actors, didn't circulate. And the American actors I liked, such as Billy Holden, I never saw much. He was in Palm Springs and I don't go to Palm Springs. I see Frank Sinatra occasionally. He sort of adopted me, and every year he sends a telegram on Mother's Day."

—To J.A. Trachtenberg in *Women's Wear Daily*, 1982

"Do I miss the Hollywood life? People always ask me that. What Hollywood life? I never traveled with the mob. I've been to only one movie star's home, Kirk Douglas's—and that was for all of ten minutes. All actors are freaks, and I guess I'm the freak's freak. If

I walked into a restaurant [in Hollywood], people held their breath—they waited for me to walk up and sock someone. In Maryland, I'm not an actor. I'm just another farmer. I like it that way."

—To Sheila Graham in the *New York World Telegram and Sun*, 1965

"I was a guest at Eleanor Roosevelt's place. I saw this pink night-gown and just for a gag, put it on over my clothes. Noel Coward walks in and says, 'My dear, you look simply di-vine!' and kisses my hand. Next time I see Eleanor at a party she says loudly, 'Why Bob, last time we met you were in a pink nightgown being kissed by Noel Coward!' What could I do but admit it?"

—In *Starspeak: Hollywood on Everything* by Doug McClelland, 1987

"You can't go to the john in this town without someone slipping up on you with a gold spoon. I guess it's OK. If you want your nose anesthetized. I don't know what they're up to, really. As far back as I can remember, aside from a few pleasant experiences, a Hollywood party to me is a bunch of pretty people standing around waiting for a warm body to drop."

—To Joseph McBride in *Daily Variety*, 1977

On Studio Accounting:

"The trouble is, I can't say no to these bastards . . . . I don't even like acting. But every time I turn around, someone calls me. The other day John Huston rang up . . . That's why I bought a place in Maryland. It's not easy to reach and the little men from MCA can't drop by on their way from the studio to the office. I'm in this for the money. But ever since I got on this percentage deal, I haven't seen a kopeck. All the companies have accountants. They come, bringing a stack of figures with them. The picture has grossed $14 million, but by the time they're finished explaining, you're almost thanking them for not charging you for your services . . . . If I'm not involved between pages 35 and 79 of the script, great, then I can take off. But you know what they do? They turn around and rewrite the thing so that I'm in every scene. I'm a luck-less child."

—To *Newsweek*, 1959

ON 'THAT CHAMPIONSHIP SEASON':

"It was the most competitive group of actors I've ever worked with. They were all fighting for time on the screen. I was taught to get it done and get out of there. They would take a three-word ex-clamation and stretch it into four reels. Somebody told me Martin Sheen always looks like he's quietly, desperately going mad. He gets unbelievably carried away. One day on the set I was supposed to hold up this trophy, to show him it all counted, and he just went berserk. They had to carry him off . . . . After we finished shoot-ing, Cannon Films, the distributor, hosted a party. [Bruce] Dern of-fered to help with the decorations. Well, he arranged it so that his picture was the first thing you saw as you entered and the last thing you saw as you left. In fact, his pictures outnumbered every-body else's by three to one."

—To J.A. Trachtenberg in *Women's Wear Daily*, 1982

ON SEEING A PSYCHIATRIST:

[Sarcastically] "Yeah, I'm really a three-year-old girl. I weep all the time. [Then:] I can't stop to indulge myself in sadness, wear a black arm band and widow's weeds. But I haven't known any great enthusiasm since infancy. One time my family said, 'You've got to be crazy.' So they sent me to a psychiatrist. He had me take this test, where they hold up cards and you say what the pictures look like. The doctor finally gave up and said, 'What's your prob-lem?' I told him I didn't have any, but that my family had sent me to see him. So the doctor asked me whether I thought of going home and telling my family what they could do in their hats. And that was the last time I went."

—To William Wolf, Metropolitan Sunday Newspaper Syndicate, 1970

ON AILMENTS WHILE MAKING 'THE WINDS OF WAR':

"I turned up one day on the set in Los Angeles and was diagnosed as having the Thai flu and a temperature of 104. I went home feeling awful. Then when I returned to Zagreb in Yugoslavia it was 20 degrees below freezing and I was really feeling rough. I had picked up another virus. I told director Dan Curtis, 'I'm dying.' He said, 'Yes, Bob, just go over there and stand in front of the camera.' I was sweating, so much that my uniform had become shiny. Finally, they called a doctor and admitted that my condition was serious. I developed pleurisy, which really ripped up my lungs. I was coughing everywhere and one day I choked and sprayed blood all over the snow. Curtis thought it must be a trick. He said, 'Bob, how did you do that?' Next day, I slipped into a ditch and almost broke my shoulder. In the end, it was clear I couldn't go on. So, they had to use a stand-in for weeks."

—To Ivan Waterman, *Today* (London), 1989

ON HIS NOSE AND BOXING:

"I've managed to break [my nose] many times—about four. The first time was when I was four years old. I fell on it. Then I fell another time and I've had it banged up in fights. The last time was when I was 20 years old. I woke up one morning and found my nose was clear over on my cheek. I set it myself. Broke it in a fight. Thirty-five dollars. That was the purse. And the guy murdered me. The promoter wouldn't let me lie down; he was a tough guy. The other fighter ended up breaking my nose, cutting my eyelids and busting one of my ribs. That was about the end of my fighting career."

—To Bob Thomas of the Associated Press, year unknown

ON 'WAR AND REMEMBRANCE':

"Me sit through 18 hours of *War and Remembrance* or whatever the hell it is? No thanks. I've only actually sat through four movies in ten years. There's nothing in my contract that says I have to see the stuff. I clocked in and I clocked out. Whether or not people enjoy my performance is really not my department . . . . The highlight of the whole experience came the day Dan Curtis said, 'That's it. It's a wrap.' . . . I leave the publicity to [co-star Jane

Seymour]. She's more conscious of her image than I am. I'm fold-
ing up my tent and going home to do my laundry."

—To Victor Davis in *Mail on Sunday*, London, 1989

ON DEBORAH KERR:

"I envy you the time spent with Deborah in sharing her humors
and perspectives. It is often lamentable that the association of
friends is limited to professional endeavors which occasion a void
upon completion. She is a lady of such remarkable and tolerant
perception that the resultant communication is a source of joy, in
that even the obscure intention finds appreciation in her cheerful
translation. One feels 'understood,' and, thus encouraged by her
understanding, inspired to assist her own happiness. She makes it
so much easier—so much clearer, and so much more fun. Long
may she wave."

—In a letter to Eric Braun, author of *Deborah Kerr*, 1978

ON MARILYN MONROE:

"Marilyn Monroe was always filled with sly humor. On *River of
No Return* she'd jokingly say, 'What a set! A girl doesn't get
much action around here!' Once, when she'd said something of
the kind, my stand-in piped up, 'What about a round-robin?'
Marilyn didn't know what that was. 'You and me and Mitch,' he
said. 'Ooooooh, that would kill me!' Marilyn replied. 'Nobody's
died from it yet,' he told her. 'I bet they have,' she said. 'But in
the papers it says the girl died from natural causes.'"

—In *Starspeak: Hollywood on Everything* by Doug McClelland, 1987

ON POLITICS:

"There are three times in life when it's useless trying to hold a man
to anything he says—when he's madly in love, drunk or running
for office."

—In *Starspeak: Hollywood on Everything* by Doug McClelland, 1987

ON DIETING:

"I never diet. I was outside the Beverly Hills Hotel one day when

I bumped into Gina Lollobrigida. She was going on the Johnny Carson talk show live that night and says to me, 'How on earth do you keep that figure? Is it some special diet?' I tell her, 'No, lady, by isometric farting.' She went on the show that night and, sure enough, the talk got around to diet. She's got no sense of humor, that dame, and she says, 'I saw Robert Mitchum today, and he keeps his figure by isometric farting.' Carson nearly fell off his chair."

—In *Starspeak: Hollywood on Everything* by Doug McClelland, 1987

ON WOMEN:

"I don't have any really close men friends. I'm more or less a loner anyway. I do get along well with women. But too often, in general social intercourse, it is very difficult for me because by and large the women I meet feel they have to perform. And they feel put down if some evidence of their being sexually attractive is not there."

—To Joan Dew Schmitt, *You*, 1971

ON HOWARD HUGHES:

"He summoned me once to his hotel in Vegas. I walked into his room and he said, 'Wait a minute, Bob, I have to make a phone call first.' He walked into the next room, and that's the last I ever saw of him. Strange fellow."

—Reported from the San Francisco Film Festival
by Herb Michelson in *Daily Variety*, 1983

ON THE MARYLAND FARM:

"If I could outlast some of the movies I've made, the rest is easy, that's for mother sure . . . . [The Maryland farm] is where I'll finally sit on the porch with a shotgun across my knee and aim at anything that looks like it's going to make me work."

—To Sidney Skolsky in the *Los Angeles Times*, 1959

"[The farm] is 12 miles by land and five minutes by water from

Easton in Talbot County . . . where the only topics for discussion are hunting, fishing and drinking."

—To Hedda Hopper, *Chicago Tribune*, 1961

On Katharine Hepburn:

"If I put out some phony reform story, then fall from grace, I'd look like a liar . . . . But when I spilled my problem to her, she said, 'It's not as though you were an actor. Synthetic motion picture personalities can't hope to cope with some of these situations that arise.' There went my illusions about Miss Hepburn."

—To Hedda Hopper, *Chicago Tribune*, 1949

Response to Sour Apple Award as "Least Co-operative Actor" of 1949 from the Hollywood Women's Press Club:

"Your gracious award becomes a treasured addition to a collection of inverse citations. These include prominent mentions in several ten worst-dressed Americans lists and a society columnist's ten most desirable male guests list, which happily was published on the date I was made welcome at the county jail."

—In the *Los Angeles Herald and Express*, 1950

Response to Charges of Anti-Semitism in an 'Esquire' Interview :

"I'm sorry there's such an unnecessary flap . . . . I was just putting him on . . . . When they finally do corner me, I either tell them what I think they want to hear or else I invent a whole new beginning. I occasionally say something outrageous so they'll say, 'He's not well, let's leave him alone.' . . . I think anyone who knows me, knows my only objections are to injustice and general discrimination."

—Reported by Henry Unger, *Los Angeles Herald-Examiner*, 1983

On His Rounder's Reputation:

"But the public and many movie producers are sold on the idea that I live 90 percent of my life in a bar with a pair of broads around my neck and my right hand cocked for anyone who

breathes hard in my direction . . . . "[Favorite role is] *Camille*: I'd just love to lie there and cough for about 20 reels."
> —To Dorothy Manners, *Los Angeles Herald-Examiner*, 1964

ON CONVERSATIONAL DIPLOMACY:

"I'll take either side of an argument to keep it going."
> —To Sidney Skolsky, *Citizen-News* (Hollywood), 1964

ON THE MITCHUM RAMBLE:

"People think I have an interesting walk like John Wayne . . . . Hell, man, I'm just trying to hold my gut in."
> To Earl Wilson in the *Los Angeles Herald-Examiner*, 1971

ON VIRTUES:

"I don't know what they are, but I lack them. More than that, I *feel* the lack of them . . . . I think I help. I idle away a moment for people . . . . Say I'm a whore with a heart of gold."
> —To *The Observer*, London, 1969

ON HIS CAREER:

"I always thought I had as much inspiration and as much tenderness as anyone in the business. I always thought I could do better. But you don't get to do better. You get to do more."
> —To James W. Seymour Jr. in *People Weekly*, 1983

COMMENTARY ON MITCHUM

FROM FILMMAKERS

JOHN HUSTON:
[Director, *Heaven Knows, Mr. Allison*
and *The List of Adrian Messenger*]

"I had been told that Bob Mitchum was difficult. Nothing could have been further from the truth. He was a delight to work with and he gave a beautiful performance [in *Heaven Knows, Mr. Allison*]. He is one of the finest actors I've ever had anything to do with. His air of casualness or, rather, his lack of pomposity is put down to a lack of seriousness, but when I say a fine actor, I mean an actor of the caliber of Olivier, Burton and Brando. In other words, the very best in the field. He simply walks through most of his pictures with his eyes half open because that's all that's called for, but he is capable of playing *King Lear*.

"In one scene Bob had to crawl through the grass on his elbows like a snake—the Army crawl . . . . We did it three or four times. Finally, I said, 'That's it!' Bob got up and turned around, and he was blood from the neck down. He had been crawling over stinging nettles. 'Jesus Christ, Bob!' I said, and asked him why he did it. 'That's what you wanted,' he answered. And that was the whole size of it."

—In *An Open Book* by John Huston, 1980

". . . a rarity among actors, hard-working, noncomplaining, amazingly perceptive, one of the most shockingly underrated stars in the business."

—To Lloyd Shearer in *Parade*, 1961

WILLIAM A. WELLMAN:

[Director, *The Story of G.I. Joe* and *Track of the Cat*]

"There are only a few stars left who I would go out to see in a picture, but I never fail to see Mitchum. There's something about Mitchum that just thrills me to death. I think he's one of the finest, most solid and real actors we have in the world."

—In *The Robert Mitchum Story: 'It Sure Beats Working'*
by Mike Tomkies, 1972

EDWARD DMYTRYK:

[Director, *Crossfire, Till the End of Time* and *Anzio*]

"He was born with what we call film-style acting. A really fine film actor does not give a performance. He creates a person. And is that person. Mitchum was one of the very best at that . . . . He knew people, common people—I think that's one thing that endears him to people. He gives that feeling."

—In *Robert Mitchum: The Reluctant Star,* Cinemax, 1991

HOWARD HAWKS:

[Director, *El Dorado*]

"It was the first time I'd worked with Robert Mitchum. I enjoyed it. The first time I work with a good actor I have fun finding things for them to do . . . . John Wayne said I give all the fireworks to the other guys . . . You remember that scene in the bathtub? Well, it was Mitchum's idea that when the girl walked past, *he'd* pull the hat over *his* eyes. I laughed as hard as anybody. You can hear the crew laughing on the soundtrack, because nobody knew he was going to do it. These things are just marvelous."

—To David Austen in *Films and Filming,* 1968

". . . I said, 'You know, you're the biggest fraud I've ever met in all my life.' He grinned and said, 'Why?' I said, 'You pretend you don't care a damn thing about a scene, and you're the hardest working so-and-so I've ever known.' He said, 'Don't tell anybody.'"

—To Joseph McBride in *Hawks on Hawks,* 1982

CHARLES LAUGHTON:

[Director, *The Night of the Hunter*]

"He has great talent. He'd make the best Macbeth of any actor living. All of this tough talk is a blind, you know. He's a literate, gracious, kind man, with wonderful manners and he speaks beautifully—when he wants to. He's a very tender man and a very great gentleman. You know, he's really terribly shy . . . . He's one of my very favorite people in the world. I can't praise him too much."

—To Helen Lawrensen in *Esquire*, 1964

RAOUL WALSH:

[Director, *Pursued*]

"Robert Mitchum impressed me as being one of the finest natural actors I ever met . . ."

—In *Each Man in His Time* by Raoul Walsh, 1974

MERVYN LEROY:

[Director, *The Human Comedy* and *Thirty Seconds Over Tokyo*]

"You're either the lousiest actor in the world or the best; I can't make up my mind which."

—In *The Tough Guys* by James Robert Parish, 1976

STANLEY KRAMER:

[Director, *Not as a Stranger*]

"Bob, in my opinion, is one of the finest actors in the motion picture business . . . . I cannot praise too highly Bob's talents."

—To Dee Phillips in *Photoplay*, 1955

"Robert Mitchum—Mitchum who eats pickled eels for breakfast—and takes joy in having the feminine actors smell his breath thereafter. That's a separate problem. That seems to be a hygenics problem that somebody should deal with. This is a business of personalities and people so that everybody isn't really normal."

—To James Powers in *Dialogue on Film*, 1973

LLOYD BACON:

[Director, *She Couldn't Say No*]

"He has the greatest natural sense of timing a line of anybody I have seen work before the cameras. He does naturally what most actors and actresses strive for years to attain without success."

— From an unpublished section of a feature article, 1954

RICHARD FLEISCHER:

[Director, *His Kind of Woman* (uncredited) and *Bandido*]

"We started over. Vincent Price threw a party on the stage. He was celebrating his first year on the picture [*His Kind of Woman*]. Mitchum took to drink. Who could blame him? The picture was finally getting to him . . . . Disaster. Bob was drunk . . . . We tried it again. Bob put much more violence into the action this time. The stunt men went flying. The situation became clear. Mitchum was in a drunken, macho mood . . . . It turned into a real brawl. I started yelling, "Cut! Goddamn it. Cut!" It was about as effective as using a squirt gun to douse a warehouse fire. It ended when the stunt men got thrown into the heavy poker table, which toppled over onto the terrified doctor . . . . I was boiling.

"'Bob,' I said quietly, slowly and clearly, ' I don't know if you're trying to make a complete fool of yourself, or of me, but you have succeeded in doing both.' The grenade went off. 'That does it!' he screamed. 'That does it! I'm not taking any more of this shit! I've had it with you and this fucking picture and with this whole god-damn thing!' and he went on a rampage. He started with the lighting equipment. He smashed every lamp on the set. Every piece of furniture he completely demolished . . . . reduced to rubble. He kicked down every door. He put his foot through every wall . . . . There was nothing I could do except stand there and watch and hope the fury would finally drain out of him. It didn't. It went on and on. Everybody was riding his coattails . . . Stinking directors riding on his back . . . And fuck Howard Hughes, too.

"Eventually he went to his dressing room . . . . 'Get [the set] fixed,' I [said] . . . . I didn't sleep that night . . . . I got to the studio early . . . . Mitchum looked into the mirror. My reflection glared back at him. Slowly he raised both hands and covered his face. 'Oh my God,' he said. Then he slid out of the chair and onto the floor and rolled under the couch . . . disappeared completely. 'Bob,' I said, 'come out.' His right arm appeared . . . . 'I can't,' he said. 'I'm too ashamed. I can't face you. Please, go away.'

"'Come on out. I have something to say to you . . . .' He crawled out and stood up. I suddenly realized what a big man he was. 'Don't say anything,' he said, holding out his hands as if to fend me off. 'I feel bad enough about yesterday.' I started into my prepared speech . . . 'You're a bully and a—' but Bob interrupted. 'Look,' he said, 'I'm sorry about what happened. I apologize. What more can I say?' I felt like a full-rigged sailing vessel that had run into a sudden calm.

"'Bob,' I said, 'you're a son-of-a-bitch.'"

"'I know.'

"We shook hands and finished the picture."

—In *Just Tell Me When to Cry: A Memoir* by Richard Fleischer, 1993

"I know one of my big surprises with him was when I was trying to get a close-up of him reacting to something and I said, 'Action!' And nothing happened. So I cut and said, 'You're supposed to react.' 'I did react.' 'Well, I didn't see it!' He said, 'Well, it's the best I can do.' I thought, 'Jesus, he's pretty snotty.' We run the dailies the next day and by God you look at the screen and he is reacting. It's on the screen and I couldn't see it."

—To Christ Petit and Chris Wicking in *Time Out* (London), 1977

OTTO PREMINGER:
[Director, *Angel Face* and *River of No Return*]

"Marilyn [Monroe] didn't question [speech coach] Natasha [Lytess]'s judgment. She rehearsed her lines with such grave ar-tic-yew-lay-shun that her violent lip movements made it impossible to photograph her. Natasha applauded her on her marvelous pronunciation, which inspired Marilyn to exaggerate even more [on *River of no Return*]. I pleaded with her to relax and speak naturally but she paid no attention . . . . there was nothing I could do. Monroe was the top box office attraction.

"Robert Mitchum saved the situation. During rehearsals, he ignored her studied affectation. Then, just as I was ready to shoot, he would slap her sharply on the bottom and snap, 'Now stop that nonsense! Let's play it like human beings. Come on!' He managed to startle her and she dropped, at least for the moment, her Lytess mannerisms."

—In *Preminger: An Autobiography,* 1977

FRED ZINNEMANN:
[Director, *The Sundowners*]

"He's one of the finest of instinctive actors in the business, almost in the same class as Spencer Tracy."

—To Bill Davidson in *The Saturday Evening Post,* 1962

ROBERT PARRISH:
[Director, *Fire Down Below* and *The Wonderful Country*]

"He'll give a creative performance if believes in what he's doing. If he doesn't, that's where he differs from other guys. They'll say, 'We can't do this, it's terrible.' But he just hits the marks. If you say, 'Mitch, that's not very good,' he'll say, 'I'm paid to say it, not to write it.' He crawls into a cocoon. Talk to Huston or Zinnemann. I'm sure they'd tell you he's about the best movie star in the world. I certainly think so . . . but with the right to part. . . . I know how difficult it can be to crack that turtle shell of his."

—To Christ Petit and Chris Wicking in *Time Out* (London), 1977

VINCENTE MINNELLI:
[Director, *Undercurrent* and *Home From the Hill*]

"Few actors I've worked with bring so much of themselves to a picture, and *none* do it was such total lack of affectation as Mitchum does."

—In *I Remember It Well* by Vincente Minnelli and Hector Arce, 1974

DARRYL F. ZANUCK:

[Producer, *The Longest Day*]

". . . Bob Mitchum had to get out of a landing craft and race across a beach for 2,000 yards. He had to keep up with a regiment of trained GIs. He had to duck 97 marked explosion points and without stopping or 'cutting' he had to flop down at the foot of a bunker and read his dialogue while explosions went off practically under him."

—Writing in *The New York Times*, 1962

BURT KENNEDY:

[Director, *Young Bill Young* and *The Good Guys and the Bad Guys*]

"Robert Mitchum is very professional and one of the finest actors I have worked with. I did two pictures in a row with him. He's amazing in that if you listen to him, he sounds like he's a little crazy, but he's not at all. He's one of the brightest guys I know."

—In *Hollywood Trail Boss* by Burt Kennedy, 1997

DAVID LEAN:

[Director, *Ryan's Daughter*]

"He is a master of stillness. Other actors act. Mitchum is. He has true delicacy and expressiveness, but his forte is in his indelible identity. Simply by being there, Mitchum can make almost any other actor look like a hole in the screen."

—To Grover Lewis in *Rolling Stone*, 1973

PETER YATES:

[Director, *The Friends of Eddie Coyle*]

"Mitchum was extraordinary on our film. He's that way if he respects the film. If he really sees that you're working on the film you had said you were going to make, he'll be right in there with you, doing his best."

—To Jerry Roberts for Copley News Service, 1987

SYDNEY POLLACK:
[Director, *The Yakuza*]

"My fascination with him comes from the tension between his own sensitivity and delicacy and his cultural sense of what is macho, because you can feel these two elements at war . . . . Mitchum, like a lot of guys who grew up at the time he grew up, had certain ideas of what masculinity is and what is appropriate behavior for a man. Acting, like dancing—certain areas of the arts—seemed inappropriate to certain men. It seemed to them like a slightly sissified profession. It certainly seemed that way to Mitchum . . . . He used to drink Scotch in a water glass with no ice, with just a little plain tap water as a chaser. He'd drink it the way you drink coffee, just sip slowly on it all day. And he would never pass out or never get falling down drunk—he'd reach this certain level and talk all day—just tell the most incredible range of stories.

"I found him to be like a very, very powerful and lazy horse. He wants to walk as slow as possible and wants to get away with doing as little as possible. You used to really have to push him. He won't offer of the full emotional nature of a performance, at least he didn't for me, until you went after him a little bit . . . . He's full of feeling, which he just keeps at bay most of the time. Every once in a while, there's an opportunity in the acting for it to come out."
—In *Robert Mitchum: The Reluctant Star,* Cinemax, 1991

DICK RICHARDS:
[Director, *Farewell, My Lovely*]

"In the novels [Philip Marlowe] doesn't trust anyone enough to make him a friend . . . . Well, that's where Bob Mitchum came in. He played Marlowe like a man of his age. He's tired. Marlowe is tough, smart, but fallible. He can say, almost at the end, 'Now, I get it.' It's nearly too late. But he knows how to get information . . . . Oh [Mitchum] liked the role. But he worried how he would be accepted playing Marlowe. Bob Mitchum is a great sardonic character. That's the way I wanted him to play

Marlowe. And, of course, he had always wanted to play Marlowe. We talked over the role quite a bit. We agreed what kind of guy Marlowe was."

—To Jon Tuska in *The Detective in Hollywood,* 1978

DAN CURTIS:

[Director and Producer, *The Winds of War* and *War and Remembrance*]

"He's the biggest pro in the world."

—To James W. Seymour Jr. in *People Weekly,* 1983

ANDREW J. FENADY:

[Writer, executive producer, *Jake Spanner, Private Eye*]

"I sent the script to Mitchum. It was then entitled *The Old Dick*—about a retired private eye . . . I called him up. His reply . . . 'I am The Old Dick.' Mitchum is 72 . . . was in every scene. The next to last day was our 'chariot race,' a fleet of ultra-light airplanes, helicopters, chase cars, explosions with the entire cast and a battalion of extras. While running, Mitchum twisted his leg, he collapsed—his ankle swelled and turned blue. I knew if I sent him to the emergency room we wouldn't see him for weeks. 'Bob,' I asked, 'you want me to shut down the company?' 'I'll let you know.' He never did and we finished the day's work. He went home quivering with pain and said, ' . . . I'll see you tomorrow.'

"I didn't believe that he would show up. But he did. He literally could not stand. I rewrote his scenes so he could sit down. We finished at exactly midnight. Cinderella went home with a pumpkin-sized ankle. Indifferent? Casual? Jaded? Languid? Laid back? Tell it to the Marines. Not to anybody on this picture."

—In "Robert Mitchum—The Ice Man"
by Andrew J. Fenady, *Daily Variety,* 1989

FROM ACTORS

JANE GREER:
[Co-star, *Out of the Past* and *The Big Steal*]

"To the people who knew him well, the gesture of remaining himself was the greatest piece of acting Mitchum had ever done. It was the toughest job in his career. For we could see that—far from the impression given by the newspapers—Bob was intensely upset by what had happened. He was upset for himself and he was even more upset for his wife and two sons. This latter fact came out just once: when he asked the photographers not to take pictures of him behind bars, because his kids might see them. Otherwise, he did not show his extreme discomfort—and the fact that he did not was a very special sort of heroism to those who love him . . . .

"You can't make a serious statement to Mitch about himself. He can be serious, about things, about people, but he insists—tacitly—that he will not be serious about what happens to him. Thus, none of us could really tell him what we felt, especially when he came on the set early in the morning that day of this trial. We could only show our sympathy and hoping for him by a physical gesture . . . . Anything else, we knew, would have embarrassed him."

—Writing in *Silver Screen*, 1949

MYRNA LOY:
[Co-star, *The Red Pony*]

"Robert Mitchum, who played the ranch hand, was a devil, one of those men who got a great kick out of teasing me. He just about tortured me with his pranks during shooting—particularly when he had an audience. He seized one opportunity when Hedda Hopper came out to the ranch where we were shooting to interview me. As she angled for a story, Mitchum sat there on the porch watching. 'You know,' he suddenly interjected, 'at one point Myrna comes out into the corral and does a dance of the seven veils,' which he demonstrated in vivid detail, managing to fluster even a tough old bird like Hedda. Oh, yes, Bob clowned around, but when it came to actually working he was all business. He is one of those artists that make it look easy, a fine actor and intriguing man with so many sides to him. He has that smooth, masculine face, seemingly without a care in the world, yet you saw an underlying sensitivity and intelligence. And it was typical of his contradictory nature that this macho man who loved bedeviling me should ask me to sign a photograph for him at the end of the picture."

—In *Myrna Loy: Being and Becoming*
by James Kotsilibas and Myrna Loy, 1987

AVA GARDNER:
[Co-star, *My Forbidden Past*]

"If I could have gotten him into bed, I would have. I think that every girl who ever worked with Bob fell in love with him and I was no exception . . . . Dear Bob. A lovely, lovely character."

—In *Ava: My Story* by Ava Gardner, 1990

JANE RUSSELL:
[Co-star, *His Kind of Woman* and *Macao*]

"When Mitch came along, a lot of producers didn't know what to do with a guy who was just all man. He was always strong and women liked his looks a lot . . . . He has none of the nonsense of having to feel his part or go around doing exactly what that person would have been doing and staying in that mood and everything. He can just turn it on . . . . He has empathy for people and yet he's never a crybaby and he won't let you be a crybaby, either. He's an average guy and with Robert Mitchum, it's Dorothy. They have a *family*-family . . . . Sometimes he gets a little testy with high-minded producers or directors, and especially if they're trying to push around the other actors or the crew. He will very calmly go out of his way to make them fall on their faces."

—In *Robert Mitchum: The Reluctant Star,* Cinemax, 1991

ANTHONY CARUSO:

[Actor, *His Kind of Woman*]

"I made a picture—*His Kind of Woman*—with Bob. Bob wanted coffee on the set and they would bring coffee for him. And he says, 'No. I want it for everybody.' They said, 'Well, everybody's not going to have it' . . . and this was a Hughes picture. And Bob would get in his car and say, 'I'm going to go for a cup of coffee.' Now, they say, 'We have coffee on the set.' 'No, I don't like this coffee; I'm going for a cup of coffee.' Two hours later he would come back. He didn't say, 'I demand you have coffee on the set for everybody.' But every morning for three or four days he would do this. And they finally got the message. And they had coffee on the set for everybody."

—In *Robert Mitchum: The Reluctant Star,* Cinemax, 1991

STEWART GRANGER:

[Ex-husband of Jean Simmons, who co-starred in *Angel Face, She Couldn't Say No, The Grass Is Greener* and *North and South*]

"Bert rang to tell us that Jean's next film was to be a 'potboiler' called *Angel Face.* 'But there would be one good thing about it. Bob Mitchum is co-starring and he'll look after her.' . . . Bob really took Jean under his wing and, in spite of the bullying Otto Preminger who was directing it, Jean enjoyed the film. She adored Mitchum and used to tell me what a good actor he was, how funny and amusing and easygoing, he just wouldn't let things get him down. I wished I could have been more like him.

"In one scene Bob was supposed to smack Jean, and she told the really gentle Mitchum to really let go. Otto insisted on take after take and poor Jean's cheek was getting redder and redder. As Otto insisted on yet another take, Mitchum turned to him and let him have one right across the face.

"'Would you like another, Otto?' he said.

"Otto quickly agreed to print the last take."

—In *Sparks Fly Upward* by Stewart Granger, 1981

OLIVIA DE HAVILLAND:

[Co-star, *Not as a Stranger*]

"Bob's a teaser, and I did knock a beer bottle out of his hand on the set one day. But we're friends. Actually, he's a very sensitive man."

—To Howard Thompson in *The New York Times*, 1954

FRANK SINATRA:

[Co-star, *Not as a Stranger*]

"Mitchum is a savorer, a taster. He sips happiness like wine and rolls it around in his brain and gets a little high on joy. Unhappiness to Bob is something that must be swallowed . . . hopes to hell it will be over with as soon as possible . . . . Mitch has got a heart as sensitive as an open wound. He's had to develop that tough exterior to protect the vital spots—his mind and his heart."

—Writing in *Motion Picture*, 1956

LEE MARVIN:

[Actor, *Not as a Stranger*]

"The beauty of that man. He's so still. He's moving. And yet he's not moving."

—In *Movie Talk: Who Said What About Whom in the Movies* by David Shipman, 1988

DEBORAH KERR:

[Co-star, *Heaven Knows, Mr. Allison, The Grass Is Greener, The Sundowners* and *Reunion at Fairborough*]

"Someone who's quite extraordinary is Bob Mitchum. He can take a page, run his eyes down it—like that—and he knows it. He must have a photographic memory."

—To Jon Whitcomb in *Cosmopolitan*, 1961

"This sort of macho thing about him being so tough—it's partly true. But underneath all that there's a gentleness you would never

expect . . . . The public knowledge of him as a sleepy-eyed crea-
ture who really didn't care about anything—all untrue. He cares
tremendously."

—In *Robert Mitchum: The Reluctant Star,* Cinemax, 1991

GEORGE HAMILTON:

[Co-star, *Home From the Hill*]

"He is a bit embarrassed about being the great actor he is. And he
is a great actor. But he covers it up . . . . [He is] one of the kind-
est, nicest men I've ever met."

—To Tom Cherwin in *Movie World,* 1971

SHIRLEY MACLAINE:

[Co-star, *Two for the Seesaw* and *What a Way to Go!*]

"Mitchum had been a childhood hero of mine, a broad-shouldered,
barrel-chested, macho, gentle giant of a man who resorted to violence only when profoundly provoked. I loved those qualities in
him. What I wasn't prepared for was how much of an under-
achiever he was. I was fascinated by a man who seemed to have
no ambition, no dreams to fulfill, no drive to prove anything to
anybody. It was a case of opposites attracting when he walked into
the small office on the Goldwyn lot. I stood up and looked into his
face. He shook my hand.

"'Don't let me take up too much space,' he said. 'I'm basically
a Bulgarian wrestler. I'm not right for this part [Jerry in *Two for
the Seesaw*].'

"'You're wonderful,' I said. 'I'd admired you for so long—I
think you'll be great.'

"He lit one of his Gitane filtered cigarettes and inhaled
deeply . . . . He walked across the room with a rolling swagger and
sat down. Then he looked up at me.

"'Hey,' he said, 'I've got a broken nose, and I can change a tire
without help. I'm nothing but a goddamn mechanic. If I can be a
movie star, anyone else can be a king . . . . But why you want me
for this part is your problem.'

"The die was cast. I willingly fell into the role of the rescuer, saving him from himself. It gave me something to do . . . unlock the great Mitchum so the world could witness what gold there was underneath.

"Over the three years that our relationship flourished, I found him to be a complex mystery, multifaceted, ironically witty, shy to the point of detachment, and incapable of expressing what he personally desired . . . . Perfect . . . . He became a project."

—In *My Lucky Stars: A Hollywood Memoir*
by Shirley MacLaine, 1995

POLLY BERGEN:

[Co-star, 1962 *Cape Fear, The Winds of War*
and *War and Remembrance*]

"That sort of he-man quality of Mitch's, which is real and is there—he's very much a man's man—is certainly a part of his personality, but it covers up a lot of anxiety and a certain amount of fear and terror from his childhood . . . . Mitch was not someone prepared to become a star. Mitch was only prepared to be whoever it was he was. And if that was acceptable, that was OK. And if it wasn't, that was OK, too . . . . Mitch never holds back. He always says exactly whatever he thinks. And he always pretty much does whatever he wants, and by and large does it without hurting other people. If he hurts anybody, it's himself . . . . There is no persona to Mitch. Mitch does not put on another persona like so many of us do when we're in the public eye . . . . I don't think there's a self-involved bone in Mitch's body. I don't think he cares how you shoot him. I don't think he cares where the camera is. I don't think he cares where the lights are. I think he only cares at that very moment of actually doing the scene and allowing it to be an experience he's going through . . . .

"Mitch just simply never played the movie star game. I mean, can you picture the head of some studio saying to Mitchum, 'OK, kid, look, now I want you to go to this premier tonight and I want you to pick up so and so and I want you to act like a movie star.' Mitchum would probably either say no, or punch him out. It would be one or the other."

—In *Robert Mitchum: The Reluctant Star*, Cinemax, 1991

JACK HAWKINS:

[Co-star, *Rampage*]

"But for Bob [making *Rampage*] would have been a grisly experience. He drove the production company to the verge of insanity. He had a running gag about losing his script, which never failed to produce a flutter of anxiety . . . . He is a superbly professional actor, but for some reason he tries to disguise this."

—In *Anything for a Quiet Life* by Jack Hawkins, 1974

JOHN MILLS:

[Co-star, *Ryan's Daughter*]

"I had never met Robert Mitchum before and I enjoyed acting with him. He has, in my opinion, always been a very underestimated actor; I didn't need to work with him to discover just how good he was. He is also one of the most unselfish actors; with the strange half-animal character I was playing, it was sometimes difficult to hit crucial marks, and on one particular occasion, during a wild scene outside the public house on Rose's wedding night, when Michael is being pushed to and fro while in the circle of revelers, and as I landed against Bob's shoulder I felt him unobtrusively turn me round until I was in exactly the right position for the camera to zoom in on a close-up."

—In *Up in the Clouds, Gentleman Please* by John Mills, 1981

ALI MACGRAW:

[Co-star, *The Winds of War*]

"There's tremendous danger in Bob's face and physical presence. There's an unpredictability; there's a don't-mess-with-me—and you never, never know which part of that personality is going to surface . . . . He's the real thing. This is no guy pretending to be a tough guy, or playing intelligent or smoldering to indicate sexuality. I think he's whole—he's whole . . . . He's among a very small handful of particularly men actors who project intelligence, tremendous sexuality, danger, vulnerability—hidden, except for brief chosen moments—and mystery . . . . When I think about the films I have seen in my lifetime and my sense of who is really going to count, there are going to be a handful in that time capsule. And for my money, Mitchum is going to be one of them."

—In *Robert Mitchum: The Reluctant Star,* Cinemax, 1991

Victoria Tennant:
[Co-star, *The Winds of War*]

"I was nervous . . . . I knew Robert could wipe the floor with me if he didn't like me, and that thought was scary . . . . But he couldn't have been kinder or more considerate. I wanted to rehearse a lot and he just said, 'Whenever you want me, I'll be there'—and this is the man who is supposed to treat acting as a joke. It was clear to me right away that he thought a good deal about the role and the nature of his relationship with this young woman. The age difference between us is great. It was in the book. But he looks so handsome in his uniform, and he has such presence that it's easy to see why this young woman would be interested in him."

—To Roderick Mann in *The Los Angeles Times,* 1983

From Critics and Journalists

David Thomson:
"How can I offer this hunk as one of the best actors in the movies? . . . The intriguing ambiguity in Mitchum's work [is] the idea of a man thinking and feeling beneath a calm exterior—there is no need to put 'acting' on the surface. And for a big man, he is immensely agile, capable of unsmiling humor, menace, stoicism, and above all, of watching other people as though he were waiting to make up his mind. Of course, Mitchum has been in bad films, when he slips into the weariness of someone who has read the script, but hopes it may be rewritten. But since the war, no American actor has made more first-class films, in so many differ-

ent moods . . . . He stays busy, in movies that are wretchedly beneath his classical status . . . .

"Untouchable."

—In *A Biographical Dictionary of Film,* 1994

JIM TROMBETTA:

"In fact, Mitchum has never dominated an era or a mood the way superstars generally do. He's never been that central. He's much more elusive, with something radically uncommitted in his nature, especially when it comes to the grand schemes of others . . . . He doesn't need you to root for him. At his lowest ebb, he's still too real for that . . . . In the 'booze and broads' sweeps, big Bob is a well-advertized second-to-none . . . . Mitchum's loyalty is to the characters he creates, never to the film he's in. He's more like a mercenary than patriot . . ."

—"Hipster Saint" profile in *The Catalog of Cool* by Gene Sculatti, 1982

JAMES AGEE:

"Many things in [*The Story of G.I. Joe*] itself move me to tears . . . . The closing scene seems to me a war poem as great and as beautiful as any of Whitman's . . . . It would be impossible . . . to say enough in praise of the performances of Bob Mitchum as the captain and Freddie Steele as the sergeant . . . . It seems to me a tragic and eternal work of art."

—In *The Nation,* 1945

KAY PROCTOR:

"Latching onto Bob Mitchum, currently the hottest male bet in Hollywood, is something like walking into a cage of circus lions; you never can be sure just what's going to happen. . . . Mitchum is neither willful nor rebellious, and certainly there's no malice in him. He's just a nonconformist."

—In *Motion Picture,* 1946

BLAKE LUCAS:

"*Pursued* is one of the first postwar films to observe that the quest for identity is the central crisis faced by man in the modern world . . . . The key to [director Raoul] Walsh's interpretation . . . is the actor chosen to play Jeb, and in Mitchum, the director has found the most sympathetic Rand imaginable . . . . the restraint and visual expressiveness which have distinguished him in all of his major parts are never more evident than under Walsh's direction. The character always seems capable of dealing with the complexities which challenge him, so that his moments of passivity, in which Mitchum demonstrates an understanding of the camera's power to register the subtlest emotions—never imply a surrender of will. It is remarkable that Mitchum is brought to maturity as an actor so early in his career as a result of a Walsh's perceptiveness . . ."

—In *Magill's Survey of Cinema*

THYRA SAMTER WINSLOW:

"That's Mitchum. A curious mixture of naiveté, sophistication, adventure, indiscretion, simplicity, modesty, conceit, exhibitionism, introversion, extraversion, understanding and doubt. A complex, interesting and amusing personality."

—In *Photoplay*, 1947

JUDITH M. KASS:

"The resignation and self-disgust of the Mitchum antihero found its most successful realization in *Out of the Past*. Although Mitchum has played many roles which depend on his ennui and sexual languor for their impact, this film is the only one in which these facets coalesce around a character worthy of the film noir designation. *Out of the Past* holds for Mitchum the perfect balance of bitterness, entrapment and death, which typifies this type of character . . . . the fascination of Mitchum's performance is derived from the tension between his sleepy-eyed, sexy persona and the voluptuous self-indulgence with which he succumbs to Kathie Moffett's witchery. When she tells him she did not take Whit's

$40,000, he replies, 'Baby, I don't care,' and kisses her. It seems he has been waiting all his life, not only for her, but to yield to a force capable of overriding his inertia. He is the most willing victim in the history of the genre."

—In *Magill's Survey of Cinema*

CAMERON SHIPP:

". . . oversized young man of 31 with a corrugated nose, swamp-green eyes, a tight mouth and an elliptical face which sometimes gives him the appearance of a hungry Bing Crosby . . . . He talks with the racy vocabulary of a renegade Harvard professor who has taken up barkeeping . . . . 'Listen,' he says, 'I'm in the gravy. It's very fine gravy. But don't think I don't realize that I'm just here between trains.'"

—In "Movie Menace" in *Collier's*, 1948

ROBERT RUARK:

"I don't quite savvy all this sudden bleeding over the plight of Robert Mitchum, a droopy-eyed actor who seems to have been caught by the cops on a reefer binge with a couple of blonds."

—In the *Los Angeles Times*, 1948

RICHARD SCHICKEL:

"Robert Mitchum [was] then thought to be a dangerous guy, because he had once been busted on a marijuana rap. Well, he was dangerous, but not for the reasons people think he was. He was dangerous because he was a smart, cynical, honorable man who passed his life in a state of perpetual disgust with the hypocrisy, venality and stupidity of life. Especially public life. Most especially movie star public life."

—In *Matinee Idylls: Reflections on the Movies*, 1999

CARRIE RICKEY:

"World-weary, battered, unpretentious, Mitchum epitomized postwar masculinity. Here was the conquering hero conquered by self-doubt, who never feared reprisal for confessing this weakness . . . . Mitchum could defend himself with a truly terrifying physical strength. A typical Mitchum character never dictated good and evil, because all he could see through those heavy-lidded eyes were shades of gray. Mitchum precociously gave ambivalence a good name, anticipating a '60s ethos. A swaggerer nonetheless, Mitchum was a hipster John Wayne, never suggesting might makes right though he'd acknowledge that it sure helps. Cast against type very rarely during his 40 years of screen sleepwalking, he was the brick men could rely on, the hooligan who could be chastened by Susan Hayward's wide eyes in *The Lusty Men*, by Deborah Kerr's nun in *Heaven Knows, Mr. Allison*. He had a sense of sexual and professional protocol. Self-reliant, he expected the same of others, and he never seduced a woman who made herself unavailable."

—In *The Village Voice*, 1982

BARBARA LINET:

"[Susan Hayward] did not get along with her chief co-star, Robert Mitchum. The script [*The Lusty Men*] called for a great deal of antagonism between her character, Louise, and Mitchum's Jeff, and the emotion required no great acting ability on either part. Although respectful of his professionalism, Susan was turned off by Bob's boisterous behavior and off-color language. She was not amused when, seeing her walk by on her way to the set, he'd bellow, 'There goes the old gray mare.' She was even less amused when Mitchum tried to liven up their working hours by eating raw garlic before their intimate scenes. Soon her complaints reached the top. [Howard] Hughes was sorry. He couldn't control Mitchum's mischievous behavior—nobody could at that time— but he could and did make certain that both on the lot and on location Susan was otherwise accorded a treatment usually reserved for visiting royalty."

—In *Susan Hayward: Portrait of a Survivor* by Barbara Linet, 1980

MIKE TOMKIES:

"He walked onto the set [of *White Witch Doctor*], turned to the director and said, 'What am I supposed to say?' [Henry] Hathaway was furious and shouted at him, 'We've got six pages to shoot and you don't even know your lines?' Mitchum said, 'Just tell me what I'm supposed to say and I'll say it.' In a suddenly tense atmosphere, no one dared to bring Mitchum's lines to him and Hathaway shook his head in disbelief. 'You must be kidding,' he said. Mitchum said, 'Will somebody please bring me the script so I can find out which scene by the rock this is?' Finally he got a script. He glanced briefly over the lines, then said, 'I'm ready.' Hathaway glared at him, then said, 'All right, you sonuvabitch. Action!'

"Mitchum was absolutely letter-perfect. It was the last scene shot in the film and after it was over there was a silence on the set. Then Hathaway turned to Mitchum and said, 'Bob, you're the most wonderful guy I ever worked with in my life.' To which Mitchum replied, 'What do you want for these prices? Bums?' Later Henry Hathaway was overheard speaking on the phone to Darryl F. Zanuck, then the powerful head of the Fox studio, and he was saying, 'This sonuvabitch is the most phenomenal actor I've ever seen. He glanced through the script and did six pages of dialogue—four in solid African—letter-perfect, with every nuance."

—In *The Robert Mitchum Story: 'It Sure Beats Working,'* 1972

BLAKE LUCAS:

"[*The Night of the Hunter*] remains unexpected and strange after 25 years; far from being a simple curiosity, however, it is an important achievement, reflecting directly the influence of the silent cinema in a highly personal way . . . . Robert Mitchum is cast against type as Powell, although he played villains in . . . *Track of the Cat* and *Cape Fear*. In each of the three films, Mitchum plays a character who is not simply a bad man, but a metaphor for evil, and Powell is easily the most complex of these roles because of the character's mocking, self-conscious irony. While Mitchum is generally credited for his ability to underplay, the character of Powell calls for a theatricality associated with [director Charles] Laughton himself. Mitchum demonstrates a flair for this theatricality without giving up the restraint that distinguishes him; his performance proves him to be one of the cinema's most outstanding actors."

—In *Magill's Survey of Cinema*

CECIL SMITH:

"Robert Mitchum's middle name is trouble . . . . You can paraphrase the old Shakespeare line—some men are born to trouble, some achieve trouble and some have trouble thrust upon them. Mitch qualifies in each department."

—In the *Los Angeles Times*, 1956

RICHARD THOMPSON:

"[*Thunder Road*] shrinks from art straight toward its own truth. It transcends the limits of art because it is uncompromised by any elevated artistic intent: it exists at the white-hot juncture of fact and legend. The film's being is completely determined by the anti-art genius of Robert Mitchum . . . . It was not made for critics. The film exists for a postwar subculture built on adolescence, cars, roads, night, windows rolled down, sleeves rolled up . . . . It is a work whose charm is open only to those to have first-hand knowledge of the world it depicts . . . . *Thunder Road* is a private myth irradiating the street corners of a lost existence with the savor of true existentialism . . . . The unique and subtle charm of this movie, and the source of its lasting underground reputation, lies . . . in the realization of the road as its own poetry."

—In *December* magazine, 1969

RICHARD GEHMAN:

"[He is] Hollywood's foremost apostle of outrageous obstreperousness. . . . [After being commended by a reporter for not cursing]: 'Goddamn but I'll be a sonuvabitch if it don't beat the hell out of me, lady.'"

—In *True: The Men's Magazine*, 1962

HELEN LAWRENSEN:

"It's pretty impossible to quote any conversation with him verbatim, not just because of the hair-raising language but also because he often talks in an elliptical or cryptic style, with snatches of disconnected or outwardly irrelevant phrases . . . . He doesn't care whether you understand it or not . . . . He can make an interviewer feel like a nincompoop."

—In *Esquire*, 1963

'TIME' MAGAZINE:

"All three films do nothing to disturb the widespread image of Mitchum as a handsome side of beef, a kind of swaggering, heavy-lidded Victor Mature. That may be the public's view of Mitchum, but Hollywood knows better. At 51, after 64 pictures, Mitchum is still a star to contend with. More than that, he is one of the most respected professionals in the business, a no-nonsense actor who is never late on the set and knows his lines cold. Directors, writers and other stars admire the force and the surprising nuances he can bring to even the tackiest one-dimensional role. Just about the only one who continually puts down Mitchum is Mitchum himself."

—In a profile of the actor, 1968

TIM TYLER:

"Just then his public relations man comes in and says, 'Bob, the Heart Association wants you to do a TV testimonial. Wanna do it?' And Mitchum hardens up, 'Tell them I wanna see their books.' 'Should I tell them no, Bob?' 'No, just tell them I wanna see their books.' The PR guy shuffles off, wondering how he's going to tell the head of the Heart Association that Bob Mitchum wants to see their books.

"Mitchum has sunk back into his role. So I get up to go. He shakes [hands], which is more than he was willing to do on the way in. He sees me to the front door, past the musical chimes and out. It's still raining. I imagine that he's glad to see me go. I was destroying his image for a while. I get in my car and he says with a sad smile, 'Well—back into limbo.' And I suddenly realize, though he'd never admit it, that the sonofabitch actually enjoyed talking to me."

—In the *Los Angeles Times* and *San Francisco Chronicle,* 1970

GARY ARNOLD:

". . . The barrel chest has become so pronounced that you're reminded of operatic tenors . . . . slowly, as you adjust to his tempo, you realize that you're in the presence of an unusually witty man, gifted monologuist and impressionist and satirist. Behind that sleepy look, there's an alert and civilized intelligence."

—In the *Washington Post,* 1970

JOHN BELTON:

"What distinguishes Mitchum from other major stars is that he changes, constantly eluding categorization. Mitchum continues to grow within his craft, renewing himself with each role. Tough and vulnerable, cynical and sentimental, heroic and antiheroic, Mitchum embodies many contradictory qualities. He remains an enigmatic anarchist."

—In *Robert Mitchum* (Pyramid Publications), 1976

MOLLY HASKELL:

"Mitchum's age and iconographic wrinkles that he brings to any role are, in a sense, the keys in which [*Farewell, My Lovely*] has been composed. Aware of the resonance built into an older movie star's mere presence, today's writers and directors are learning how to exploit this gift from the medium. By simply rack-focusing on Mitchum in an occasional close-up, his face filling half the screen, [director Dick] Richards evokes an entire biography, a sense of the past, of weariness and reflection.

"The film adds another meaning to the 'farewell' of the title by becoming a twilight movie, a Trent's Last Case, into which the voice-over monologue, so familiar a device in the '40s, will fit as a kind of meditation on the genre. We are persuaded by Mitchum that this is the way Marlowe would look and think and feel if he were grown old, and if the funny, haunting saga of the lovesick gorilla and his two-faced woman were his last assignment. We sense that those eyes—a perennial 'cover' suggesting the sophistication and concealing the true innocence that is also Marlowe's—are about to shut all the way for the big sleep."

—In *The Village Voice*, 1975

JANET MASLIN:

". . . Oh you know the type. Mr. Mitchum knows the type, too, so intimately that he manages to lend unexpected weight and dignity to moments of no consequence at all. This is the flimsiest movie [*The Amsterdam Kill*] Mr. Mitchum has made in some time, but for that very reason his performance is particularly arresting . . . . There's something impressive about the imperturbability with which he marches through the most potentially embarrassing situations."

—In *The New York Times*, 1977

RODERICK MANN:

"Mitchum has journeyed down the crazy years with considerable style and aplomb, always slightly out of step with his peers, most of whom long since succumbed to respectability and matching socks. A character he started out, a character he remains."

—In the *Los Angeles Times*, 1978

CHARLES MICHENER:

"Tall, big-bellied at 65, Mitchum has something none of the others quite have—presence. When he ambles outside during a lunch break [on *That Championship Season*], a crowd of Scrantonians who have stood quietly all day behind a rope chant his name. Between shots on the set, he sits in his high canvas chair, a half-awake lion gazing at something known only to himself. In his unmistakable voice, as enveloping and bottomless as a coal mine, he answers questions with a profane and terse eloquence that seems to come right off the screen. Did he ever see the play? 'No. I don't go to movies or plays. I've seen only one movie in ten years—*Star Wars*. I was ankle-deep in popcorn and pot.' . . . Isn't the coach a bit different for him? 'Oh, yeah. He's sort of a pivotal blowhard.' Watching the young actors rehearse, he says, 'This is like working with an English company; all these guys talk about is acting. I come from the school where all we talked about was overtime and screwing.'"

—In *Newsweek*, 1982

HERMAN WOUK:

"Every reader of *The Winds of War* . . . has his own vision of Capt. Victor Henry. For the viewers of the serial, he can only be Robert Mitchum. That is declared at once. Mr. Mitchum does not look like my own mental picture of Pug Henry. His Pug is taller than Mrs. Henry . . . which subtly alters the whole texture of that marriage . . . .in the scraps of film I saw, I was much taken with Mr. Mitchum's naval officer. He caught Pug's essential sadness, his integrity, his authority and his taciturn droll intelligence."

—Writing in *The New York Times*, 1981

HARRY F. WATERS:

"Even now, Robert Mitchum's chest gets wherever he's going about five seconds before he does. That's fortunate, for the sooner he arrives on the scene the better . . . . Never before has a miniseries [*The Winds of War*] . . . been so dependent on one sexagenarian actor for its muscle and pulse . . . . Mitchum, never one to volunteer excessive exertion, gives no more than his part requires, and yet that's more than enough."

—In *Newsweek*, 1983

JOHN J. O'CONNOR:

"Robert Mitchum . . . manages to carry the art of acting to the extremes of minimalism. He moves like an imposing battleship. His heavy-lidded eyes are nearly always at half-mast. His reactions [in *The Winds of War*] are rarely more than carefully restrained. He seems to be in a constant state of amusement at the human condition. In fact, Mr. Mitchum is completely miscast physically as far as the character in the novel is concerned . . . Mr.

Mitchum is 65, tall and still very much the leading man type . . . .
At one point he is described as Sphinx-like. Mr. Mitchum cap-
tures that aspect to perfection and gradually his imposing presence becomes the essential anchor for the overall drama . . . .
played with monumental solidity by Robert Mitchum . . ."

—In *The New York Times,* 1983

PETER RAINER:

"Mitchum is like a relic from the vainglorious past—a postwar
era when men were sultry and sullen and had cigarettes slanting
out of the corners of their tight, tough-guy mouths. Trenchcoats
were their second skin, and they always seemed hungover from
booze and despair. They knew how to treat women—with rough
tenderness and suspicion—and they knew how to handle men,
too. This is the hardboiled code that most of Mitchum's characters subscribe to, and it still has its vast appeal. If Mitchum is a
relic, he's a living relic."

—In the *Los Angeles Herald-Examiner,* 1983

BOB THOMAS:

"Other stars may perform their mea culpas in public, but
Mitchum remains Mitchum—unregenerate, nonapologetic, a rare
and endangered species . . . . A Mitchum interview is always wide-
ranging, sometimes unintelligible and often libelous."

—For the Associated Press, 1985

ROGER EBERT:

"Although you can't 'see' Mitchum acting at many moments in
any given film, the range of his various performances is astonish-
ing. He can be tough, gentle, heroic, indifferent; Irish, English,
Australian, Mexican; a big-city private eye, a two-bit hood. Each
performance is done with such quiet assurance, with such an apparent knowledge on his part about why he's in the film and where
his character stands, that the acting is invisible, just as John Ford
said film editing should be."

—In *Close-Ups: The Movie Star Book* Edited By Danny Peary, 1989

CHRONOLOGY

August 6, 1917: Born Robert Charles Durman Mitchum at Bridgeport, Connecticut.

February 1919: Father, James Thomas Mitchum, killed in railroad accident at Charleston, South Carolina.

1925: Boyhood poems published in *The Bridgeport Post-Telegram*, which also ran a feature article about the young writer at age 8.

1926: Sent with brother Jack Mitchum to live with relatives on a farm at Woodside, Delaware.

1928: Runs away from home for the first time with boyhood pal Manuel Barque.

1929: Bob and Jack sent to Philadelphia to live with their sister, Annette (known as Julie).

1930–31: Boys live with their mother and her third husband, Hugh Cunningham-Morris, in Manhattan. At age 13, Bob contributes radio dialogue for his sister Julie's character of Aunt Cappy Ricks on her show on WMCA radio.

1932: Boys sent to live with relatives at Rising Sun, Delaware. After self-accelerated studies, Bob completes high school curriculum at age 14, voted valedictorian of the senior class at Felton High School, Felton, Delaware, but leaves on another journey with Barque prior to graduation.

Summer 1932: Employment on salvage ship Sagamore, out of Fall River, Massachusetts.

Summer 1933: During first train-riding hobo experience, arrested for vagrancy at Savannah, Georgia, sentenced to Chatham County Camp No. 1, Brown Farm, Pipemaker Swamp chain gang. Escapes after about 30 days back to Delaware, contracting blood poisoning and gangrene from the shackle. Recovers in the care of his mother.

Autumn 1933: Meets Dorothy Spence at Voshall's Mill Pond, local swimming hole at Camden, Delaware.

1934: First transcontinental freight hop, to visit sister Annette at Long Beach, California.

Mid-1930s: Works as a punch-press operator, Toledo, Ohio; as a Civilian Conservation Corps (CCC) laborer, Chico, California; longshoreman, Long Beach; fill-in prizefighter or "bum fighter," Redding, California; coalminer, Libertyville, Pennsylvania; generally subsists on the hobo's road.

August 1937: Stage debut in *Rebound* for the Long Beach Players Guild.

1938–39: Writes children's plays *Smiler's Dragon* and *The Moss Green Bird*, staged by the Long Beach Players Guild. Writes installments of radio show *Calling All Girls* starring Peggy Fears and Patsy Kelly. Writes songs and risqué stage material for cabaret singers Nan Blackstone, Belle Barth and female impersonator Rae Bourbon.

Summer 1939: Writes *Refugees*, performed by Benny Rubin, introduced by Orson Welles, for the Jewish Relief Fund, Hollywood Bowl.

Autumn 1939: Hired by astrologer Carroll Righter as an assistant for an Eastern Seaboard tour.

March 16, 1940: Marries Dorothy Spence at Dover, Delaware.

1940: Employment as a sheet-metal worker for Lockheed Aircraft, Burbank, California.

May 8, 1941: Son James (Josh or Jim) Mitchum born.

June 1942: Hired by producer Harry "Pop" Sherman and star William Boyd as an actor and stunt man for Hopalong Cassidy westerns filmed at Kernville, California.

1943: Film debut in *Hoppy Serves a Writ*. Appears in 19 films during the year.

October 16, 1943: Son Christopher Mitchum born.

May 25, 1944: Signs a seven-year contract with RKO Radio Pictures.

1944: First star billing, in *Nevada*.

April 6–7, 1945: Jailed for being "in an intoxicated condition on private property" by Judge Cecil Holland as his Army induction day loomed.

April–October 1945: Duty as private first class, U.S. Army, stationed at Camp Roberts and Fort MacArthur.

February 1946: Received Academy Award nomination for best supporting actor of 1945 for his performance in *The Story of G.I. Joe*.

January 6, 1947: Network radio debut, *Lux Radio Theatre*, CBS, recreating his role of Billy Tabeshaw in *Till the End of Time*.

Fall 1947: Mitchum's business manager Paul Behrmann could not provide a satisfactory explanation for the disappearance of the Mitchums' savings, as much as $50,000. Mitchum refused to prosecute, but Dorothy Mitchum testified against Behrmann in another case in which the accountant bilked a client.

August 31, 1948: Arrested with three others at 8443 Ridpath Drive, Laurel Canyon. Charged with possession of marijuana and conspiracy, igniting Hollywood scandal.

February 9, 1949: Sentenced to 60 days in jail on the conspiracy conviction. Some of time spent at Wayside Honor Farm near Castaic, California.

March 30, 1949: Released from jail.

Summer 1949: Mitchums move to 1639 Mandeville Canyon Road, West Los Angeles.

January 31, 1951: Judge Clement D. Nye reviews the marijuana case, enters a "not guilty" plea in place of Mitchum's earlier plea of *nolo contendere,* and expunges the case from the records.

November 8, 1951: Knocks out soldier and prizefighter Bernard Reynolds, one of the world's top 10 heavyweights, in a barroom brawl near Colorado Springs, Colorado.

March 3, 1952: Daughter Petrine Mitchum born.

1954: RKO contract expires, opens up business offices at 9200 Sunset Boulevard and free-lances acting services. Makes *River of No Return* near Calgary, Canada, with Marilyn Monroe and *Track of the Cat* at Mount Rainier, Washington.

January 12, 1955: Fired off *Blood Alley* in San Rafael, California, for alleged pranks in one of the movies' most widely reported dismissals.

March 8, 1955: Forms DRM Productions (named for Dorothy and Robert Mitchum), which enters into a five-picture deal with United Artists.

May 9, 1955: Sues *Confidential,* scandal rag, for $1 million for the salacious and apochryphal story, "Robert Mitchum . . . The Nude Who Came to Dinner." Magazine forced to suspend publication.

June–August 1955: Mitchums vacation in Sweden and France during shooting on *Foreign Intrigue.* Releases of *The Night of the Hunter* and *Not as a Stranger* gain him prestige as an actor.

October 23, 1955: Sings two songs in first network television appearance, on *Stage Show* on CBS.

1956: Co-produces *Bandido* in Mexico.

1957: Release of long-playing album, "Robert Mitchum— Calypso Is Like So" and two films made back-to-back on the Caribbean island of Tobago, *Heaven Knows, Mr. Allison* and *Fire Down Below*.

1958: Produces and stars in and writes the original story and songs for *Thunder Road*, filmed at Asheville, North Carolina.

September 1958: Recording of "The Ballad of Thunder Road" reaches No. 62 on the pop charts.

1959: Produces and stars in *The Wonderful Country*, filmed in Durango, Mexico. Family moves to the 300-acre Belmont Farms, Eastern Shore district, Maryland.

1960: First involvement with horse breeding. Renames DRM Productions as Talbot Productions (for Talbot County, Maryland). Shoots *The Sundowners* in Australia.

December 1960: Named best actor of the year by the National Board of Review for his performances in *Home From the Hill* and *The Sundowners*.

1962: His strong performances drive much of the action in *The Longest Day* and *Cape Fear*.

1965: Trip to Kenya to make *Mister Moses*.

Spring 1966: Tours American bases in Vietnam on a morale-boosting mission for the U.S. State Department.

Spring 1967: Second civilian tour of Vietnam.

1967: Family moves to Cole Porter's old home, Rockingham Avenue, Brentwood, California.

1968: The Mitchums move to 268 Saint Pierre Road, Bel Air, California.

May 13, 1968: Recording of "Little Old Wine Drinker Me" peaks at No. 9 on the country music chart and cracks the top 100 on the pop music chart.

1969: Spends most of the year in Dingle, Ireland, making *Ryan's Daughter*.

1973: Critical acclaim for *The Friends of Eddie Coyle*.

1974: Mitchum's horse, Don Guerro, wins annual Quarter Horse Running Aged Stallion in "Champion of Champions" race.

1975: Critical acclaim for *Farewell, My Lovely*. Cast by Elia Kazan in *The Last Tycoon*.

1976: Lake Forest School District in Delaware, which encompassed Mitchum's defunct alma mater of Felton High, confers on him his diploma 44 years after he finished his studies.

1978: The Mitchums move to Montecito, California.

1980: The Los Angeles Film Critics Association bestows Mitchum with its annual Career Achievement Award.

December 8, 1980: Television movie acting debut, *Nightkill*.

February 6, 1983: Debut installment, *The Winds of War*.

February 7, 1983: Appears on the cover of *Time* magazine.

October 5, 1983: Los Angeles Mayor Tom Bradley proclaims "Robert Mitchum Day."

January 16, 1984: Received the 1,775th star on the Hollywood Walk of Fame at 6240 Hollywood Boulevard.

Summer 1987: Replaces the ailing John Huston in *Mr. North*.

November 14, 1987: Guest host, *Saturday Night Live*.

November 13, 1988: Debut installment, *War and Remembrance*.

1989: Accepted People's Choice Award for best miniseries for *War and Remembrance* on network telecast.

1989: Is host and narrator for the TNT feature-length documentary *John Huston: The Man, the Movies, the Maverick*.

February 2, 1990: Mitchum's mother, Ann Harriet Gunderson Mitchum Morris, dies at age 96.

1990: Stars in TV sitcom, *A Family for Joe.*

March 16, 1990: 50th wedding anniversary celebrated, L'Ermitage, Beverly Hills, California.

1991: Appearance in Martin Scorsese's *Cape Fear* remake. The documentary *Robert Mitchum: The Reluctant Star* airs on Cinemax.

1992: Recipient of the Cecil B. De Mille Award for career achievement at the Golden Globe Awards.

1992–94: Plays continuing character in the Family Channel series *African Skies.*

1996: Appears in Jim Jarmusch's *Dead Man.*

July 1, 1997: Dies of complications from lung cancer and emphysema at his Montecito home.

1999: Posthumously named No. 23 on the American Film Institute's top 25 male stars of the century.

February 28, 2000: Debut of the "Robert Mitchum" installment of E! Entertainment television's *Mysteries and Scandals.*

FILMOGRAPHY

Key to abbreviations:
D=Director.
W=Screenplay or Teleplay Writer.
P=Producer.
Cam=Cinematographer or Director of Photography or
Cameraman.

FEATURE FILMS

1. *HOPPY SERVES A WRIT* (1943) United Artists. **D:** George Archainbaud. **W:** Gerald Geraghty. **P:** Harry Sherman. **Cam:** Russell Harlan. **Cast:** William Boyd, Andy Clyde, Jay Kirby, Victor Jory, George Reeves, Forbes Murray, Jan Christy, Bob Mitchum (as Rigney). A Hopalong Cassidy western.

2. *BORDER PATROL* (1943) United Artists. **D:** Lesley Selander. **W:** Michael Wilson. **P:** Harry Sherman. **Cam:** Russell Harlan. **Cast:** William Boyd, Andy Clyde, Jay Kirby, Russell Simpson, George Reeves, Pierce Lyden, Cliff Parkinson, Duncan Renaldo, Bob Mitchum (as Henchman). A Hopalong Cassidy western.

3. *THE LEATHER BURNERS* (1943) United Artists. **D:** Joseph E. Henabery. **W:** Jo Pagano. **P:** Harry Sherman. **Cam:** Russell Harlan. **Cast:** William Boyd, Andy Clyde, Jay Kirby, Victor Jory, George Givot, George Reeves, Shelley Spencer, Bob Mitchum (as Randall). A Hopalong Cassidy western.

4. *FOLLOW THE BAND* (1943) Universal. **D:** Jean Yarbrough. **W:** Warren Wilson, Dorothy Bennett. **P:** Paul Malvern. **Cam:** Elwood Bredell. **Cast:** Eddie Quillan, Mary Beth Hughes, Leon Errol, Anne Rooney, Samuel S. Hinds,

Bob Mitchum (as Tate Winters). A backstage musical featuring novelty acts.

5. *COLT COMRADES* (1943) United Artists. **D:** Lesley Selander. **W:** Michael Wilson. **P:** Harry Sherman. **Cam:** Russell Harlan. **Cast:** William Boyd, Andy Clyde, Jay Kirby, George Reeves, Gayle Lord, Earle Hodgins, Victor Jory, Douglas Fowley, Bob Mitchum (as Bart). A Hopalong Cassidy western.

6. *THE HUMAN COMEDY* (1943) Metro-Goldwyn-Mayer. **D/P:** Clarence Brown. **W:** Howard Estabrook. **Cam:** Harry Stradling. **Cast:** Mickey Rooney, James Craig, Frank Morgan, Fay Bainter, Donna Reed, Van Johnson, Frank Craven, Dorothy Morris, Barry Nelson, Don DeFore, Bob Mitchum (as Horse). The adaptation of William Saroyan's novel about home-front problems in a small California town during World War II.

7. *WE'VE NEVER BEEN LICKED* (1943) Universal. **D:** John Rawlins. **W:** Norman Reilly Raine, Nick Grinde. **P:** Walter Wanger. **Cam:** Milton Krasner. **Cast:** Richard Quine, Anne Gwynne, Martha O'Driscoll, Noah Beery Jr., William Frawley, Harry Davenport, Samuel S. Hinds, Bob Mitchum (as Panhandle Mitchell). A youth discovers patriotism at Texas A&M University.

8. *BEYOND THE LAST FRONTIER* (1943) Republic. **D:** Howard Bretherton. **W:** John K. Butler, Morton Grant. **P:** Louis Gray. **Cam:** Bud Thackery. **Cast:** Eddie Dew, Smiley Burnette, Lorraine Miller, Bob Mitchum (as Trigger Dolan), Ernie Adams. A Texas Ranger infiltrates a criminal gang.

9. *BAR 20* (1943) United Artists. **D:** Lesley Selander. **W:** Morton Grant, Norman Houston, Michael Wilson. **P:** Harry Sherman. **Cam:** Russell Harlan. **Cast:** William Boyd, Andy Clyde, George Reeves, Dustine Farnum, Victor Jory, Douglas Fowley, Bob Mitchum (as Richard Adams). A Hopalong Cassidy western.

10. *DOUGHBOYS IN IRELAND* (1943) Columbia. **D:** Lew Landers. **W:** Howard J. Green. **P:** Jack Fier. **Cam:** L.W. O'Connell. **Cast:** Kenny Baker, Jeff Donnell, Lynn Merrick, Guy Bonham, Red Latham, Wamp Carlson, Bob Mitchum (as Ernie Jones). A World War II musical about GIs stationed in Ireland.

11. *CORVETTE K-225* (1943) Universal. **D:** Richard Rosson. **W:** John Rhodes Sturdy. **P:** Howard Hawks. **Cam:** Tony Gaudio. **Cast:** Randolph Scott, James Brown, Ella Raines, Barry Fitzgerald, Andy Devine, Fuzzy Knight, Noah Beery Jr., Thomas Gomez, Murray Alper, James Flavin, Robert Mitchum (as Sheppard), Charles McGraw, Peter Lawford. The title escort ship serves in the North Atlantic during the early days of World War II.

12. *AERIAL GUNNER* (1943) Paramount. **D:** William Pine. **W:** Maxwell Shane. **P:** William Pine, William Thomas. **Cam:** Fred Jackman Jr. **Cast:** Chester Morris, Richard Arlen, Lita Ward, Jimmy Lydon, Dick Purcell, Bob Mitchum (as Sergeant). Two gunner trainees fight over a girl prior to World War II combat exploits.

13. *THE LONE STAR TRAIL* (1943) Universal. **D:** Ray Taylor. **W/P:** Oliver Drake. **Cam:** William Sickner. **Cast:** Johnny Mack Brown, Tex Ritter, Fuzzy Knight, Jennifer Holt, Bob Mitchum (as Ben Slocum), Earle Hodgins. A falsely jailed rancher sets out on parole to find the culprits who framed him.

14. *FALSE COLORS* (1943) United Artists. **D:** George Archainbaud. **W:** Bennett Cohen. **P:** Harry Sherman. **Cam:** Russell Harlan. **Cast:** William Boyd, Andy Clyde, Jimmy Rogers, Tom Seidel, Claudia Drake, Douglass Dumbrille, Bob Mitchum (as Rip Austin), Glenn Strange, Pierce Lyden. A Hopalong Cassidy western.

15. *THE DANCING MASTERS* (1943) Twentieth Century-Fox. **D:** Malcolm St. Clair. **W:** Scott Darling. **P:** Lee Marcus. **Cam:**

Norbert Brodine. **Cast:** Stan Laurel, Oliver Hardy, Trudy Marshall, Robert Bailey, Margaret Dumont, Allan Lane, Matt Briggs, Bob Mitchum (as Mickey), Nestor Paiva. Laurel and Hardy get involved with the "Arthur Hurry School of Dancing."

16. *RIDERS OF THE DEADLINE* (1943) United Artists. **D:** Lesley Selander. **W:** Bennett Cohen. **P:** Harry Sherman. **Cam:** Russell Harlan. **Cast:** William Boyd, Andy Clyde, Jimmy Rogers, Richard Crane, Frances Woodward, William Halligan, Bob Mitchum (as Drago). A Hopalong Cassidy western.

17. *GUNG HO!* (1943) Universal. **D:** Ray Enright. **W:** Lucien Hubbard. **P:** Walter Wanger. **Cam:** Milton Krasner. **Cast:** Randolph Scott, Grace MacDonald, Alan Curtis, Noah Beery Jr., J. Carrol Naish, David Bruce, Peter Coe, Bob Mitchum (as Pigiron Matthews), Rod Cameron, Sam Levene, Milburn Stone, Richard Lane. A U.S. Marine Raider battalion is trained in rough tactics, then fights the Battle of Makin in the Gilbert Islands.

18. *MINESWEEPER* (1943) Paramount. **D:** William Berke. **W:** Edward T. Lowe, Maxwell Shane. **Cam:** Fred Jackman Jr. **Cast:** Richard Arlen, Jean Parker, Russell Hayden, Guinn "Big Boy" Williams, Emma Dunn, Douglas Fowley, Frank Fenton, Bob Mitchum (as Chuck). A service train-and-fight film set during World War II.

19. *CRY HAVOC* (1943) Metro-Goldwyn-Mayer. **D:** Richard Thorpe. **W:** Paul Osborne. **P:** Edwin Knopf. **Cam:** Karl Freund. **Cast:** Margaret Sullavan, Ann Sothern, Joan Blondell, Fay Bainter, Marsha Hunt, Ella Raines, Connie Gilchrist, Heather Angel, Dorothy Morris, William Bishop, Frances Gifford, Bob Mitchum (as Groaning Man). American women volunteers help U.S. nurses treat the wounded during the Battle of Bataan.

20. *JOHNNY DOESN'T LIVE HERE ANYMORE* (1944)

Monogram. **D:** Joe May. **W:** Philip Yordan, John Kafka. **P:** Maurice King. **Cam:** Ira Morgan. **Cast:** Simone Simon, James Ellison, William Terry, Minna Gombell, Chick Chandler, Alan Dinehart, Gladys Blake, Robert Mitchum (as CPO Jeff Daniels). A woman sublets a flat and finds that 12 men also have keys to the place.

21. *WHEN STRANGERS MARRY* (1944) Monogram. **D:** William Castle. **W:** Philip Yordan, Dennis Cooper. **P:** Maurice King, Franklin King. **Cam:** Ira Morgan. **Cast:** Dean Jagger, Kim Hunter, Robert Mitchum (as Fred), Neil Hamilton, Neil Lubin, Milton Kibbee, Dewey Robinson, Claire Whitney, Dick Elliott, Lee "Lasses" White, Rhonda Fleming. A young bride arrives in New York City and suspects that her husband is a serial killer.

22. *THIRTY SECONDS OVER TOKYO* (1944) Metro-Goldwyn-Mayer. **D:** Mervyn LeRoy. **W:** Dalton Trumbo. **P:** Sam Zimbalist. **Cam:** Harold Rosson. **Cast:** Spencer Tracy, Van Johnson, Robert Walker, Phyllis Thaxter, Tim Murdock, Robert Mitchum (as Bob Gray), Scott McKay, Gordon McDonald, Horace "Stephen" McNally, Steve Brodie, Blake Edwards, Hazel Brooks. "Doolittle's Raid," the first American attack on Japan in World War II, is secretly planned and carried out.

23. *THE GIRL RUSH* (1944) RKO Radio. **D:** Gordon Douglas. **W:** Robert E. Kent. **Cam:** Nicholas Musuraca. **Cast:** Wally Brown, Alan Carney, Frances Langford, Vera Vague, Robert Mitchum (as Jimmy Smith), Paul Hurst, Rita Corday, Bert LeBaron. Vaudevillians bring showgirls to a corrupt gold-mining town.

24. *MR. WINKLE GOES TO WAR* (1944) Columbia. **D:** Alfred E. Green. **W:** Waldo Salt, George Choey, Louis Solomon. **P:** Jack Moss. **Cam:** Joseph Walker. **Cast:** Edward G. Robinson, Ruth Warrick, Ted Donaldson, Bob Haymes, Robert Armstrong, Richard Gaines, Jeff Donnell, Bob Mitchum (as

Corporal). A henpecked bank clerk is drafted into the Army for World War II.

25. *NEVADA* (1944) RKO Radio. **D:** Edward Killy. **W:** Norman Houston. **P:** Herman Schlom. **Cam:** Harry J. Wild. **Cast:** Robert Mitchum (as Jim "Nevada" Lacy), Anne Jeffreys, Guinn "Big Boy" Williams, Nancy Gates, Richard Martin, Craig Reynolds, Harry Woods. A man escapes his own lynching for murder and fingers the real culprits in this adaptation of a Zane Grey story.

26. *WEST OF THE PECOS* (1945) RKO Radio. **D:** Edward Killy. **W:** Norman Houston. **P:** Herman Schlom. **Cam:** Harry J. Wild. **Cast:** Robert Mitchum (as Pecos Smith), Barbara Hale, Richard Martin, Thurston Hall, Rita Corday, Russell Hopton, Bill Williams, Harry Woods. A woman escapes from a stagecoach holdup and masquerades as a boy in this Zane Grey adaptation.

27. *THE STORY OF G.I. JOE* (1945) United Artists. **D:** William A. Wellman. **W:** Leopold Atlas, Guy Endore, Philip Stevenson. **Cam:** Russell Metty. **Cast:** Burgess Meredith, Robert Mitchum (as Lieutenant/Captain Walker), Freddie Steele, Wally Cassell, Jimmy Lloyd, Jack Reilly, Bill Murphy, William Self, Billy Benedict. Correspondent Ernie Pyle joins "Charlie" Company of the U.S. Infantry, which fights in Italy in World War II.

28. *TILL THE END OF TIME* (1945) RKO Radio. **D:** Edward Dmytryk. **W:** Allen Rivkin. **P:** Dore Schary. **Cam:** Harry J. Wild. **Cast:** Dorothy McGuire, Guy Madison, Robert Mitchum (as Billy Tabeshaw), Bill Williams, Tom Tully, William Gargan, Jean Porter, Johnny Sands, Blake Edwards. G.I.s return from World War II and readjust to civilian life, including Billy Tabeshaw, a former rodeo rider whose war wounds prohibit that profession.

29. *UNDERCURRENT* (1946) Metro-Goldwyn-Mayer. **D:** Vincente Minnelli. **W:** Edward Chodorov. **P:** Pandro S.

Berman. **Cam:** Karl Freund. **Cast:** Katharine Hepburn, Robert Taylor, Robert Mitchum (as Michael Garroway), Edmund Gwenn, Marjorie Main, Jayne Meadows, Clinton Sundberg. A newlywed learns that her airplane manufacturer husband harbors a deep hatred of his brother, Michael, who's secretly hiding out on a ranch.

30. *THE LOCKET* (1946) RKO Radio. **D:** John Brahm. **W:** Sheridan Gibney. **P:** Bert Granet. **Cam:** Nicholas Musuraca. **Cast:** Laraine Day, Brian Aherne, Robert Mitchum (as Norman Clyde), Gene Raymond, Sharyn Moffett, Ricardo Cortez, Henry Stephenson, Reginald Denny, Queenie Leonard, Martha Hyer. A groom learns on his wedding day that his wife-to-be is a kleptomaniac who drove artist Norman Clyde to suicide.

31. *PURSUED* (1947) Warner Bros. **D:** Raoul Walsh. **W:** Niven Busch. **P:** Milton Sperling. **Cam:** James Wong Howe. **Cast:** Teresa Wright, Robert Mitchum (as Jeb Rand), Judith Anderson, Dean Jagger, Alan Hale, John Rodney, Harry Carey Jr., Clifton Young, Ray Teal, Lane Chandler. Spanish-American War veteran Jeb Rand returns to the New Mexico ranch where he was raised an orphan and marries his childhood sweetheart.

32. *CROSSFIRE* (1947) RKO Radio. **D:** Edward Dmytryk. **W:** John Paxton. **P:** Adrian Scott. **Cam:** J. Roy Hunt. **Cast:** Robert Young, Robert Mitchum (as Sergeant Peter Kelley), Robert Ryan, Gloria Grahame, Paul Kelly, Sam Levene, Jacqueline White, Steve Brodie, George Cooper, Richard Benedict, Lex Barker. A Jew is murdered in New York and three soldiers become suspects during a nightlong police investigation.

33. *DESIRE ME* (1947) Metro-Goldwyn-Mayer. **D:** George Cukor, Mervyn LeRoy, Jack Conway, Victor Saville (none was credited). **W:** Marguerite Roberts, Zoe Akins. **P:** Arthur Hornblow Jr. **Cam:** Joseph Ruttenberg. **Cast:** Greer Garson,

Robert Mitchum (as Paul Aubert), Richard Hart, Florence Bates, Morris Ankrum, George Zucco. Paul Aubert returns to Normandy from battle to find his wartime pal pursuing his wife.

34. *OUT OF THE PAST* (1947) RKO Radio. **D:** Jacques Tourneur. **W:** Geoffrey Homes (aka Daniel Mainwaring), Frank Fenton (uncredited). **P:** Warren Duff. **Cam:** Nicholas Musuraca. **Cast:** Robert Mitchum (as Jeff Bailey), Jane Greer, Kirk Douglas, Rhonda Fleming, Richard Webb, Steve Brodie, Virginia Houston, Paul Valentine. A detective hired to find a racketeer's moll foolishly falls in love with her and is played for a sap.

35. *RACHEL AND THE STRANGER* (1948) RKO Radio. **D:** Norman Foster. **W:** Waldo Salt. **P:** Richard H. Berger. **Cam:** Maury Gertsman. **Cast:** Loretta Young, William Holden, Robert Mitchum (as Jim Fairways), Gary Gray, Tom Tully, Sara Haden, Frank Ferguson, Walter Baldwin. On the Ohio frontier in 1820, a remarried widower and footloose woodsman Jim Fairways become rivals for the recent bride while the Shawnees threaten.

36. *BLOOD ON THE MOON* (1948) RKO Radio. **D:** Robert Wise. **W:** Lillie Hayward. **P:** Theron Warth. **Cam:** Nicholas Musuraca. **Cast:** Robert Mitchum (as Jim Garry), Barbara Bel Geddes, Robert Preston, Walter Brennan, Phyllis Thaxter, Frank Faylen, Harry Carey Jr., Tom Tully, Charles McGraw, Chris-Pin Martin, Iron Eyes Cody. A hired gun watches as his cattlemen employers bully homesteaders, forcing his change of allegiance.

37. *THE RED PONY* (1949) Republic. **D:** Lewis Milestone. **W:** John Steinbeck. **Cam:** Tony Gaudio. **Cast:** Myrna Loy, Robert Mitchum (as Billy Buck), Louis Calhern, Sheppard Strudwick, Peter Miles, Margaret Hamilton, Patty King, Beau Bridges. In John Steinbeck's own adaptation of his classic novel, a sensitive young boy raises a colt and is be-

friended by pragmatic ranch hand Billy Buck while his parents' marriage deteriorates.

38. *THE BIG STEAL* (1949) RKO Radio. **D:** Don Siegel. **W:** Geoffrey Homes, Gerald Drayson Adams. **P:** Jack J. Gross. **Cam:** Harry J. Wild. **Cast:** Robert Mitchum (as Duke Halliday), Jane Greer, William Bendix, Patric Knowles, Ramon Novarro, Don Alvarado, John Qualen, Dorothy Mitchum. Duke Halliday, who's chased by a U.S. army captain into Mexico, teams with a bus passenger who's in turn pursuing a man who swindled her.

39. *HOLIDAY AFFAIR* (1949) RKO Radio. **D/P:** Don Hartman. **W:** Isobel Lennart. **Cam:** Milton Krasner. **Cast:** Robert Mitchum (as Steve Mason), Janet Leigh, Wendell Corey, Gordon Gebert, Griff Barnett, Esther Dale, Henry O'Neill, Henry "Harry" Morgan, Chick Chandler. Steve Mason is fired by a department store during Christmas season and asks the single-parent widow who feels guilty about his fate to bail him out of jail.

40. *WHERE DANGER LIVES* (1950) RKO Radio. **D:** John Farrow. **W:** Charles Bennett. **P:** Irving Cummings. **Cam:** Nicholas Musuraca. **Cast:** Robert Mitchum (as Jeff Cameron), Faith Domergue, Claude Rains, Maureen O'Sullivan, Charles Kemper, Ralph Dumke, Billy House, Jack Kelly, Jack Kruschen, Ray Teal, Harry Shannon. Medical intern Jeff Cameron is convinced by his scheming girlfriend that he killed her father.

41. *MY FORBIDDEN PAST* (1950) RKO Radio. **D:** Robert Stevenson. **W:** Marion Parsonnet. **P:** Robert Sparks, Polan Banks. **Cam:** Harry J. Wild. **Cast:** Robert Mitchum (as Dr. Mark Lucas), Ava Gardner, Melvyn Douglas, Lucille Watson, Janis Carter, Gordon Oliver, Basil Ruysdael, Clarence Muse. In 1890 New Orleans, a scheming heiress in hot romantic pursuit of the married Dr. Lucas comes to his aid when he's accused of killing his wife.

42. *HIS KIND OF WOMAN* (1951) RKO Radio. **D:** John Farrow, Richard Fleischer (uncredited). **W:** Frank Fenton. **P:** Howard Hughes, Robert Sparks. **Cam:** Harry J. Wild. **Cast:** Robert Mitchum (as Dan Milner), Jane Russell, Vincent Price, Raymond Burr, Tim Holt, Charles McGraw, Jim Backus, Marjorie Reynolds, Mamie Van Doren. Gambler Dan Milner accepts a job at a Mexican resort, where he courts a singer and is kidnapped by mobsters.

43. *THE RACKET* (1951) RKO Radio. **D:** John Cromwell, Nicholas Ray (uncredited). **W:** William Wister Haines, W.R. Burnett. **P:** Edmund Grainger. **Cam:** George E. Diskant. **Cast:** Robert Mitchum (as Captain Thomas McQuigg), Robert Ryan, Lizabeth Scott, Ray Collins, Joyce MacKenzie, Robert Hutton, Virginia Houston, William Conrad, Les Tremayne, Iris Adrian. Former boyhood chums become mobster and police captain.

44. *MACAO* (1952) RKO Radio. **D:** Josef von Sternberg, Nicholas Ray (uncredited). **W:** Bernard C. Schoenfeld, Stanley Rubin, Walter Newman (uncredited), Robert Mitchum (uncredited). **P:** Alex Gottlieb, Jerry Wald (uncredited). **Cam:** Harry J. Wild. **Cast:** Robert Mitchum (as Nick Cochran), Jane Russell, William Bendix, Thomas Gomez, Gloria Grahame, Brad Dexter, Philip Ahn. Mistaken identity in the Portuguese protectorate's nightclubs includes Nick Cochran for a rackets-busting agent.

45. *ONE MINUTE TO ZERO* (1952) RKO Radio. **D:** Tay Garnett. **W:** Milton Krims, William Wister Haines. **P:** Edmund Grainger. **Cam:** William E. Snyder. **Cast:** Robert Mitchum (as Colonel Steve Janowski), Ann Blythe, William Talman, Charles McGraw, Margaret Sheridan, Richard Egan, Stuart Whitman, John Mallory (aka John Mitchum). In the Korean War, an Army officer orders artillery strikes against refugees.

46. *THE LUSTY MEN* (1952) RKO Radio. **D:** Nicholas Ray.

W: Horace McCoy, David Dortort, Robert Mitchum (uncredited), Nicholas Ray (uncredited). **P:** Jerry Wald, Norman Krasna. **Cam:** Lee Garmes. **Cast:** Susan Hayward, Robert Mitchum (as Jeff McCloud), Arthur Kennedy, Arthur Hunnicutt, Frank Faylen, Carol Nugent, Burt Mustin, Sheb Wooley, John Mitchum. On the rodeo circuit, a bronc-busting star falls for his protégé's wife.

47. *ANGEL FACE* (1952) RKO Radio. **D/P:** Otto Preminger. **W:** Frank Nugent, Oscar Millard. **Cam:** Harry Stradling. **Cast:** Robert Mitchum (as Frank Jessup), Jean Simmons, Mona Freeman, Herbert Marshall, Leon Ames, Barbara O'Neil, Kenneth Tobey, Griff Barnett, Jim Backus. An unbalanced heiress plots her stepmother's demise while wooing the family chauffeur, but doesn't count on her father in the vicinity during the deadly act.

48. *WHITE WITCH DOCTOR* (1953) Twentieth Century-Fox. **D:** Henry Hathaway. **W:** Ivan Goff, Ben Roberts. **P:** Otto Lang. **Cam:** Leon Shamroy. **Cast:** Susan Hayward, Robert Mitchum (as Lonni Douglas), Walter Slezak, Mashood Ajala, Joseph C. Narcisse, Timothy Carey, Elzie Emanuel, Michael Ansara. In the 1907 Congo, a female missionary and adventurer Lonni Douglas debate their avocations and fall in love on a jungle trek.

49. *SECOND CHANCE* (1953) RKO Radio. **D:** Rudolph Mate. **W:** Oscar Millard, Sydney Boehm. **P:** Sam Weisenthal. **Cam:** William Snyder. **Cast:** Robert Mitchum (as Russ Lambert), Linda Darnell, Jack Palance, Sandro Giglio, Rodolfo Hoyos Jr., Reginald Sheffield, Roy Roberts, Fortunio Bonanova, Milburn Stone, Dan Seymour. Prizefighter Russ Lambert, barnstorming in South America, falls in love with a mob moll fleeing the U.S.

50. *SHE COULDN'T SAY NO* (1954) RKO Radio. **D:** Lloyd Bacon. **W:** D.D. Beauchamp, William Powers, Richard Flournoy. **P:** Robert Sparks. **Cam:** Harry J. Wild. **Cast:**

Robert Mitchum (as Doc), Jean Simmons, Arthur Hunnicutt, Edgar Buchanan, Wallace Ford, Raymond Walburn, Burt Mustin, Dabbs Greer, Jimmy Hunt. A philanthropist returns to Progress, Arkansas, to repay the townsfolk for financing her girlhood operation.

51. *RIVER OF NO RETURN* (1954) Twentieth Century-Fox. **D:** Otto Preminger. **W:** Frank Fenton. **P:** Stanley Rubin. **Cam:** Joseph LaShelle. **Cast:** Robert Mitchum (as Matt Calder), Marilyn Monroe, Rory Calhoun, Tommy Rettig, Murvyn Vye, Douglas Spencer, Don Beddoe, Arthur Shields, Ed Hinton. An ex-con frontier rancher, his son and an abandoned dance hall girl escape hostile Indians down a whitewater river on a makeshift raft.

52. *TRACK OF THE CAT* (1954) Warner Bros. **D:** William A. Wellman. **W:** A.I. Bezzerides. **P:** Robert Fellows. **Cam:** William Clothier. **Cast:** Robert Mitchum (as Curt Bridges), Teresa Wright, Diana Lynn, Tab Hunter, Beulah Bondi, William Hopper, Carl Switzer. Trapped by a blizzard in a mountain cabin, the Bridges family ruminates on their emotional tangles while brooding elder son Curt goes into the drifts to hunt a marauding cougar.

53. *NOT AS A STRANGER* (1955) United Artists. **D/P:** Stanley Kramer. **W:** Edna Anhalt, Edward Anhalt. **Cam:** Franz Planer. **Cast:** Olivia DeHavilland, Robert Mitchum (as Dr. Lucas Marsh), Frank Sinatra, Broderick Crawford, Charles Bickford, Gloria Grahame, Lee Marvin, Myron McCormick, Lon Chaney Jr., Harry Morgan, Whit Bissell, Mae Clarke. The ambitious and unscrupulous Lucas Marsh ruthlessly transcends his low origins.

54. *THE NIGHT OF THE HUNTER* (1955) United Artists. **D:** Charles Laughton. **W:** James Agee, Charles Laughton (uncredited). **P:** Paul Gregory. **Cam:** Stanley Cortez. **Cast:** Robert Mitchum (as Preacher Harry Powell), Shelley Winters, Lillian Gish, Billy Chapin, Sally Jane Bruce, Peter

Graves, James Gleason, Don Beddoe, Corey Allen. A West Virginia preacher murders a woman and pursues her fleeing children to steal $10,000.

55. *THE MAN WITH THE GUN* (1955) United Artists. **D:** Richard Wilson. **W:** N.B. Stone Jr. **P:** Samuel Goldwyn Jr. **Cam:** Lee Garmes. **Cast:** Robert Mitchum (as Clint Tollinger), Jan Sterling, Karen Sharpe, Henry Hull, Emile Meyer, John Lupton, Ted De Corsia, Leo Gordon, Angie Dickinson, Stafford Repp, Barbara Lawrence. A drifting Old West town-tamer finds his wife has become the local madam of corrupted Sheridan City.

56. *FOREIGN INTRIGUE* (1956) United Artists. **D/W/P:** Sheldon Reynolds. **Cam:** Bertil Palmgrem. **Cast:** Robert Mitchum (as Bishop), Genevieve Page, Ingrid Tulean (Thulin), Frederick O'Brady, Gene Deckers, Inga Tidblad, John Padovano, Peter Copley. A press agent finds that his dead boss was one of four magnates who had contracted with Hitler to betray their nations, and tracks blackmail information in postwar Stockholm and Paris.

57. *BANDIDO* (1956) United Artists. **D:** Richard Fleischer. **W:** Earl Felton. **P:** Robert L. Jacks, Robert Mitchum (uncredited). **Cam:** Ernest Laszlo. **Cast:** Robert Mitchum (as Wilson), Ursula Thiess, Gilbert Roland, Zachary Scott, Rodolfo Acosta, Henry Brandon, Douglas Fowley, Jose I. Torvay, Victor Junco. During the 1916 Mexican Revolution, mercenary Wilson eventually throws in with a rebel band to defeat a corrupt gunrunner.

58. *HEAVEN KNOWS, MR. ALLISON* (1957) Twentieth Century-Fox. **D:** John Huston. **W:** John Lee Mahin. **P:** Buddy Adler, Eugene Frenke. **Cam:** Oswald Morris. **Cast:** Deborah Kerr, Robert Mitchum (as Mr. Allison), Fusamoto Takasimi, Noboru Yoshida, Anna Sten, U.S. Marines of Trinidad Base. A novice Catholic nun and a U.S. Marine forge a friendship while stranded in a cave on a Japanese-held island during World War II.

59. *FIRE DOWN BELOW* (1957) Columbia. **D:** Robert Parrish.
W: Irwin Shaw. **P:** Irving Allen, Albert R. Broccoli. **Cam:**
Desmond Dickinson. **Cast:** Rita Hayworth, Robert Mitchum
(as Felix Bowers), Jack Lemmon, Herbert Lom, Bonar
Colleano, Bernard Lee, Edric Connor, Anthony Newley,
Peter Illing, Joan Miller. A Caribbean cargo boat captain and
his naive first mate both become enamored of a weary
beauty seeking a safe harbor.

60. *THE ENEMY BELOW* (1957) Twentieth Century-Fox. **D/P:**
Dick Powell. **W:** Wendell Mayes. **Cam:** Harold Rosson.
Cast: Robert Mitchum (as Captain Murrell), Curt Jurgens,
David Hedison, Theodore Bikel, Russell Collins, Kurt
Kreuger, Frank Albertson, Biff Elliott, Doug McClure, Ralph
Manza. In the South Atlantic in World War II, a Navy de-
stroyer captain engages a German U-boat commander in a
cat-and-mouse battle.

61. *THUNDER ROAD* (1958) United Artists. **D:** Arthur Ripley.
W: James Atlee Phillips, Walter Wise, Robert Mitchum (orig-
inal story). **P:** Robert Mitchum. **Cam:** Alan Stensvold, David
Ettinson. **Cast:** Robert Mitchum (as Luke Doolin), Gene
Barry, Jacques Aubuchon, Keely Smith, Trevor Bardette,
Sandra Knight, Jim Mitchum, Betsy Holt, Mitchell Ryan,
Peter Breck, Jerry Hardin, Robert Porterfield. A folk-heroic
North Carolina moonshiner evades federal authorities and
mobsters to deliver his goods.

62. *THE HUNTERS* (1958) Twentieth Century-Fox. **D/P:** Dick
Powell. **W:** Wendell Mayes. **Cam:** Charles G. Clarke. **Cast:**
Robert Mitchum (as Major Clive Seville), Robert Wagner,
Richard Egan, May Britt, Lee Philips, John Gabriel, Stacy
Harris, Victor Sen Yung, Nobu McCarthy, Keye Luke, Ron
Ely. During the Korean War, World War II veteran Clive
Seville proves himself among younger pilots and has an af-
fair with one of their wives.

63. *THE ANGRY HILLS* (1959) Metro-Goldwyn-Mayer. **D:** Robert Aldrich. **W:** A.I. Bezzerides. **P:** Raymond Stross. **Cam:** Stephen Dade. **Cast:** Robert Mitchum (as Mike Morrison), Stanley Baker, Elisabeth Mueller, Gia Scala, Theodore Bikel, Sebastian Cabot, Peter Illing, Leslie Philips, Donald Wolfit, Marius Goring. American correspondent Mike Morrison in Nazi-occupied Greece is suspected of carrying a list of Allied agents.

64. *THE WONDERFUL COUNTRY* (1959) United Artists. **D:** Robert Parrish. **W:** Robert Ardrey. **P:** Chester Erskine, Robert Mitchum (uncredited). **Cam:** Floyd Crosby, Alex Phillips. **Cast:** Robert Mitchum (as Martin Brady), Julie London, Gary Merrill, Pedro Armendariz, Jack Oakie, Albert Dekker, Charles McGraw, Leroy "Satchel" Paige. Martin Brady works as a liaison between Texas Rangers and Mexican independents.

65. *HOME FROM THE HILL* (1960) Metro-Goldwyn-Mayer. **D:** Vincente Minnelli. **W:** Irving Ravetch, Harriet Frank Jr. **P:** Edmund Grainger. **Cam:** Milton Krasner. **Cast:** Robert Mitchum (as "Captain Wade" Hunnicutt), Eleanor Parker, George Peppard, George Hamilton, Everett Sloan, Luana Patten, Anne Seymour, Dub Taylor, Denver Pyle, Guinn "Big Boy" Williams, Burt Mustin. Texas land baron Wade Hunnicutt's failures as a father reflect on his legitimate and illegitimate sons.

66. *THE NIGHT FIGHTERS* (1960) United Artists. **D:** Tay Garnett. **W:** Robert Wright Campbell. **P:** Raymond Stross. **Cam:** Stephen Dade. **Cast:** Robert Mitchum (as Dermot O'Neil), Anne Heywood, Dan O'Herlihy, Cyril Cusack, Richard Harris, Niall MacGinnis, Marianne Benet, Eileen Crowe, Hilton Edwards, T.P. McKenna. A shiftless boozer joins the Irish Republican Army, then becomes disillusioned with its brutal methods.

67. *THE GRASS IS GREENER* (1960) Universal. **D:** Stanley

Donen. **W:** Hugh Williams, Margaret Williams. **P:** James Ware. **Cam:** Christopher Challis. **Cast:** Cary Grant, Deborah Kerr, Robert Mitchum (as Charles Delacro), Jean Simmons, Moray Watson. Texas millionaire Charles Delacro falls in love with a castle matron on his visit to the British Isles, a circumstance that leads her urbane husband into a duel of words, then pistols.

68. *THE SUNDOWNERS* (1960) United Artists. **D/P:** Fred Zinnemann. **W:** Isobel Lennart. **Cam:** Jack Hildyard. **Cast:** Deborah Kerr, Robert Mitchum (as Paddy Carmody), Peter Ustinov, Michael Anderson Jr., Glynis Johns, Dina Merrill, Chips Rafferty, Wylie Watson, Lola Brooks. A nomadic sheep drover and his family, "Sundowners" in Australian vernacular, face the possibility of settling down when their son's racing colt becomes a winner.

69. *THE LAST TIME I SAW ARCHIE* (1961) Universal. **D/P:** Jack Webb. **W:** William Bowers. **Cam:** Joseph MacDonald. **Cast:** Robert Mitchum (Archie Hall), Jack Webb, Martha Hyer, France Nuyen, Joe Flynn, James Lydon, Del Moore, Louis Nye, Don Knotts, Richard Arlen, Robert Strauss, Harvey Lembeck, James Mitchum, Don Drysdale. In the last days of World War II a classic goldbrick artist impersonates a general to catch a spy.

70. *CAPE FEAR* (1962) Universal. **D:** J. Lee Thompson. **W:** James R. Webb. **P:** Gregory Peck (uncredited). **Cam:** Sam Leavitt. **Cast:** Gregory Peck, Robert Mitchum (as Max Cady), Polly Bergen, Lori Martin, Martin Balsam, Telly Savalas, Jack Kruschen, Barrie Chase, Ward Ramsey. In a small North Carolina town, recently released ex-con Max Cady terrorizes the family of the lawyer whose testimony sent him to prison for years.

71. *THE LONGEST DAY* (1962) Twentieth Century-Fox. **D:** Andrew Marton, Ken Annakin, Bernhard Wicki, Darryl F. Zanuck (uncredited). **W:** Cornelius Ryan, Romain Gary,

James Jones, David Pursall, Jack Seddon. **P:** Darryl F. Zanuck. **Cam:** Jean Bourgoin, Henri Persin, Walter Wottitz. **Cast:** John Wayne, Robert Mitchum (as General Norman Cota), Henry Fonda, Richard Burton, Robert Ryan, Rod Steiger, Robert Wagner, Richard Beymer, Mel Ferrer, Roddy McDowall, Eddie Albert, Red Buttons, Sal Mineo, Stuart Whitman, Edmond O'Brien. A kaleidoscopic look at the Allied invasion of Normandy in World War II, with Cota's troops taking Omaha Beach.

72. *TWO FOR THE SEESAW* (1962) United Artists. **D:** Robert Wise. **W:** Isobel Lennart. **P:** Walter Mirisch. **Cam:** Ted McCord. **Cast:** Robert Mitchum (as Jerry Ryan), Shirley MacLaine, Edmond Ryan, Elisabeth Fraser, Eddie Firestone, Billy Gray, Vic Lundin, Virginia Whitmore. In the adaptation of the William Gibson play, a Nebraska lawyer who's separated from his wife has a fling in Greenwich Village with a Bronx free spirit and aspiring dancer.

73. *THE LIST OF ADRIAN MESSENGER* (1963) Universal. **D:** John Huston. **W:** Anthony Veiller. **P:** Edward Lewis. **Cam:** Joseph MacDonald. **Cast:** George C. Scott, Kirk Douglas, Dana Wynter, Clive Brook, Herbert Marshall, John Huston, Burt Lancaster, Robert Mitchum (as Jim Slattery), Frank Sinatra, Tony Curtis, Gladys Cooper, Marcel Dalio. In England, a U.S. intelligence officer deciphers clues to collar a serial killer.

74. *RAMPAGE* (1963) Warner Bros. **D:** Phil Karlson. **W:** Robert I. Holt, Marguerite Roberts. **P:** William Fadiman. **Cam:** Harold Lipstein. **Cast:** Robert Mitchum (as Harry Stanton), Jack Hawkins, Elsa Martinelli, Sabu, Cely Carrillo, Emile Genest, Stefan Schnabel, David Cadiente. An American game trapper teams with a hunter in Malaysia to capture a tiger/leopard hybrid and the two become rivals for the hunter's consort.

75. *MAN IN THE MIDDLE* (1964) Twentieth Century-Fox. **D:**

Guy Hamilton. **W:** Keith Waterhouse. **P:** Walter Seltzer. **Cam:** Wilkie Cooper. **Cast:** Robert Mitchum (as Lieutenant Colonel Barney Adams), Trevor Howard, France Nuyen, Keenan Wynn, Barry Sullivan, Alexander Knox, Sam Wanamaker, Gary Cockrell, Edward Underdown. A U.S. Army lawyer in 1944 India is assigned to defend a racist American accused of 11 murders.

76. *WHAT A WAY TO GO!* (1964) Twentieth Century-Fox. **D:** J. Lee Thompson. **W:** Betty Comden, Adolph Green. **Cam:** Leon Shamroy. **Cast:** Shirley MacLaine, Paul Newman, Robert Mitchum (as Rod Anderson), Dean Martin, Gene Kelly, Dick Van Dyke, Bob Cummings, Reginald Gardiner, Margaret Dumont. A young woman yearning domesticity marries a succession of wealthy husbands who die in a variety of ways.

77. *MISTER MOSES* (1965) United Artists. **D:** Ronald Neame. **W:** Charles Beaumont, Monja Danischewsky. **P:** Frank Ross. **Cam:** Oswald Morris. **Cast:** Robert Mitchum (as Joe Moses), Carroll Baker, Ian Bannen, Alexander Knox, Raymond St. Jacques, Orlando Martins, Reginald Beckwith. An adventurer in Africa is urged by a missionary's daughter to lead a group of Masai tribespeople out of an area to be flooded by a new dam.

78. *THE WAY WEST* (1967) United Artists. **D:** Andrew V. McLaglen. **W:** Ben Maddow, Mitch Lindemann. **P:** Harold Hecht. **Cam:** William H. Clothier. **Cast:** Kirk Douglas, Robert Mitchum (as Dick Summers), Richard Widmark, Sally Field, Lola Albright, Michael Whitney, Stubby Kaye, William Lundigan, Jack Elam, Harry Carey Jr., John Mitchum, Patric Knowles, Roy Glenn. A wagon train bound for Oregon in 1843 is beset by squabbles.

79. *EL DORADO* (1967) Paramount. **D/P:** Howard Hawks. **W:** Leigh Brackett. **Cam:** Harold Rosson. **Cast:** John Wayne, Robert Mitchum (as Sheriff J.P. Harrah), James Caan,

Charlene Holt, Paul Fix, Arthur Hunnicutt, Christopher George, Ed Asner, Michele Carey, R.G. Armstrong, Jim Davis, John Mitchum. A gunman helps sober up drunk sheriff J.P. Harrah to stop a land baron and his henchmen from stealing water rights.

80. *ANZIO* (1968) Columbia. **D:** Edward Dmytryk. **W:** Harry A.L. Craig. **P:** Dino De Laurentiis. **Cam:** Giuseppe Rotunno. **Cast:** Robert Mitchum (as Dick Ennis), Peter Falk, Earl Holliman, Arthur Kennedy, Robert Ryan, Mark Damon, Reni Santoni, Giancarlo Giannini, Patrick Magee, Arthur Franz, Anthony Steel. Cynical correspondent Dick Ennis observes the title World War II battle, in which American indecision allowed the Germans to retrench.

81. *VILLA RIDES* (1968) Paramount. **D:** Buzz Kulik. **W:** Robert Towne, Sam Peckinpah. **P:** Ted Richmond. **Cam:** Jack Hildyard. **Cast:** Yul Brynner, Robert Mitchum (as Lee Arnold), Charles Bronson, Grazia Buccella, Herbert Lom, Alexander Knox, Fernando Rey, Frank Wolff, John Ireland, Jill Ireland. Gun-runner Lee Arnold is captured by Pancho Villa's group in 1912 and, in lieu of execution, is conscripted into aiding the rebels.

82. *FIVE CARD STUD* (1968) Paramount. **D:** Henry Hathaway. **W:** Marguerite Roberts. **P:** Hal B. Wallis. **Cam:** Daniel L. Fapp. **Cast:** Dean Martin, Robert Mitchum (as Reverend Rudd), Inger Stevens, Roddy McDowall, Katherine Justice, John Anderson, Yaphet Kotto, Denver Pyle, Whit Bissell, Ted De Corsia, Roy Jenson. A gambler tries to discern why six poker players who lynched a seventh are mysteriously murdered one by one.

83. *SECRET CEREMONY* (1968) Universal. **D:** Joseph Losey. **W:** George Tabori. **P:** John Heyman, Norman Priggen. **Cam:** Gerry Fisher. **Cast:** Elizabeth Taylor, Mia Farrow, Robert Mitchum (as Albert), Peggy Ashcroft, Pamela Brown. A disturbed young heiress befriends a prostitute, who learns that

the girl is being ripped off by her antique store-owning aunts and that she had had a sexual relationship at age 13 with her stepfather, Albert.

84. *YOUNG BILLY YOUNG* (1969) United Artists. **D/W:** Burt Kennedy. **P:** Max E. Youngstein. **Cam:** Harry Stradling Jr. **Cast:** Robert Mitchum (as Ben Kane), Angie Dickinson, Robert Walker Jr., David Carradine, Jack Kelly, John Anderson, Deana Martin, Paul Fix, Willis Bouchey, Christopher Mitchum. A lawman seeking his son's murderer is deputized and assigned to arrest wild youth Billy Young, but instead befriends and mentors him.

85. *THE GOOD GUYS AND THE BAD GUYS* (1969) Warner Bros. **D:** Burt Kennedy. **W:** Ronald M. Cohen. **P:** Ronald M. Cohen, Dennis Shryack. **Cam:** Harry Stradling Jr. **Cast:** Robert Mitchum (as James Flagg), George Kennedy, David Carradine, Martin Balsam, John Carradine, Tina Louise, Lois Nettleton, Douglas V. Fowley, Marie Windsor. A New Mexico lawman and his old nemesis team up uneasily to prevent a train robbery.

86. *RYAN'S DAUGHTER* (1970) Metro-Goldwyn-Mayer. **D:** David Lean. **W:** Robert Bolt. **P:** Anthony Havellock-Allan. **Cam:** Freddie Young. **Cast:** Robert Mitchum (as Charles Shaughnessy), Sarah Miles, Trevor Howard, John Mills, Christopher Jones, Leo McKern, Barry Foster, Marie Kean, Gerald Sim, Barry Jackson, Archie O'Sullivan. A middle-aged schoolteacher in a 1916 Irish village patiently waits out his young wife's affair with a soldier.

87. *GOING HOME* (1971) Metro-Goldwyn-Mayer. **D/P:** Herbert B. Leonard. **W:** Lawrence Marcus. **Cam:** Fred Jackman. **Cast:** Robert Mitchum (as Harry K. Graham), Brenda Vaccaro, Jan-Michael Vincent, Jason Bernard, Sally Kirkland, Lou Gilbert, Josh Mostel, Carol Gustafson, Big Tim Wallace. Harry Graham, an ex-con who murdered his

wife, tries to mend his relationship with his son, whose testimony convicted him.

88. *THE WRATH OF GOD* (1972) Metro-Goldwyn-Mayer. **D/W:** Ralph Nelson. **P:** William S. Gilmore Jr. **Cam:** Alex Phillips. **Cast:** Robert Mitchum (as Father Oliver Van Horne), Frank Langella, Rita Hayworth, Victor Buono, John Colicos, Ken Hutcheson, Gregory Sierra, Paul Pritchett, Ralph Nelson. An excommunicated priest boozes and fornicates his way through Central America until he's blackmailed into being an assassin.

89. *THE FRIENDS OF EDDIE COYLE* (1973) Paramount. **D:** Peter Yates. **W/P:** Paul Monash. **Cam:** Victor J. Kemper. **Cast:** Robert Mitchum (as Eddie "Fingers" Coyle), Peter Boyle, Richard Jordan, Steven Keats, Alex Rocco, Joe Santos, Mitchell Ryan, James Tolkan, Kevin O'Morrison. An aging Massachusetts hoodlum runs guns to an illegal dealer and turns informer to try to avoid a prison term for a hijacking job.

90. *THE YAKUZA* (1975) Warner Bros. **D/P:** Sydney Pollack. **W:** Paul Schrader, Robert Towne. **Cam:** Okazaki Kozo, Duke Callaghan. **Cast:** Robert Mitchum (as Harry Kilmer), Takakura Ken, Brian Keith, Richard Jordan, Herb Edelman, Kishi Keiko, Okado Eiji, James Shigeta, Christina Kokubo, Go Eiji. Former private eye Harry Kilmer is hired by an old Army pal to find the latter's daughter, the victim of a mob kidnapping in Japan.

91. *FAREWELL, MY LOVELY* (1975) Avco Embassy. **D:** Dick Richards. **W:** David Zelag Goodman. **P:** George Pappas, Jerry Bruckheimer. **Cam:** John Alonzo. **Cast:** Robert Mitchum (as Philip Marlowe), Charlotte Rampling, John Ireland, Sylvia Miles, Harry Dean Stanton, Jack O'Halloran, Anthony Zerbe, Jim Thompson, Sylvester Stallone. Private eye Philip Marlowe is hired to find a missing taxi dancer in 1940s Los Angeles.

92. *MIDWAY* (1976) Universal. **D:** Jack Smight. **W:** Donald S. Sanford. **P:** Walter Mirisch. **Cam:** Harry Stradling Jr. **Cast:** Charlton Heston, Henry Fonda, Robert Mitchum (as Admiral William F. "Bull" Halsey), Glenn Ford, Cliff Robertson, James Coburn, Toshiro Mifune, Robert Wagner, Robert Webber, Hal Holbrook, Christopher George, Dabney Coleman, Ed Nelson, Edward Albert, Christina Kokubo, James Shigeta, Tom Selleck, Monte Markham. Admiral Chester Nimitz directs the defense of U.S. Naval positions during the crucial World War II battle.

93. *THE LAST TYCOON* (1976) Paramount. **D:** Elia Kazan. **W:** Harold Pinter. **P:** Sam Spiegel. **Cam:** Victor Kemper. **Cast:** Robert De Niro, Robert Mitchum (as Pat Brady), Jack Nicholson, Ingrid Boulting, Tony Curtis, Jeanne Moreau, Ray Milland, Theresa Russell, Dana Andrews, Anjelica Huston, John Carradine, Lew Ayres, Donald Pleasance, Peter Strauss. Mercurial movie studio head Monroe Stahr deals with unionization in Hollywood and falls in love in this adaptation of the F. Scott Fitzgerald novel.

94. *THE AMSTERDAM KILL* (1977) Columbia. **D:** Robert Clouse. **W:** Robert Clouse, Gregory Teifer. **P:** André Morgan. **Cam:** Alan Hume. **Cast:** Robert Mitchum (as Quinlan), Bradford Dillman, Leslie Nielsen, Richard Egan, Keye Luke, George Cheung, Chan Sing. Quinlan, a former U.S. Drug Enforcement Agency operative and former drug addict, accepts the job of attempting to break up a Dutch heroin-trafficking ring to clear his name.

95. *THE BIG SLEEP* (1978) United Artists. **D/W:** Michael Winner. **P:** Elliott Kastner, Michael Winner. **Cam:** Richard Paynter. **Cast:** Robert Mitchum (as Philip Marlowe), Sarah Miles, James Stewart, Richard Boone, Oliver Reed, John Mills, Candy Clark, Joan Collins, Edward Fox, Richard Todd, Harry Andrews, Colin Blakely. Privaye eye Philip Marlowe is hired independently by a London tycoon and his daughter to protect another daughter.

96. *MATILDA* (1978) American-International. **D:** Daniel Mann. **W:** Albert S. Ruddy, Timothy Galfas. **P:** Albert S. Ruddy. **Cam:** Jack Woolf. **Cast:** Elliott Gould, Robert Mitchum (as Duke Parkhurst), Harry Guardino, Clive Revill, Roy Clark, Karen Carlson, Lionel Stander, Art Metrano, Gary Morgan, Larry Pennell, Lenny Montana. A New York theatrical agent who's down on his luck decides to promote a boxing kangaroo.

97. *BREAKTHROUGH* (1978) Maverick Pictures International. **D:** Andrew V. McLaglen. **W:** Tony Williamson. **P:** Achim Sellus, Alex Winitzky. **Cam:** Tony Imi. **Cast:** Richard Burton, Robert Mitchum (as Colonel Rogers), Rod Steiger, Curt Jurgens, Helmut Griem, Klaus Loewitsch, Michael Parks, Veronique Vendell. Near World War II's end in this sequel to Sam Peckinpah's *Cross of Iron*, a German sergeant saves the life of American Colonel Rogers, who was lost behind enemy lines.

98. *AGENCY* (1979) Jensen Farley. **D:** George Kaczender. **W:** Noel Hynd. **P:** Robert Lantos, Stephen J. Roth. **Cam:** Miklos Lente. **Cast:** Robert Mitchum (as Ted Quinn), Lee Majors, Valerie Perrine, Saul Rubinek, Alexandra Stewart, Hayward Morse, Anthony Parr, Michael Kirby, Pierre Sevigny, Julie London. An advertising executive intends to gain political clout by producing television programming containing subliminal propaganda.

99. *THAT CHAMPIONSHIP SEASON* (1982) Cannon. **D/W:** Jason Miller. **P:** Menahem Golan, Yorum Globus. **Cam:** John Bailey. **Cast:** Robert Mitchum (as Coach Delaney), Bruce Dern, Stacy Keach, Martin Sheen, Paul Sorvino, Arthur Franz, Michael Bernosky, Joseph Kelly, James M. Langan. The 25th reunion of a Pennsylvania state champion high school basketball team provides the opportunity for the "boys" to emotionally open up.

100. *MARIA'S LOVERS* (1985) Cannon. **D:** Andrei

Konchalovsky. **W:** Gerard Brach, Andrei Konchalovsky, Marjorie David. **P:** Menahem Golan, Yorum Globus. **Cam:** Juan Ruiz Anchia. **Cast:** Nastassja Kinski, John Savage, Robert Mitchum (as Old Man Bibic), Keith Carradine, Vincent Spano, John Goodman, Anita Morris, Bud Cort, Bill Smitrovich. In a small postwar Pennsylvania town, beautiful Maria is wooed by several suitors.

101. *THE AMBASSADOR* (1985) Cannon. **D:** J. Lee Thompson. **W:** Max Jack. **P:** Menahem Golan, Yorum Globus. **Cam:** Adam Greenberg. **Cast:** Robert Mitchum (as Peter Hacker), Ellen Burstyn, Rock Hudson, Fabio Testi, Donald Pleasance, Heli Goldenberg, Michal Bat-Adam, Ori Levy. The efforts of the American ambassador in Tel Aviv to settle Arab-Israeli disputes are complicated by his wife's affair with a radical PLO leader.

102. *MR. NORTH* (1988) Samuel Goldwyn. **D:** Danny Huston. **W:** Janet Roach, John Huston, James Costigan. **P:** Steven Haft, Skip Steloff. **Cam:** Robin Vidgeon. **Cast:** Anthony Edwards, Robert Mitchum (as James McHenry Bosworth), Lauren Bacall, Anjelica Huston, Harry Dean Stanton, Mary Stuart Masterson, Virginia Madsen, David Warner. In 1926 Newport, R.I., a young man demonstrates the power to bodily store electricity.

103. *SCROOGED* (1988) Paramount. **D:** Richard Donner. **W:** Mitch Glazer, Michael O'Donoghue. **P:** Richard Donner, Art Linson. **Cam:** Michael Chapman. **Cast:** Bill Murray, Robert Mitchum (as Preston Rhinelander), John Forsythe, John Glover, Bobcat Goldthwaite, David Johansen, Carol Kane, Alfre Woodard, Buddy Hackett, John Houseman. The Charles Dickens Christmas story is comically updated to the world of television.

104. *BELIEVED VIOLENT* (1990) Candice Productions. **D:** Georges Lautner. **W:** Sergio Gobbi, Gilles Lambert. **P:** Sergio Gobbi. **Cam:** Yves Rodallec. **Cast:** Michael Brandon,

Sophie Duez, Robert Mitchum (Professor Forrester), Francis Perrin, Marie Laforet, Mario Adorf, Marc De Jonge. An insurance agent investigates when Paris scientist Forrester is kidnapped for his committed-to-memory secret formula for a new discovery.

105. *CAPE FEAR* (1991) Universal. **D:** Martin Scorsese. **W:** Wesley Strick. **P:** Barbara De Fina. **Cam:** Freddie Francis. **Cast:** Robert De Niro, Nick Nolte, Jessica Lange, Juliette Lewis, Robert Mitchum (as Lieutenant Elgart), Gregory Peck, Martin Balsam, Joe Don Baker, Illeana Douglas, Fred Dalton Thompson. In the remake of the '62 movie, an ex-con terrorizes the family of the lawyer who helped send him to prison.

106. *MIDNIGHT RIDE* (1992) Cannon. **D:** Robert Bralver. **W:** Russell V. Manzatt, Robert Bralver. **P:** Joan Weidman. **Cam:** Roberto D'Ettorre Piazzoli. **Cast:** Michael Dudikoff, Mark Hamill, Robert Mitchum (as Dr. Hardy), Savina Gersak. A serial killer kidnaps the wife of a policeman and goes on a murderous spree.

107. *TOMBSTONE* (1993) Hollywood (Disney). **D:** George Pan Cosmatos. **W:** Kevin Jarre. **P:** Sean Daniel. **Cam:** William A. Fraker. **Cast:** Kurt Russell, Val Kilmer, Michael Biehn, Sam Elliott, Bill Paxton, Powers Boothe, Dana Delaney, Charlton Heston, Stephen Lang, Harry Carey Jr., Billy Bob Thornton, Michael Rooker, Billy Zane, Terry O'Quinn, Joanna Pacula, Christopher Mitchum, Pedro Armendariz Jr., Frank Stallone, Robert Mitchum (narrator). The Earp brothers and Doc Holliday fight the battle of the O.K. Corral and clean up Tombstone, Arizona.

108. *WOMAN OF DESIRE* (1993) Nu Image. **D:** Robert Ginty. **W:** Anthony Palmer. **P:** Danny Lerner. **Cam:** Hanro Mohr. **Cast:** Jeff Fahey, Bo Derek, Robert Mitchum (as Walter J. Hill), Steven Bauer, Thomas Hall, John Matshikiza, Warrick Grier, Todd Jenson, Michael McCabe. A hard-luck dude is

framed for the murder of a playgirl's wealthy boyfriend during a yacht trip.

109. *BACKFIRE!* (1994) A-pix Entertainment. **D/W:** A. Dean Bell. **P:** J. Christian Ingvordsen. **Cam:** Richard Connors. **Cast:** Josh Mosby, Robert Mitchum (as Marshal Marc Marshall), Kathy Ireland, Telly Savalas, Shelley Winters, Mary McCormack, John Christian, Michelle Miller, Tracy Douglass, Jeffrey Howard. A comedy about a man joining an all-female fire department.

110. *THE SUNSET BOYS* (1995, aka *PAKTEN*) Yellow Cottage, Norsk Film. **D:** Leidulv Risan. **W:** Arthur Johansen, Leidulv Risan, Allan Oberholzer. **P:** Aage Aaberge. **Cam:** Axel Block. **Cast:** Robert Mitchum (as Ernest Bogan), Cliff Robertson, Erland Josephson, Espen Skjonberg, Hanna Schygulla, Nadja Tiller, Ingrid van Bergen, Bodil Kjer. Four aging men make a pact to send each of the others off with a mutual burial rite while they search for the World War II era former lover of one of them.

111. *DEAD MAN* (1996) Miramax. **D/W:** Jim Jarmusch. **P:** Demetra J. MacBride. **Cam:** Robby Muller. **Cast:** Johnny Depp, Gary Farmer, Lance Henrikson, Michael Wincott, Billy Bob Thornton, Robert Mitchum (as John Dickinson), Mili Avital, Iggy Pop, Crispin Glover, John Hurt, Gabriel Byrne, Alfred Molina, Steve Buscemi, Jared Harris, Eugene Byrd. An accountant heads west in 1875 and is confused for poet William Blake by a new best friend and for a killer by bounty hunters.

112. *JAMES DEAN: RACE WITH DESTINY* (1997) Capstone. **D:** Mardi Rustam. **W:** Dan Sefton. **Cast:** Casper Van Dien, Carrie Mitchum, Diane Ladd, Mike Connors, Casey Kasem, Robert Mitchum (as George Stevens), Monique Parent, Justin William Root. A fact-based look at the mercurial rise and death of the title actor and his relationship with the actress Pier Angeli.

TELEVISION MOVIES & MINISERIES

1. *NIGHTKILL* (1980) NBC. **D:** Ted Post. **W:** Joane Andre. **P:** Richard Hellman, David Gil. **Cam:** Anthony Richmond. **Cast:** Jaclyn Smith, Robert Mitchum (as Donner/Rodriguez), Mike Connors, James Franciscus, Fritz Weaver, Sybil Danning, Tina Menard, Michael Anderson Jr. The mysterious Donner stalls an heiress/lover plot to murder her husband in Scottsdale, Arizona.

2. *ONE SHOE MAKES IT MURDER* (1982) CBS. **D:** William Hale. **W:** Felix Culver. **P:** Mel Ferrer. **Cam:** Terry K. Meade. **Cast:** Robert Mitchum (as Harold "Shill" Schillman), Angie Dickinson, Mel Ferrer, Jose Perez, John Harkins, Howard Hesseman, Asher Brauner. A former San Diego policeman is hired to find a gambler's wife, an unfaithful possible suicide.

3. *THE WINDS OF WAR* (1983 miniseries) ABC. **D/P:** Dan Curtis. **W:** Herman Wouk. **Cam:** Charles Correll, Steven Larner. **Cast:** Robert Mitchum (as Captain Victor "Pug" Henry), Ali MacGraw, Jan-Michael Vincent, John Houseman, Polly Bergen, Lisa Eilbacher, David Dukes, Topol, Ralph Bellamy, Peter Graves, Jeremy Kemp, Victoria Tennant, Edmond Purdom, Andrew Duggan, Scott Brady, Richard X. Slattery, Barbara Steele, Barry Morse, John Dehner, George Murdock, Ben Piazza, Charles Lane, Ron Rifkin. In the years 1939–41, globetrotting military attache Pug Henry advises world leaders as Nazi Germany and the Japanese increase Axis control.

4. *A KILLER IN THE FAMILY* (1983) ABC. **D:** Richard T. Heffron. **W:** Sue Grafton, Steven Humphrey, Robert Aller. **P:** Robert Aller. **Cam:** Hanania Baer. **Cast:** Robert Mitchum (as Gary Tyson), James Spader, Lance Kerwin, Eric Stoltz, Stuart Margolin, Salome Jens, Lynn Carlin, Arliss Howard, Catherine Mary Stewart. Based on the true story of Gary

Tyson in 1978 Arizona, a father is sprung from prison by his three sons.

5. *THE HEARST & DAVIES AFFAIR* (1985) ABC. **D:** David Lowell Rich. **W:** Alison Cross, David Solomon. **P:** Paul Pompian. **Cam:** Charles Wheeler. **Cast:** Robert Mitchum (as William Randolph Hearst), Virginia Madsen, Fritz Weaver, Doris Belack, Laura Henry, George Touliatos, Caroline Yeager. At age 52, the title newspaper tycoon falls in love with the 18-year-old chorus girl who became silent screen star Marion Davies.

6. *REUNION AT FAIRBOROUGH* (1985) Home Box Office. **D:** Herbert Wise. **W:** Albert Ruben. **P:** William Hill. **Cam:** Tony Imi. **Cast:** Robert Mitchum (as Carl Hostrup), Deborah Kerr, Red Buttons, Judi Trott, Barry Morse, Shane Rimmer, Ed Devereaux. A wealthy, divorced World War II veteran returns to the English town where he was stationed in wartime and looks up his old flame, who reveals a secret to him.

7. *PROMISES TO KEEP* (1985) CBS. **D:** Noel Black. **W:** Phil Penningroth. **P:** Robert A. Papazian, Milton Sperling. **Cam:** Dennis A. Dalzell. **Cast:** Robert Mitchum (as Jack Palmer), Christopher Mitchum, Bentley Mitchum, Claire Bloom, Tess Harper, Merrit Butrick, Paul Mantee. A dying rancher looks up the California seaside family that he abandoned 30 years ago.

8. *NORTH AND SOUTH* (1985 miniseries) ABC. **D:** Richard T. Heffron. **W:** Douglas Heyes, Paul F. Edwards, Kathleen A. Shelley, Patricia Green. **P:** Paul Freeman. **Cam:** Steven Larner. **Cast:** Patrick Swayze, James Read, Kirstie Alley, Georg Stanford Brown, David Carradine, Lesley-Anne Down, Johnny Cash, Robert Mitchum (as Patrick Flynn), Elizabeth Taylor, Jean Simmons, Hal Holbrook, Robert Guillaume, Morgan Fairchild, Forest Whitaker, Mitchell Ryan, John Anderson. Pennsylvania and South Carolina

plebes at West Point forge a friendship that becomes increasingly tested by events leading to the Civil War.

9. *THOMPSON'S LAST RUN* (1986) CBS. **D:** Jerrold Freedman. **W:** John Carlen. **P:** Jennifer Faulstich. **Cam:** Hal Trussell. **Cast:** Robert Mitchum (as John Thompson), Wilford Brimley, Kathleen York, Guy Boyd, Susan Tyrrell, Royce Wallace, Benjamin Gregory. Safecracker John Thompson is sprung from jail by his niece, who wants him to pinpoint his loot stash.

10. *WAR AND REMEMBRANCE* (1988–89 miniseries) ABC. **D:** Dan Curtis. **W:** Earl W. Wallace, Dan Curtis, Herman Wouk. **P:** Barbara Steele. **Cam:** Dietrich Lohman. **Cast:** Robert Mitchum (as Victor "Pug" Henry), Jane Seymour, Victoria Tennant, John Gielgud, Hart Bochner, Polly Bergen, Sharon Stone, Michael Woods, Robert Morley, Barry Bostwick, Sami Frey, Topol, Ian MacShane, Leslie Hope, Peter Graves, Ralph Bellamy, E.G. Marshall, Jeremy Kemp, Nicholas Pryor, Robert Stephens, Mike Connors, Howard Duff, Nina Foch, Pat Hingle, Eddie Albert, Brian Blessed, Peter Vaughn, R.G. Armstrong, G.D. Spradlin. In this sequel to *The Winds of War*, Pug Henry gets a brief cruiser command after Pearl Harbor and his far-flung family tries to survive the war, particularly his daughter-in-law, a Jew hiding from the Nazis, whose death camps are discovered.

11. *THE BROTHERHOOD OF THE ROSE* (1989 miniseries) NBC. **D/P:** Marvin J. Chomsky. **W:** Gy Waldron. **Cam:** James Bartle. **Cast:** Robert Mitchum (as John Eliot), Peter Strauss, David Morse, Connie Selleca, James B. Sikking, M. Emmet Walsh, James Hong, Nick Enright. A CIA agent who raised two orphans to be spies orders the death of one of them, triggering a battle of wits.

12. *JAKE SPANNER, PRIVATE EYE* (1989) USA Network. **D:** Lee H. Katzin. **W:** Andrew J. Fenady. **P:** Syd Vinnedge, John Vinnedge. **Cam:** Hector Figueroa. **Cast:** Robert Mitchum (as

Jake Spanner), Ernest Borgnine, John Mitchum, Stella Stevens, Richard Yniguez, Jim Mitchum, Dick Van Patten, Edie Adams, Sheree North, Kareem Abdul-Jabbar, Nita Talbot, Clive Revill. An ex-private eye is coaxed into tracking down the kidnapped granddaughter of a rackets boss he sent to jail 25 years earlier.

13. *A FAMILY FOR JOE* (1990) NBC. **D:** Jeffrey Melman. **W:** Arnold Margolin. **P:** Arnold Margolin, Sonny Grosso, Larry Jacobson. **Cam:** Paul Lohman. **Cast:** Robert Mitchum (as Joe Whitaker), Chris Furth, Maia Brewton, Jarrad Paul, Jessica Player, Barbara Babcock, David Nelson, John Mitchum, Janet MacLachlan, Richard X. Slattery. A cranky, homeless man is coerced into posing as the grandfather to siblings who would otherwise be split up into foster homes. Pilot for same-name sitcom.

14. *WAITING FOR THE WIND* (1991) Syndicated. **D:** Don Schroeder. **W:** Douglas Lloyd McIntosh. **P:** Jeffrey Zeitlin. **Cam:** Bill Dickson. **Cast:** Robert Mitchum (as Walter), Rhonda Fleming, Zachary Bostrom, Jameson Parker, Shelbey Bradley, Fred Pinkard. A landlocked Kansas farmer dying of cancer has always dreamed of sailing his sailboat, parked in the backyard.

Television Series

1. *A FAMILY FOR JOE* (1990) NBC. **D:** Alan Rafkin. **W:** Arnold Margolin, Oliver Goldstick, Phil Rosenthal, David A. Caplan, Brian LaPan. **P:** Hollis Rich, Mady Julian, Bob Birnbaum. **Creator:** Arnold Margolin. **Cast of Regulars:** Robert Mitchum (as Joe Whitaker), Juliette Lewis, David Lascher, Jessica Player, Ben Savage, Barry Gordon. Series based on the TV movie pilot of the same name depicts a cranky ex-merchant marine and formerly homeless old man posing as the grandfather of an orphaned family to keep it together. Ran for 14 episodes.

2. *AFRICAN SKIES* (1992–94) Family Channel. **D:** Doug Rotstein. **P:** Franklin/Waterman Entertainment, Atlantis Films Ltd. **Cast of Regulars:** Catherine Bach, Robert Mitchum (as Sam Dutton), Simon James, Raimund Harmstorf, Rouxnet Brown, Nakedi Ribane. A widowed American executive takes a position with an African company and occasionally is advised by her father-in-law, Sam Dutton. Ran for nine episodes.

DOCUMENTARIES

1. *A MOVEABLE SCENE* (1968) Syndicated. **P:** Airlie Productions, George Washington University Medical Center. This installment of *The Distant Drummer* series, about rising drug abuse by America's youth, was narrated by Robert Mitchum.

2. *AMERICA ON THE ROCKS* (1973) Syndicated. **D/P:** Frank Kavanaugh, Airlie Productions, George Washington University Medical Center. This half-hour special on the use and abuse of alcohol in America was narrated by Robert Mitchum.

3. *HOWARD HUGHES: THE INSIDE STORY* (1983) Home Box Office. **P:** Tom McDermott, Wrather Entertainment. This special chronicles the tycoon's passions: aviation, movies, golf, wealth, beautiful women. Interviewed on-camera are Robert Mitchum, Jane Russell, Pat O'Brien, Kathryn Grayson, Anne Francis.

4. *THE ENTREPRENEURS* (1986) Syndicated. This documentary series intended to profile America's great entrepreneurs, such as King Gillette and Wally "Famous" Amos, but only one or two installments aired in major markets. Robert Mitchum narrates.

5. *MARILYN MONROE: BEYOND THE LEGEND* (1986) Cinemax. **D/P:** Gene Feldman, Wombat Productions. A look back at the career of the tragic beauty features on-camera interviews with Robert Mitchum, Joshua Logan, Shelley

Winters, Sheree North, Celeste Holm, Susan Strasberg. Richard Widmark narrates.

6. *CHANDLER* (1986) PBS. **D/P:** David Thomas. This British-produced documentary and dramatization (with actor Robert Stephens) about crime novelist Raymond Chandler features on-camera interviews with Robert Mitchum, John Houseman, Neil Morgan, James Ellroy, Frank MacShane, Matthew Bruccoli, George V. Higgins. Mitchum reads Chandler passages.

7. *BROKEN NOSES* (1988) Syndicated. **D:** Bruce Weber. This documentary about child boxer Andy Minsker features music by Julie London, Gerry Mulligan, Chet Baker, Robert Mitchum.

8. *REMEMBERING MARILYN* (1988) ABC. **D/P:** Andrew Solt. A documentary on Marilyn Monroe features on-camera interviews with Robert Mitchum, Robert Wagner, Don Murray, Gloria Steinem, Susan Strasberg. Lee Remick hosts and narrates.

9. *HOLLYWOOD: THE GOLDEN YEARS* (1988) Arts & Entertainment Network. This British-made documentary on RKO Radio Pictures features on-camera interviews with Robert Mitchum, Jane Greer, Stewart Granger. Ed Asner hosts and narrates.

10. *WILLIAM HOLDEN: THE GOLDEN BOY* (1989) Cinemax. **D/P:** Gene Feldman, Wombat Productions. The title actor's life, films and untimely death are recalled. On-camera interviewees include Robert Mitchum, Robert Wagner, Cliff Robertson, Blake Edwards, Glenn Ford. Richard Kiley narrates.

11. *JOHN HUSTON: THE MAN, THE MOVIES, THE MAV-ERICK* (1989) TNT. **D/W:** Frank Martin. **P:** Joni Levin. This look at the career and life of the great director includes on-screen interviews with Paul Newman, Anjelica Huston, Michael Caine, Lauren Bacall, Arthur Miller. Robert Mitchum hosts and narrates.

12. *THE GOLDEN YEARS?* (1989) PBS. **P:** David Davis. This Seattle-produced documentary looks at the abuse of the elderly in America's nursing homes. Robert Mitchum narrates.

13. *THE EYES OF WAR* (1989) Syndicated. **D/P/W:** Peter Foges, Vestron Television. The first of a planned eight-part series of two-hour specials documenting the history of World War II was the only one completed. Robert Mitchum narrates.

14. *ROBERT MITCHUM: THE RELUCTANT STAR* (1991) Cinemax. **D/P:** Gene Feldman, Suzette Winter, Wombat Productions. This chronologically arranged documentary discusses the life and career of Robert Mitchum. He's interviewed on-camera and clips of his films are shown. Also interviewed are Deborah Kerr, Jane Russell, Jane Greer, Sydney Pollack, Edward Dmytryk, John Mitchum, Christopher Mitchum, Ali MacGraw, Polly Bergen and Sarah Miles. Mitchum talks about Howard Hughes, William A. Wellman, Raoul Walsh, John Huston and others.

15. *WILD BILL: HOLLYWOOD MAVERICK* (1996) TNT **D/W:** Todd Robinson. **P:** Kenneth A. Carlson, William A. Wellman Jr. This feature on the life and career of director William A. Wellman includes clips and interviews with Clint Eastwood, James Garner, Robert Mitchum, Gregory Peck, Sidney Poitier, Nancy Reagan, Robert Redford, Martin Scorsese, James Whitmore, Richard Widmark, Robert Wise and others.

16. *ROBERT MITCHUM* (2000) E! Entertainment Television. **P:** Nick Cates, Lynne Morgan. This installment of the *Mysteries & Scandals* series keys off the marijuana scandal using clips and interviews with Bentley Mitchum, Sydney Pollack, Dan Curtis, George Hamilton, Joan Collins, Charles Champlin, James Robert Parish, Bob Thomas, James Bacon, Anthony Caruso, Jerry Roberts, agent Mike Greenfield and his assistant Toni Hayes and lawyer Michael Genelin. A.J. Benza narrates.

INDEX

ABC–TV, 33, 238, 239, 240, 243
Academy Awards (and nominations), 28, 48, 75, 161, 207
Academy of Motion Picture Arts and Sciences, 126
Aerial Gunner, 121, 214
African Skies, 211, 242
Agee, James, 27, 194, 223
Agency, 24, 234
Agnew, Spiro T., 65
Ainsworth, Alan ("Cupid"), 120
Akins, Zoe, 166, 218
Albert, Eddie, 240
Aldrich, Robert, 141, 226
Allegheny County, Pa., Workhouse, 17, 18, 19
Allen, Irving, 137, 225
Alonzo, John, 232
Ambassador, The, 235
America on the Rocks (documentary), 242
American Film Institute (AFI), 149, 211
American-Hawaiian docks, 22, 101, 118
American-International, 234
Amsterdam Kill, The, 24, 202, 233
Anderson, Dame Judith, 103, 218
Anderson, George, 164
Anderson, Michael Jr., 227, 238
Andrews, Dana, 233
Andrews, Harry, 233
Angel Face, 23, 28, 69, 181, 188, 222
Angry Hills, The, 24, 141, 159, 226
Anhalt, Edward, 223
Anniston, Ala., 37–38
Anton, Cecil, 137–138
Anything for a Quiet Life (book), 192
Anzio, 178, 230
Arce, Hector, 165, 182
Archainbaud, George, 212, 214
Arizona, 70, 94, 105, 152
Armstrong, Louis, 169
Arnold, Gary, 201
Arts & Entertainment Network, 243
Ashcroft, Dame Peggy, 230
Asheville, N.C., 139, 209
Asner, Edward, 230, 243
Associated Press, 165, 172, 204
astrology, 120–121, 206
Atlantic City, 29
Austen, David, 178
Australia, 47, 118, 135, 209
auteur theory, 72
Ava: My Story (book), 187
Avco Embassy, 232
Ayres, Lew, 233

Bacall, Lauren ("Betty"), 133, 235, 244
Bach, Catherine, 242

Backfire!, 237
Bacon, James, 165, 244
Bacon, Lloyd, 180, 222
Baker, Carroll, 229
Baker, Joe Don, 236
Baker, Kenny, 87, 214
Baker, Stanley, 226
Bakersfield, Calif., 122
"The Ballad of Thunder Road" (song), 209
Balsam, Martin, 227, 231, 236
Bandido, 141, 142, 180, 208, 224
Banff River, 125
Bannen, Ian, 229
Bar 20, 213
Bardette, Trevor, 140, 225
Barque, Manuel, 115, 116, 205
Barry, Gene, 225
Barth, Belle, 206
Batjac Productions, 132
Baur, Harry, 77
Baxter, Warner, 71
Beaumont, Hugh, 120
Beery, Noah Jr. ("Ted"), 87, 213, 214, 215
Beery, Wallace, 160
Behrmann, Paul, 127–128, 207
Bel Air, Calif., 99, 209
Bel Geddes, Barbara, 166, 219
Believed Violent, 24, 235–236
Bell, A. Dean, 237
Bellamy, Ralph, 238, 240
Belmont Farms, 209
Belton, John, 201
Bendix, William, 220, 221
Bergen, Polly, 110, 191, 227, 238, 240, 244
Berman, Pandro S., 217
Bessemer, Ala., 117
Betty Ford Rehabilitation Center, 30
Beverly Hills, Calif., 67, 134, 143, 211
Beverly Hills Courthouse, 134–135
Beverly Hills Hotel, 143
Beverly Wilshire Hotel, 147
Beyond the Last Frontier, 213
Bezzerides, A.I., 223, 226
Bickford, Charles, 223
Big Sky, The, 104
Big Sleep, The (1978), 9, 26, 152, 158, 233
Big Steal, The, 90, 186, 220
Bikel, Theodore ("Theo"), 139, 225, 226
Biographical Dictionary of Film, A, 194
Black, Noel, 239
Black Warrior River, 117
Blackfoot Indians, 22, 115
Blackstone, Nan, 120, 206
Blondell, Joan, 215
Blood Alley, 30, 94–95, 131, 132, 208
Blood on the Moon, 23, 90, 166–167, 219

Bloom, Claire, 239
Bogart, Humphrey, 11, 24, 74, 133, 138, 152–153, 157
Bolt, Robert ("Bobby"), 62, 66, 148, 231
Boone, Richard ("Dick"), 152, 233
Border Patrol, 212
Borgnine, Ernest, 240
Boston, 97, 154
Botticelli, Sandro, 84
Bourbon, Rae, 206
boxing *see* prizefighting
Boyd, William ("Bill"), 42, 102, 122, 207, 212, 213, 214, 215
Boyle, Hal, 74
Boyle, Peter, 97
Brackett, Leigh, 229
Bradley, Tom, 210
Brahm, John, 218
Brahms, Johannes, 88
Bralver, Robert, 236
Brando, Marlon, 21, 22, 57, 167, 177
Braun, Eric, 173
Bravo (cable network), 99
Breakthrough, 234
Brennan, Walter, 167, 219
Brentwood, Calif., 209
Bridge on the River Kwai, The, 149
Bridgeport, Calif., 126–127
Bridgeport, Conn., 34, 54, 100, 126, 205
Bridgeport Post-Telegram, 100, 205
Bridges, Harry, 118, 119
Briggs, Johnny, 61
Brimley, Wilford, 240
Broccoli, Albert R. ("Cubby"), 137, 225
Brodie, Steve, 123, 216, 218, 219
Broken Noses (documentary), 243
Bronfman family, 148
Bronson, Charles, 230
Brotherhood of the Rose, The, 240
Brown, Christy, 48–50
Brown, Clarence, 213
Brown, Geoff, 167
Brown, Johnny Mack, 214
Brown, Pamela, 230
Brown Farm (Chatham County, Ga.), 35, 205
Bruce, Sally Jane, 133–134, 223
Bruckheimer, Jerry, 232
Bryant, Charlsie, 106
Brynner, Yul, 230
Bryson, John, 20
Buchwald, Art, 166
Buetel, Jack, 143
Build My Gallows High (novel), 103
Buono, Victor, 151, 159
Burke, Johnny, 140
Burr, Raymond, 129, 221
Burstyn, Ellen, 235
Burton, Richard, 22, 73, 138, 177, 228, 234
Buscemi, Steve, 237
Busch, Niven, 92
Buttons, Red, 228, 239

CBS Radio, 207

CBS–TV, 208, 238, 239, 240
Caan, James, 229
Cabeen, Boyd, 88
Cagney, James, 57
Caine, Michael, 244
Calgary, 125, 208
Calhoun, Rory, 223
Calling All Girls (radio show), 120, 206
Camden, Del., 39, 206
Camille, 176
Cannes Film Festival, 166
Cannon Group, The, 171, 234, 236
Cape Fear (1962), 23, 28, 33, 57, 94, 110, 142, 191, 198, 209, 227
Cape Fear (1991), 24, 110, 210, 236
Carey, Harry Jr., 218, 219, 229, 236
Carpenter, Scott, 64–65
Carradine, David, 231, 239
Carradine, John, 231, 233
Carradine, Keith, 235
Carson, Johnny, 174
Caruso, Anthony, 188, 244
Castaic, Calif., 51, 207
Cat Ballou, 29
Cat People (1942), 103
Catalog of Cool, The (book), 194
Cavett, Dick, 33
Cecil B. De Mille Award (Golden Globes), 211
Centaur, The (novel), 86
Champlin, Charles, 13, 99–113, 158, 244
Champlin on Film (TV series), 99
Chandler (documentary), 243
Chandler, Raymond, 74, 243
Chapin, Billy, 133, 223
Chapman, Michael, 235
Charles, Ray, 151
Charleston, S.C., 22, 55, 115, 205
Chatham County, Ga., 205
Chicago Daily News, 162
Chicago Sun-Times, 14, 163
Chicago Tribune, 167, 175
Chico, Calif., 118, 206
Chivas Regal, 149
Chomsky, Marvin J., 240
Chulay, Cornell, 13
Cinemax (cable network), 178, 184, 187, 188, 189, 192, 193, 211, 242, 243
Citizen-News (Hollywood), 176
Civilian Conservation Corps (CCC), 206
Clark, Bobby, 104
Cleopatra (1963), 112
Close-Ups: The Movie Star Book, 204
Clothier, William, 223, 229
Clouse, Robert, 233
Coburn, James, 233
cocaine, 170
Cody, Iron Eyes, 219
Coleman, George, 132–133
Collier's, 196
Collins, Joan, 233, 244
Colorado Springs, 131, 208
Colt Comrades, 213
Columbia Pictures, 87, 214, 216, 225, 230, 233

Columbia University, 57
Comden, Betty, 229
Confidential, 51–52, 80, 208
Connecticut, 100, 205
Connors, Mike ("Touch"), 237, 238, 240
Conrad, Joseph, 149
Conway, Jack, 141, 218
Corsica, 150
Cortez, Stanley, 223
Corvette K-225, 214
Cosmopolitan, 189
Coward, Noel, 169, 170
Crawford, Broderick ("Brod," "The Crawdad"), 134–135, 151, 223
Cromwell, John, 221
Crosby, Bing, 196
Crosby, Floyd, 226
Crossfire, 23, 178, 218
Crowther, Bosley, 30
Crowther, Bruce, 26
Cry Havoc, 215
Cukor, George, 90, 141, 166, 218
Cummings, Robert, 229
Cunningham-Morris, Hugh, 205
Curtis, Dan, 172, 185, 238, 240, 244
Curtis, Tony, 228, 233

DRM Productions, 142, 208, 209
Daily Mail (London), 163
Daily Telegraph (Sydney), 164
Daily Variety, 165, 170, 174
Dancing Masters, 87, 214–215
Darden, Christopher, 79
Darnell, Linda, 222
Darrach, Brad, 80, 160
David Frost Show, The, 33–56
Davidson, Bill, 162, 182
Davis, Victor, 173
Day, Elias, 119
Day, Laraine, 112, 120, 218
Day, Oranne Truitt, 119
Day-Lewis, Daniel, 48
Dead Man, 211, 237
Dean, James, 237
Deborah Kerr (book), 173
December (magazine), 199
Defiant Ones, The, 29
De Fina, Barbara, 236
DeHavilland, Olivia, 189, 223
De Laurentiis, Dino, 230
Delaware, 34–35, 37, 39, 40, 100, 101, 115, 205, 206, 210
De Niro, Robert ("Bobby"), 110, 233, 236
Depp, Johnny, 237
Depression Era *see* Great Depression
Derek, Bo, 236
Dern, Bruce, 171, 234
Desire Me, 90, 112, 141, 159, 166, 218
Detective in Hollywood, The (book), 185
Dialogue on Film (magazine), 179
Dick Cavett Show, The, 33
Dickinson, Angie, 224, 231, 238
Dickinson College, 121

Dillman, Bradford, 233
Dingle, Ireland, 20, 148, 210
Directors Guild of America (DGA), 9
Dirty Harry, 29, 41, 83, 90, 98
Distant Drummer, The (TV series), 242
Dixon, Dick, 42
Dmytryk, Edward, 10, 178, 217, 218, 230, 244
"dognapping," 117–118
Domergue, Faith, 129, 220
Don Guerro (quarter horse), 210
Donen, Stanley, 226–227
Donnell, Jeff, 87, 214
Donner, Richard, 235
Doughboys in Ireland, 87, 214
Douglas, Gordon, 158, 216
Douglas, Illeana, 236
Douglas, Kirk, 27, 31, 64, 95–96, 104, 147, 148, 163, 169, 219, 228, 229
Douglas, Melvyn, 220
Dover, Del., 40, 206
Dudikoff, Michael, 236
Dumont, Margaret, 215, 229
Durango, Mex., 141–142, 164, 209

E! Entertainment Television, 244
Each Man in His Time (book), 179
Easton, Md., 175
Eastwood, Clint, 41, 57, 244
Easy Rider, 64
Ebert, Roger, 12, 13, 14–20, 31, 136, 150, 163, 204
Edwards, Anthony, 235
Edwards, Blake, 164, 216, 217, 243
Egan, Richard, 221, 225, 233
Eglin Field, Fla., 123
Elam, Jack, 229
El Dorado, 23, 29, 33, 55, 94–95, 104–106, 153, 178, 229
Elliott, Sam, 236
Enemy Below, The, 23, 33, 138, 225
England, 45, 47
Enright, Ray, 215
Entrepreneurs, The (documentary series), 242
Ephraim, Eliot, 13
Erwin Frankel Productions, Ltd., 13, 57
Esmond, Jill, 109
Esquire, 30, 110, 155, 157, 160, 161, 168, 175, 179, 200
Evans, Vicki, 167
Eyes of War, The (documentary), 244

Fairbanks, Douglas Sr., 57
Falk, Peter, 230
Fall Guy, The (book), 141
Fall River, Mass., 100, 116, 205
Family Channel, The, 211, 242
Family for Joe, A, (TV pilot movie), 241
Family for Joe, A, (TV series), 211, 241
Farewell, My Lovely, 24, 26, 100, 184–185, 201–202, 210, 232
Farrow, John, 129, 220, 221
Farrow, Mia, 129, 230
Faulkner, William, 143

Fears, Peggy, 120, 206
Feldman, Gene, 242, 244
Fellow Traveler (play), 118–119
Fellow Traveler (film), 119
Felton, Earl, 143, 224
Felton High School (Delaware), 115, 116, 205, 210
Fenady, Andrew J., 185, 240
Fernandez, Emilio, 130
Ferrer, Mel, 228, 238
Field, Sally, 229
Fields, Sidney, 159
film noir, 12, 24, 26, 103, 204
Films and Filming (magazine), 178
Fire Down Below, 26, 47, 137, 182, 209, 225
Fisher, Gerry, 230
Five Card Stud, 82, 154, 164, 230
Five Points, N.M., 45
Fleischer, Richard, 180–181, 221, 224
Fleming, Rhonda, 216, 219, 241
Florida, 34, 39, 110, 114, 123, 152
Flynn, Errol, 136
Foch, Nina, 240
Follow the Band, 212–213
Ford, Glenn, 233, 243
Fonda, Henry ("Hank"), 112, 228, 233
Ford, John ("Jack"), 89, 204
Ford, Robin ("Danny the Moat," "Robin the Golfer"), 128–129
Foreign Intrigue, 24, 160, 208, 224
Forsythe, John, 235
Fort Benning, Ga., 44
Fort Lauderdale, Fla., 110
Fort MacArthur (San Pedro, Calif.), 43, 207
Fort Walton Beach, Fla., 123
Fowley, Douglas, 87, 213, 215, 224, 231
Fraker, William A., 236
France, 112, 208
Francis, Anne, 242
Francis, Freddie, 236
Franciscus, James, 238
Frank, Harriet Jr., 226
Frankel, Erwin, 13, 57
Frankenheimer, John, 99
Frederick, Reva, 65, 79–80, 81, 82, 92–93, 95, 97, 147
Freedman, Jerrold, 240
French Connection, The, 29,
Freud, Sigmund, 80
Freund, Karl, 215, 218
Friends of Eddie Coyle, The, 23, 26, 79, 81, 97, 99, 183, 210, 232
Frost, David, 13, 33–56

Gallaher, Jack, 61
Gardner, Ava, 26, 187, 220
Garmes, Lee, 222, 224
Garner, James, 244
Garnett, Tay, 221, 226
Garson, Greer, 112, 124, 155, 159, 166, 218
Gaudio, Tony, 214, 219
Gaydos, Steven, 13, 114
Gehman, Richard, 199

Gentle Approach, The (play), 123–124
George Washington High School (New York), 34
George Washington University Medical Center, 242
Georgia, 22, 35 36, 108, 110, 115, 118, 205
Gielgud, Sir John, 240
Giesler, Jerry, 128
Gilchrist, Roderick, 163
Ginty, Robert, 236
Girl Rush, The, 87, 158, 216
Gish, Lillian, 223
Globus, Yorum, 234, 235
Godzilla, 85
Going Home, 14, 26, 97, 153, 231–232
Golan, Menahem, 234, 235
Golden Boy, 149
Golden Globe Awards, 211
Golden Years?, The (documentary), 244
Goldwyn, Samuel, Jr., 133, 224, 235
Goldwyn, Samuel Sr., 63
Goldwyn Studios, 190
Gomez, Thomas ("Tommy"), 91, 214, 221
Gone With the Wind, 60
Good Guys and the Bad Guys, The, 183, 231
Gould, Elliott, 234
Grace, Joe, 48
Grafton, Sue, 238
Graham, Sheila, 170
Grahame, Gloria, 218, 221, 223
Grainger, Edmund, 221, 226
Granger, Stewart, 188, 243
Grant, Cary, 57, 63, 67, 227
Grass Is Greener, The, 188, 189, 226
Graves, Peter, 223–224, 240
Grayson, Kathryn, 242
Great Depression, 12, 22, 34–39, 68, 100–101, 115–121
Greece, 159
Green, Adolph, 229
Green, Alfred E., 216
Green Berets (U.S. Special Forces), 144–146
Greenfield, Mike, 244
Greenwood Press, 114
Greer, Jane ("Bettejane"), 27, 28, 89, 103, 148, 186, 219, 220, 243, 244
Gregory, Paul, 134, 223
Grey, Zane, 108, 217
Griffith, D.W., 57, 70
Group W Productions, 13, 33
Guinness, Sir Alec, 149
Gunfight, A, 64
Gunfight at the O.K. Corral, 29
Gung Ho!, 215
Gurlock, Bob, 146
Gustafson, Carol (Robert's half-sister), 231
Guthrie, A.B. Jr. ("Bud"), 104

HBO, 239
Haaren High School (New York), 34, 35, 68, 115, 116
Hackman, Gene, 29
Haifa, Israel, 46
Hale, William, 238

Half Breed, The, 143
Hall, William, 12
Halsey, Admiral William F. ("Bull"), 150
Hamill, Mark, 236
Hamilton, George, 165, 190, 226, 244
Hamilton, Guy, 229
Hardy, Oliver, 87, 215
Harlan, Russell, 212, 213, 214, 215
Harper, Tess, 239
Harris, Richard, 226
Hartman, Don, 220
Haskell, Molly, 201–202
Hathaway, Henry, 82, 198, 222, 230
Havelock-Allan, Anthony, 231
Hawaii, 118, 147, 152
Hawkins, Jack, 192, 228
Hawks, Howard, 11, 95, 104–106, 178, 214, 229
Hawks on Hawks (book), 178
Hayes, Toni, 244
Hayward, Susan, 155, 197, 222
Hayworth, Rita, 26, 47, 225
Hearst, William Randolph, 239
Hearst & Davies Affair, The, 239
Heaven Knows, Mr. Allison, 23, 28, 33, 45, 57, 126, 135–38, 153, 166, 177, 189, 197, 209, 224
Hecht, Harold, 229
Heffron, Richard T., 238, 239
Heflin, Van, 140
Helmick, Paul, 105
Henabery, Joseph E., 212
Henrikson, Lance, 237
Hepburn, Katharine ("Katie"), 88–89, 112, 124, 175, 218
Heston, Charlton, 27, 233, 236
Higgins, George V., 79, 81
High Noon, 59
Hildyard, Jack, 227, 230
Hingle, Pat, 240
His Kind of Woman, 23, 26, 27, 33, 129, 180, 187, 188, 221
Hitchcock, Alfred, 89
Ho Chi Minh Trail (Vietnam War), 145
Hoboing, 35–39, 101, 108, 117–118, 205–206
Hodgins, Earle, 122, 213, 214
Holbrook, Hal, 233, 239
Holden, William, 149, 169, 219, 243
Holiday Affair, 153, 220
Holland, Dave, 13, 107
Holland, Judge Cecil, 207
Holliman, Earl, 230
Hollywood Bowl, 206
Hollywood Pictures (Disney), 236
Hollywood: The Golden Years (documentary), 243
Hollywood Trail Boss (book), 183
Hollywood Walk of Fame, 210
Hollywood Women's Press Club, 175
Holt, Tim, 108
Home Box Office, *see* HBO
Home From the Hill, 23, 29, 33, 54–55, 94, 143, 153, 165, 182, 190, 209, 226

Homolka, Oscar, 76
Honeycutt, Kirk, 158
Hong Kong, 47
Hoover, J. Edgar, 15
Hopalong Cassidy westerns ("Hoppies"), 42–43, 58, 87, 102, 107, 122–123, 207, 212, 213, 214, 215
Hopper, Hedda, 159, 167, 175, 186
Hoppy Serves a Writ, 107, 207, 212
Hornblow, Arthur Jr., 112, 218
Hornsby, Peter, 140–141
House Un-American Activities Committee (HUAC), 119
Houseman, John, 235, 238, 243
Howard, Trevor, 48, 75, 96, 107, 149, 163, 167, 229, 231
Howard Line barges, 100
Howard Hughes: The Inside Story (documentary), 242
Howe, James Wong, 218
Hudson, Rock, 235
Hughes, Howard, 29, 91, 92, 128, 131, 174, 188, 197, 221, 242, 244
Human Comedy, The, 179, 213
Hume, Alan, 233
Hunter, Kim, 216
Hunters, The, 33, 164–165, 225
Hurt, John, 237
Huston, Anjelica, 233, 235, 243
Huston, Danny, 235
Huston, John, 9, 22, 45–47, 136–138, 155, 164, 166, 170, 177, 182, 210, 224, 228, 235, 243–244

I Remember It Well (book), 165, 182
In Old Arizona, 70
Ireland, 20, 48, 59, 66, 82, 136, 148, 163–164, 210
Ireland, Jill, 230
Ireland, John, 230, 232
Ireland, Kathy, 237

Jagger, Dean, 216, 218
Jail, *see* Mitchum, Robert: incarcerations of
Jake Spanner, Private Eye, 185, 240
James Dean: Race With Destiny, 237
Jarmusch, Jim, 211, 237
Jewish Relief Fund, 206
Jicarilla Apaches, 64
John Huston: The Man, the Movies, the Maverick (documentary), 210, 243–244
Johnny Doesn't Live Here Anymore, 215–216
Johns, Glynis, 227
Johnson, Charles, 52
Johnson, Van, 27, 213, 216
Jordan, Richard, 232
Josephson, Erland, 237
Jurgens, Curt, 225, 234
Just Tell Me When to Cry: A Memoir (book), 181

Kaczender, George, 234
Kael, Pauline, 24, 25

Kane, Carol, 235
Karlson, Phil, 228
Karpis, Alvin, 15
Kasem, Casey, 237
Kass, Judith M., 195–196
Katzin, Lee H., 240
Kazan, Elia, 210, 233
Keach, Stacy, 234
Keith, Brian, 232
Keller, Helen, 151
Kelly, Gene, 229
Kelly, Patsy, 120, 206
Kemper, Victor J., 232, 233
Ken, Takakura, 232
Kennedy, Arthur, 222, 230
Kennedy, Burt, 183, 231
Kennedy, George, 231
Kennedy, Robert (deejay), 154
Kennedy, Robert F. (U.S. attorney general), 84
Kenya, 209
Kern River, 122
Kernville, Calif., 102, 122, 207
Kerr, Deborah, 28, 45–47, 166, 173, 189, 197, 224, 227, 239, 244
Killer in the Family, A, 238–239
Killy, Edward ("Ed"), 92, 111, 217
King Lear (play), 73, 177
Kinski, Nastassja, 235
Knox, Alexander, 229, 230
Konchalovsy, Andrei, 234–235
Kotsilibas, James, 187
Kotto, Yaphet, 230
Kramer, Stanley, 69–70, 82, 93, 134, 179, 223
Krasna, Norman, 92, 222
Krasner, Milton, 213, 215, 226
Kulik, Buzz, 230

Ladd, Alan, 88, 157, 159
Ladd, Diane, 237
Lancaster, Burt, 27, 228
Lange, Jessica, 236
Langford, Frances, 158, 216
Lake Forest School District (Delaware), 116, 210
Landers, Lew, 87
Las Vegas, 174
LaShelle, Joseph, 223
Lasker, Edward, 104
Last Time I Saw Archie, The, 27, 94, 158, 227
Last Tycoon, The, 24, 210, 233
Laszlo, Ernest, 224
Laughton, Charles, 23, 52, 71, 73, 93, 111, 133–134, 179, 198, 223
Laurel, Stan, 87, 215
Laurel and Hardy, 87, 215
Laurel Canyon, 128
Lautner, Georges, 235
Lawless, Tim, see Wallace, Tim
Lawrence of Arabia, 106, 149
Lawrensen, Helen, 155, 157, 160, 179, 200
Lean, Sir David, 12, 22, 48, 58–61, 62, 66, 69, 72, 73, 75–76, 77, 96–97, 106–107, 111, 148, 149, 155, 163, 183, 231
Leather Burners, The, 212

Lee Thompson, J., 227, 229, 235
Leigh, Janet, 220
Lemmon, Jack, 225
Lennart, Isobel, 220, 227
Leonard, Herbert B., 97, 231
L'Ermitage (restaurant), 211
LeRoy, Mervyn, 90, 123, 141, 179, 216, 218
Lewin, David, 160, 162
Lewis, Grover, 80, 85–86, 183
Lewis, Juliette, 236, 241
Libertyville, Pa., 118, 206
Life (magazine), 57, 58
"L'il Abner," 155
Linet, Barbara, 197
List of Adrian Messenger, The, 177, 228
"Little Old Wine Drinker Me" (song), 52–54, 209
Lochte, Dick, 79–98
Locket, The, 112, 218
Lockheed Aircraft, 41–42, 101–102, 109, 120, 206
Logan, Joshua, 243
Lollobrigida, Gina, 174
Lom, Herbert, 225, 230
London, 96, 97, 138, 152
Lone Pine, Calif., 107–108, 113
Lone Pine Film Festival, 13, 99, 107
Lone Star Trail, The, 214
Long Beach, Calif., 22, 41, 101, 118, 206
Long Beach Players Guild, 101, 109, 119–120, 206
Long Goodbye, The, 29
Longest Day, The, 23, 25, 55, 112, 126, 183, 209, 227
Look Homeward, Angel (adaptation), 140
Los Angeles Film Critics Association, 114, 158, 210
Los Angeles Police Department (LAPD), 30, 128–129, 157
Los Angeles Free Press, 79
Los Angeles Herald and Express, 175
Los Angeles Herald-Examiner, 175, 176, 204
Los Angeles Times, 14, 30–31, 79, 99, 112, 158, 159, 161, 167, 174, 193, 196, 199, 201, 202
Los Angeles Weekly, 167
Losey, Joseph, 96, 230
Lough Drum, Ireland, 136
Love, Bessie, 165
Lower Depths, The (play), 101, 109
Loy, Myrna, 155, 186–187, 219
Lucas, Blake, 195, 198
Lucas, George, 99
Luke, Keye, 225, 233
Lusty Men, The, 23, 28, 92–93, 197, 221
Lux Radio Theatre, 207
Lyden, Pierce, 122, 212
Lytess, Natasha, 181

MCA, 170
MGM, see Metro-Goldwyn-Mayer
MacAdams, Lewis, 167
Macao, 26, 90–92, 124–125, 142, 187, 221
Macbeth (play), 179

MacDonald, Joseph, 227, 228
MacGraw, Ali, 192, 238, 244
MacLaine, Shirley, 26, 77, 190–191, 228, 229
Madsen, Virginia, 235, 239
Magill's Survey of Cinema, 195, 196, 199
Mail on Sunday (London), 173
Majors, Lee, 234
Man in the Middle, 27, 142, 167, 228–229
Man With the Gun, The, 23, 133, 224
Mandeville Canyon (West Los Angeles, Calif.),
    208
Mann, Daniel, 234
Mann, Roderick, 159, 165, 193, 202
Manners, Dorothy, 176
Margolin, Arnold, 241
Margolin, Stuart, 238
Maria's Lovers, 26, 234–235
marijuana, 14–20, 22, 50, 169
marijuana scandal, 22, 50, 128–129, 196, 207
Marilyn Monroe: Beyond the Legend (documen-
    tary), 242
Marks, Michael, 101
Marshall, E.G., 240
Marshall, Herbert, 222, 228
Martin, Dean, 52, 164, 229, 230
Martinelli, Elsa, 228
Marvin, Lee, 29, 134, 151, 152, 189, 223
Maryland, 48, 66, 94, 146–147, 162, 170,
    174–175, 209
Maslin, Janet, 202
Masterson, Mary Stuart, 235
Mate, Rudolph, 222
Matilda, 234
Matinee Idylls: Reflections on the Movies (book),
    196
Mature, Victor, 91, 126, 200
May, Joe, 216
McBride, Joseph, 13, 165, 170, 178
McClelland, Doug, 170, 173–174
McCormick, Myron, 134–135, 223
McCoy, Horace, 92, 222
McDowall, Roddy, 96, 228, 230
McGraw, Charles, 214, 219, 221
McGuire, Dorothy, 217
McKeesport, Pa., 18
McKern, Leo, 163, 231
McLaglen, Andrew V., 147, 229, 234
McQueen, Steve, 77
Melman, Jeffrey, 241
Meredith, Burgess, 88, 217
Merrill, Dina, 227
Metro-Goldwyn-Mayer (MGM), 97, 112, 143,
    149, 213, 215, 216, 217, 218, 226, 231, 232
Metty, Russell, 217
Mexico, 96, 130–131, 141–142, 164, 208, 209,
    220, 221, 224, 226
Michener, Charles, 202
Midnight Ride, 236
Midway, 149–50, 233
Mifune, Toshiro, 233
Miles, Sarah, 26, 62, 106, 148, 231, 233, 244
Miles, Sylvia, 232
Milestone, Lewis, 219

Milland, Ray, 233
Miller, Arthur, 244
Miller, Jason, 234
Mills, Mary, 148
Mills, Sir John, 67, 148, 149, 192, 231, 233
Minesweeper, 121, 215
Minnelli, Vincente, 94, 143, 165, 182, 217, 226
Miramax Films, 237
Mirisch, Walter, 149–150, 228, 233
Misfits, The, 29
Mississippi, 143
Mister Moses, 26, 209, 229
Mr. North, 210, 235
Mr. Winkle Goes to War, 216
Mitchum, Bentley, 239, 244
Mitchum, Carrie, 237
Mitchum, Christopher ("Chris"), 13, 31, 207,
    231, 236, 239, 244
Mitchum, Dorothy Spence ("Dottie"), 13, 26,
    37, 38–41, 94, 95, 96, 146–147, 161, 163,
    168–169, 187, 206, 207, 208, 211
Mitchum, James Thomas (Robert's father),
    21–22, 34, 35, 55, 100, 205
Mitchum, Jim (aka James, Robert's son), 140,
    206, 225, 227, 241
Mitchum, John ("Jack"), 41, 117, 147–148,
    205, 221, 222, 229, 230, 241, 244
Mitchum (Sater), Julie (aka Annette, Robert's sis-
    ter) 13, 101, 119, 120, 205, 206
Mitchum, Petrine, 154, 208
Mitchum, Robert: altercations involved in, 30,
    82–83, 131–133, 135–136, 163–164,
    175–176, 188, 208; and fame, 65, 136, 150,
    160, 161–162, 163, 196; as an actor 21–32,
    25, 47–48, 72–78, 86–87, 101, 109–110,
    138, 141, 154, 161–162, 166–167, 170–171,
    177–204; as a father, 55; as a horse breeder,
    209, 210; as a playwright, 118–119, 206; as
    a poet, 54, 154, 205; as a practical joker (or
    not), 155, 179, 186–187, 192, 197–198,
    199; as a radio writer, 205, 206; as a singer,
    52–54, 208, 209; as a songwriter, 120, 206;
    as a stunt man or doing own stunts, 42, 102,
    121–122, 126, 129–130, 137–38, 139,
    180–81, 183, 185; autobiography considera-
    tion by, 9, 157; birth of, 34, 205; childhood
    of, 34–35, 100, 115; commercial narration
    by, 10; chain gang stint by, 22, 35–38, 54,
    108, 205–106; death of, 9–10, 211; drinking
    by, 10, 44–45, 48–49, 79–81, 90, 134–135,
    145, 146, 149, 150–152, 163, 167, 175,
    180–181, 184, 189; exoneration of, 50, 208;
    in the Great Depression-era, 22, 34–39, 100,
    101, 108, 115–121, 169; gangrene suffered
    by, 22, 37, 206; humor of, 11, 12, 79–81,
    152–153, 162, 178; in movies about or-
    phans, 153; in the U.S. Army, 43–45; incar-
    cerations of, 11, 21, 22, 50–51, 54,
    128–129, 162, 167–68, 175, 207, 208; law-
    suit vs. *Confidential* filed by, 51, 208; mari-
    juana use by, 14–20, 21, 22, 39, 128–129,
    169; marriage of, 38–41, 206, 211; on being
    cast, 158–159; on directing, 71–72, 83;

Mitchum, Robert (*continued*): on Hollywood society, 169–170; on producers, 84, 92, 103; on the possibility of changing his name, 88, 109, 158; broken back suffered by, 138–139; pellagra suffered by, 22; prizefights by, 41, 117; on responsibility, 155–156, 160; on his nose, 172; schooling of, 34–35, 68–69, 100, 115–116; smoking by, 190; temper of, 180–181; voice of, 9, 10, 11, 12; writing by, 54, 91, 101, 142–143, 153–154
Monash, Paul, 81, 154, 232
Mono County, Calif., 127
Monogram Pictures, 216
Monroe, Marilyn, 12, 125–126, 173, 181–182, 208, 223, 242–243
Montecito, Calif., 114, 210, 211
Monterey, Calif., 112
Moreau, Jeanne, 233
Morley, Robert, 240
Morris, Ann Harriet Gunderson Mitchum (Robert's mother), 41, 54, 100, 153–154, 205, 206, 210
Morris, Hugh, *see* Cunningham-Morris, Hugh
Morris, Oswald ("Ozzie"), 45–46, 224, 229
Mosby, Aline, 168
Mosier, Earl, 123
Moss Green Bird, The (play), 206
Motion Picture (magazine), 189, 194
Mount Rainier, Wash., 133, 208
A Moveable Scene (documentary), 242
Movie Talk: Who Said What About Whom in the Movies (book), 189
Movie World (magazine), 190
Movieland (magazine), 157
Muller, Robby, 237
Murphy, Charlie, 122
Murphy, Francis, 116
Murray, Bill, 235
Murray, Don, 243
Murray, Jim, 12
Musuraca, Nicholas, 216, 218, 219, 220
My Forbidden Past, 24, 187, 220
My Left Foot, 48
My Lucky Stars: A Hollywood Memoir (book), 191
Myrna Loy: Being and Becoming (book), 187
Mysteries & Scandals (TV series), 244

NBC–TV, 33, 238, 240, 241
Namath, Joe, 66
Nashville, 52
Nation, The, 194
National Board of Review, 209
National Educational Television (NET), 58
Neame, Ronald, 229
Nelson, Ralph, 159, 232
Nevada, 108, 111, 207, 217
New Haven, Conn., 115
New Jersey, 40
New London, Conn., 153
New York Daily News, 159
New York Herald-Tribune, 166, 168
New York Sunday News, 163

New York Times, The, 14, 30, 58, 158, 183, 189, 202, 203, 204
New York World Telegram and Sun, 159, 170
Newman, Paul, 229, 244
Newsweek, 171, 203
Nicholson, Jack, 233
Nielsen, Leslie, 233
Night Fighters, The, 82, 165, 226
Night of the Hunter, The, 23, 29, 33, 57, 71, 76, 93, 111, 133–134, 153, 179, 198, 208, 223
Nightkill, 210, 238
Nixon, Richard M., 33, 66
Nolte, Nick, 236
North, Sheree, 241, 243
North and South (miniseries), 188, 239
North Carolina, 118, 139–140, 209
North Carolina Alcoholic Beverage Control Department (ABC), 139
Norway, 107, 153
Nostromo (adaptation), 149
Not as a Stranger, 23, 57, 69, 93, 134–135, 151, 179, 189, 208, 223
Nu Image, 236
Nuyen, France, 27, 227, 229
Nye, Judge Clement D., 50, 208

O'Brien, Pat, 242
Observer, The (London), 176
O'Connor, John J., 203–204
O'Dea, John, 124
O'Donoghue, Michael, 235
Ohio, 16, 17, 118, 206
Olivier, Laurence ("Larry"), 22, 109, 177
One Minute to Zero, 30, 131, 221
One Shoe Makes It Murder, 238
Open Book, An (book), 138, 177
Orange, Calif., 122
Oregon, 147
Oscars, *see* Academy Awards
O'Sullivan, Maureen, 129, 220
O'Toole, Peter, 149, 151
Out of the Past, 23, 24, 27, 28, 29–30, 89–90, 103, 148, 186, 195–196, 219
Oxford, Miss., 143

PBS, 243, 244
Palance, Jack, 129–131, 222
Palm Beach, Fla., 39
Palm Springs, Calif., 51, 135, 159, 169
Pan Cosmatos, George, 236
Parade (magazine), 162, 177
Paramount Pictures, 79, 81, 139, 157, 214, 215, 229, 230, 232, 233, 235
Parish, James Robert, 159, 179, 244
Parker, Tom ("Colonel Tom"), 139
Parker, Eleanor, 226
Parkinson, Cliff, 102, 212
Parrish, Robert ("Bob"), 154, 155, 182, 225, 226
Pat, Alice, 115
Patton, 29, 83, 98, 112–113, 164
Patton, Gen. George S. Jr., 74
Peary, Danny, 204

Peck, Gregory, 27, 28, 78, 227, 236, 244
Peckinpah, Sam, 164, 230
Pele, 66
Penn, Sean, 21
Penn Mutual Life Insurance Co., 40
Pennsylvania, 14–20, 35, 39–40, 100, 118, 121, 146, 206
Pensacola, Fla., 123
Penthouse, 80, 160
People (England), 169
People Weekly, 176, 185
People's Choice Awards (TV special), 210
Peppard, George, 79–80, 165, 226
Perrine, Valerie, 234
Petit, Chris, 181, 182
Petrified Forest, The (play), 101, 109
Philadelphia, 35, 39–40, 100, 128, 205
Philips, Lee, 165, 225
Phillips, Alex, 226, 232
Phillips, James Atlee, 225
Phillips, Dee, 179
Photoplay, 160, 161, 179, 195
Physicians & Surgeons Hospital, 101
Pickford, Mary, 63
Pine, William, 121, 214, 215
Pinter, Harold, 233
Pipemaker Swamp (Ga.), 205
Pittsburgh, 14–20
Pittsburgh Post-Gazette, 114, 164
Planer, Franz, 223
Pleasance, Donald, 233, 235
Poetry, *see* Mitchum, Robert: as a poet
Poitier, Sidney, 244
Pollack, Sydney, 26, 154, 183, 232, 244
Porter, Cole, 209
Post, Ted, 238
pot, *see* marijuana
"Pounded to Death by Gorillas," 125
Powell, Dick, 131, 138, 164, 225
Power, Tyrone, 27
Powers, James, 179
Prelutsky, Burt, 161
Preminger, Otto, 30, 69, 82, 126, 150–151, 181–182, 188, 222, 223
Preminger: An Autobiography, 182
Presley, Elvis, 139
Preston, Robert, 166, 219
Price, Vincent, 180, 221
prison, *see* Mitchum, Robert: incarcerations of
prizefighting, 41, 136–137, 172, 206
Proctor, Kay, 194
Promises to Keep, 239
psychiatry, 171
Public Broadcasting System, *see* PBS
Pulitzer Prize, 104
Pursued, 23, 28, 69–70, 89, 153, 179, 195, 218
Pyle, Ernie, 28, 217

Quine, Richard ("Dick"), 87, 213
Quinn, Anthony ("Tony"), 77

RKO Radio Pictures, 29, 61–62, 63, 68, 100, 103, 109, 111, 112, 129, 131, 143, 157, 158, 165, 168, 207, 208, 216, 217, 218, 219, 220, 221, 222, 243
Rachel and the Stranger, 110, 166, 219
Racket, The (1951), 221
Rafkin, Alan, 241
rail-riding, *see* hoboing
Raimu, 77
Rainer, Peter, 204
Rains, Claude, 129, 220
Rampage, 192, 228
Rampling, Charlotte, 232
Ravetch, Irving, 226
Ray, Nicholas ("Nick"), 91, 92–93, 151, 155, 221, 222
Reagan, Nancy, 244
Reagan, Ronald ("Ronnie"), 168
Rebound (play), 101, 109, 206
Red Pony, The (film, 1949), 186, 219
Redding, Calif., 117, 206
Redford, Robert, 244
Reed, Donna, 213
Reed, Oliver, 233
Refugees (oratorio), 206
Rehfeld, Barry, 157, 161, 168
Remembering Marilyn (documentary), 243
Remick, Lee, 243
Republic Pictures, 213, 219
Rettig, Tommy, 125, 223
Reunion at Fairborough, 189, 239
Rey, Fernando, 230
Reynolds, Bernard ("Bernie"), 30, 131–132, 208
Reynolds, Burt, 141
Reynolds, Debbie, 131
Reynolds, Sheldon, 224
Rich, David Lowell, 239
Richard III (play), 73
Richards, Dick, 184–185, 201
Richardson, Sir Ralph, 149
Rickards, Jocelyn, 48
Rickey, Carrie, 27, 196–197
Riders of the Deadline, 215
Righter, Carroll, 120–121, 206
Rin Tin Tin, 22, 43, 154
Ripley, Arthur, 140, 225
Risan, Leidulv, 237
Rising Sun, Del., 205
Ritter, Tex, 214
River of No Return, 69, 125–126, 153, 173, 181, 208, 223
Robe, The, 158
Roberson, Chuck ("Bad Chuck"), 141
Robert Mitchum (book, Belton, 1976), 201
Robert Mitchum (documentary), 244
Robert Mitchum: A Bio-Bibliography (book), 114
"Robert Mitchum — Calypso Is Like So" (LP), 209
"Robert Mitchum Day" (in Los Angeles), 210
Robert Mitchum Story, The: 'It Sure Beats Working,' (book), 169, 178, 198
Robert Mitchum: The Reluctant Star (documentary), 178, 184, 187, 188, 189, 192, 193, 211, 244

Roberts, Jerry, 114–156, 183, 244
Roberts, Marguerite, 218, 228, 230
Robertson, Cliff, 233, 237, 243
Robertson, Dale, 82
Robinson, Edward G., 216
Rogell, Sid, 129
Roland, Gilbert, 224
Rolling Stone, 80, 85–86, 183
Rooney, Mickey, 213
Rooney, Pat, 120
Roosevelt, Eleanor, 170
Rosebud, 30, 150–151
Ross, Don, 168
Ross, Frank, 158–159
Rosson, Harold, 216, 225, 229
Rotunno, Giuseppe, 230
Route 66, 97
Ruark, Robert, 196
Rubin, Benny, 206
Rubinek, Saul, 234
Ruddy, Albert S., 234
Russell, Jane, 27, 80, 91, 124–125, 168, 187,
   221, 242, 244
Russell, Kurt, 236
Russell, Theresa, 155, 233
Rustam, Mardi, 237
Ruttenberg, Joseph, 218
Ryan, Robert, 218, 221, 228, 230
Ryan's Daughter, 18, 20, 23, 33, 48, 57, 58, 67,
   75, 96–97, 106, 111, 148–149, 163, 183,
   192, 210, 231

Sabu, 228
"Sagamore" (salvage ship), 205
St. Louis Post-Dispatch, 167
Samuel Goldwyn Co., 235
San Francisco, 18, 118,, 174
San Francisco Chronicle, 201
San Francisco Film Festival, 174
San Pedro, Calif., 43
San Quentin, Calif., 127, 128
San Rafael, Calif., 208
Sand Pebbles, The, 77
Sanderson, Harold, 149
Santa Barbara, Calif., 9, 99, 107
Santa Catalina Historical Society, 124
Santa Catalina Island, Calif., 124
Santa Monica, Calif., 52
Saroyan, William, 213
Sarris, Andrew, 9, 24, 28
Sater, Julie, *see* Mitchum (Sater), Julie (aka
   Annette)
Saturday Evening Post, 162, 182
Saturday Night Live, 210
Savage, John, 235
Savalas, Telly, 227, 237
Savannah, Ga., 22, 35, 36, 108, 110, 115, 118,
   205
Saville, Victor, 141, 218
Schary, Dore, 217
Schickel, Richard, 13, 57–78, 196
Schlom, Herman, 109, 217
Schmitt, Joan Dew, 174

Schrader, Paul, 232
Schroeder, Don, 241
Schygulla, Hanna, 237
Scorsese, Martin, 211, 236, 244
Scott, George C., 29, 111, 138, 228
Scott, Randolph, 214, 215
Scranton, Pa., 202
Scrooged, 235
Sculatti, Gene, 194
Seagrams, 149
Second Chance, 129–130, 222
Secret Ceremony, 96, 230–231
Secret Love of Martha Ivers, The, 104
Selander, Lesley, 212, 213, 215
Selznick, David O., 46, 159
Seymour, James W. Jr., 176, 185
Seymour, Jane, 172–173, 240
Shaft, 97
Shakespeare, William, 84, 199
Shamroy, Leon, 222, 229
Shannon, Leonard, 127
Shaw, Irwin, 225
She Couldn't Say No, 153, 180, 188, 222
Shea, Jack, 102
Shearer, Lloyd, 162, 177
Sheen, Martin, 171, 234
Sherman, Harry ("Pop"), 42, 102, 122, 207,
   212, 213, 214, 215
Shigeta, James, 232, 233
Shipman, David, 189
Shipp, Cameron, 196
Siegel, Don, 90, 220
Silver Screen (magazine), 186
Simmons, Jean, 188, 222, 223, 227, 239
Simon, Simone, 103, 216
Simpson, O.J., 79
Sinatra, Frank, 10, 12, 53, 86, 93, 134–135,
   150, 165, 169, 189, 223, 228
Skolsky, Sidney, 174, 179
Skyline Drive (Virginia), 140
Smight, Jack, 233
Smiler's Dragon (play), 206
Smirnoff, 167
Smith, Brian Owen, 152
Smith, Cecil, 199
Smith, Jaclyn, 238
Smith, Keely, 225
Soon to Be a Major Motion Picture (book), 150
Sorvino, Paul, 234
Sothern, Ann, 215
Sound on Film (radio series), 57–58, 78
South Carolina, 34–35, 55, 100, 115, 205
Spader, James, 238
Sparks, Nev., 117
Sparks Fly Upward (book), 188
Special Forces (Green Berets), 144–146
Spiegel, Sam, 233
"Spike Africa" (schooner), 9–10
Stage Show (TV series), 208
Stallone, Sylvester, 232
Standish, Myles, 167
Stanislavski, Constantine, 167
Stanton, Harry Dean, 232, 235

Star Is Born, A (1954), 134
Star Wars, 202
Starspeak: Hollywood on Everything (book), 170, 173–174
Steele, Barbara, 238, 240
Steele, Freddie, 194, 217
Steiger, Rod, 228, 234
Steinbeck, John, 219
Stephens, Sir Robert, 240, 243
Sterling, Jan, 224
Sternberg, Josef von, *see* von Sternberg, Josef
Sternlight, Mel, 127
Steubenville, Ohio, 16
Stevens, George Sr., 89, 237
Stevens, Inger, 230
Stevens, Stella, 241
Stevenson, Robert, 220
Stewart, James, 9, 233
Stoltz, Eric, 238
Stone, Sharon, 240
Story of G.I. Joe, The, 21, 23, 28–29, 43, 57, 88, 99, 102, 141, 178, 194, 207, 217
Stradling, Harry, 213, 222
Stradling, Harry Jr., 231, 233
Strange Love of Martha Ivers, The, 104, 148
Stratford-upon-Avon, England, 73
Strauss, Peter, 233, 240
Street and Smith magazines, 164
Streetcar Named Desire, A (play), 157
Stross, Raymond, 82, 165, 226
Sullavan, Margaret, 215
Sunday Express (London), 165
Sunday People (London), 162
Sundowners, The, 23, 28, 33, 45, 47, 57, 135, 182, 189, 209, 227
Sunset Boys, The, 99, 107, 237
Susan Hayward: Portrait of a Survivor (book), 197
Susan Slept Here, 131, 161
Swayze, Patrick, 239
Sweden, 208
Sweethearts (play), 104
Switzerland, 47

TNT, 210, 243, 244
Talbot County, Md., 175, 209
Talbot Productions, 79, 83, 142, 209
Taylor, Elizabeth, 67, 96, 230, 239
Taylor, Robert ("Bob"), 112, 168, 218
Teamsters Union, 86
Tel Aviv, 46
Tennant, Victoria, 193, 238, 240
That Championship Season, 30, 171, 202, 234
Thaxter, Phyllis, 216, 219
Them Ornery Mitchum Boys (book), 147–148
They Live by Night, 92
They Shoot Horses, Don't They? (novel), 92
Thieves Like Us (novel), 92
Thirty Seconds Over Tokyo, 23, 33, 43, 57, 123, 179, 216
Thomas, Bob, 10, 172, 204, 244
Thomas, William, 121, 214, 215
Thompson, Fred Dalton, 236

Thompson, Howard, 189
Thompson, J. Lee, *see* Lee Thompson, J.
Thompson, Richard, 199
Thompson's Last Run, 240
Thomson, David, 23, 193–194
Thornton, Billy Bob, 236, 237
Three Wishes for Jamie (play), 133
Thunder Road, 23, 30, 57, 85, 93–94, 139–141, 142, 199, 209, 225
Till the End of Time (film), 45, 57, 178, 217
Till the End of Time (radio play), 207
Time (magazine), 57, 200, 210
Time Out (magazine), 181, 182
Times of London, The, 167
Tobago I., *see* Trinidad and Tobago
Today (London), 172
Todd, Richard, 233
Tojo Hideki, 41
Toledo, Ohio, 118, 206
Tombstone, 111, 236
Tomkies, Mike, 169, 178, 197–98
Toronto Star, The, 164
Tough Guys, The (book), 159, 179
Tourneur, Jacques, 89–90, 103–104, 219
Towne, Robert, 230, 232
Trachtenberg, J.A., 169, 171
Track of the Cat, 23, 26, 133, 178, 198, 208, 223
Tracy, Spencer, 23, 167, 182, 216
Tralee, Ireland, 48
Trinidad and Tobago, 45–47, 135–138, 155, 209
Trombetta, Jim, 194
True: The Men's Magazine, 199
Trumbo, Dalton, 216
Tucson, Ariz., 105, 152
Turner Network Television, *see* TNT
Tuska, Jon, 185
Twentieth Century Fox, 46, 112, 139, 198, 214, 222, 223, 224, 225, 227, 228, 229
Two for the Seesaw, 57, 77–78, 90, 190, 228
Tyler, Tim, 200–201

UCLA, 63, 140
U.S. Air Force, 108, 145–146
U.S. Army, 43–45, 144–146, 207
U.S. Bureau of Alcohol, Tobacco and Firearms (ATF), 139
U.S. Marine Corps, 45
U.S. Navy, 135–136
U.S. Special Forces (Army), 144–146
U.S. State Department, 84, 209
USA Network, 240
USS Kitty Hawk, 149
Undercurrent, 88, 112, 182, 217
Unger, Henry, 175
United Artists, 208, 212, 213, 214, 215, 217, 223, 224, 225, 226, 227, 228, 229, 231, 233
Universal Pictures, 68, 212, 213, 214, 215, 226, 227, 228, 230, 233
Up in the Clouds, Gentlemen Please (book), 192
Updike, John, 86
Ustinov, Peter, 78, 227

INDEX

Vaccaro, Brenda, 231
Valentine, Paul, 104, 219
Van Dyke, Dick, 229
Victorville, Calif., 103
Vietnam War, 84, 95, 143–146, 147, 150, 209
Villa, Pancho, 89, 230
Villa Rides, 230
Village Voice, The, 197, 202
Vincent, Jan-Michael, 97, 231, 238
vodka, 79–81, 134–135, 167
Voice in the Wind, 140
von Sternberg, Josef, 90–92, 124–125
Voshall's Mill Pond (Camden, Del.), 206

WMCA Radio (New York), 205
WNET–New York (TV), 33
Wagner, Robert, 225, 228, 233, 243
Waiting for the Wind, 241
Wald, Jerry, 91, 92–93, 221, 222
Walker, Joseph, 216
Walker, Paul, 52
Walker, Robert ("Bobby"), 123, 216
Walker, Robert Jr., 231
Wallace, Tim ("Big Tim"), 14–20, 86, 231
Wallis, Hal B., 230
Walsh, Raoul, 69–71, 89, 111–112, 155, 179,
    195, 218, 244
Walt Disney Co., 141
Wanger, Walter, 213, 215
War and Remembrance, 25, 30, 100, 172–173,
    185, 191, 210, 240
Warner, David, 235
Warner, Jack, 132
Warner Bros., 157, 218, 223, 228, 231, 232
Warren, Steve, 161
Washington, D.C., 37, 117–118
Washington Post, The, 201
Wassermann tests, 45
Watergate scandal, 84
Waterman, Ivan, 172
Waters, Harry F., 203
Way West, The, 24, 95–96, 104, 147, 229
Wayne, John ("Duke"), 12, 27, 29, 55, 90,
    94–95, 105–106, 112, 132, 141, 161, 176,
    178, 197, 228, 229
Wayside Honor Farm, 22, 51, 207
Weaver, Fritz, 238, 239
Webb, Jack, 94, 227
Weisenthal, Sam, 222
Welles, Orson, 206
Wellman, William A. ("Wild Bill"), 21,23, 30,
    88, 103, 132–133, 178, 217, 223, 244
Wellman, William A. Jr., 244
West of the Pecos (1945), 217
We've Never Been Licked, 87, 213
Wexford, Ireland, 48
What a Way to Go!, 153, 190, 229
When Strangers Marry, 23, 216

Where Danger Lives, 129, 220
White Witch Doctor, 24, 82, 125, 197–198, 222
Whitman, Walt, 194
Whitmore, James, 244
Wicking, Chris, 181, 182
Widmark, Richard, 27, 95, 147, 229, 243, 244
Wight Stadium, 137
Wild, Harry J., 91, 217, 220, 221, 222
Wild Bill: Hollywood Maverick (documentary),
    244
Wild Bunch, The, 164
Wild Rovers, 164
Wilkes-Barre, Pa., 146
Wilkins, Paul, 101, 102
William Holden: The Golden Boy (documen-
    tary), 243
Williams, Guinn ("Big Boy"), 215, 217, 226
Wilson, Earl, 176
Wilson, Richard, 224
Winds of War, The, 25, 100, 150, 171–172, 185,
    191, 192, 193, 203, 210, 238, 240
Winner, Michael, 233
Winslow, Thyra Samter, 195
Winters, Shelley, 71, 93, 134, 223, 237, 243
Wise, Herbert, 239
Wise, Robert ("Bobby"), 77, 90, 219, 228, 244
Wise, Walter, 225
Wolf, William, 171
Woman of Desire, 236–37
Women's Wear Daily, 169, 171
Wonderful Country, The, 23, 141–142, 182,
    209, 226
Woodard, Alfre, 235
Woodside, Del., 205
Wordsworth, William, 124
Works Progress Administration (WPA), 115
Wouk, Herman, 203, 238, 240
Wrath of God, The, 97, 159, 232
Wright, Teresa, 103, 218, 223
Wynn, Keenan, 229
Wynter, Dana, 228

Yakuza, The, 24, 26, 28, 183, 232
Yale University Law School, 160
Yates, Peter, 154, 183, 232
You (magazine), 174
Young, Freddie, 66, 231
Young, Loretta, 109–110, 166, 219
Young, Robert, 143, 218
Young Billy Young, 183, 231
Youngstein, Max E., 231
Yugoslavia, 172

Z Channel, 99
Zagreb, Yugoslavia, 172
Zanuck, Darryl, F., 112, 183, 198, 227–128
Zimbalist, Sam, 216
Zinnemann, Fred, 23, 59, 182, 227